Systemic Humiliation in America

Daniel Rothbart
Editor

Systemic Humiliation in America

Finding Dignity within Systems of Degradation

Editor
Daniel Rothbart
School for Conflict Analysis and Resolution
George Mason University
Arlington, VA, USA

ISBN 978-3-030-09981-7   ISBN 978-3-319-70679-5   (eBook)
https://doi.org/10.1007/978-3-319-70679-5

This Palgrave Macmillan imprint is published by Springer Nature
The registered company is Springer International Publishing AG
The registered company address is: Gewerbestrasse 11, 6330 Cham, Switzerland

PREFACE

"Why can't they treat us like human beings?" he asked me.

He was a Sudanese peacemaker and referring to the violent treatment that his people—the Fur tribe—had endured as a result of decades of conflict with their government. He knew about many forms of violence—the bombs and bullets, the tactics of political oppression, and policies that foster extreme poverty. He knew also about an intangible sort of violence that is particularly corrosive to the soul of his people. This is a violence of orchestrated denigration that warps the self-image of the Fur, making them feel inferior and disgraced for being born as descendants of slaves. This is a violence of large-scale humiliation manufactured as part of the government's divide-and-rule strategy in the conflict-ridden nation, implemented in government-sponsored campaigns to denigrate tribal culture, remove references to the past tribal glories from history textbooks, and severely limit their access to the channels of political power.

My conversation led to my reflection later about the kinds of violence occurring today in the United States. Could the violence of manufactured humiliation be orchestrated in this country for purposes of disciplinary control? A memory of the conversation with the peacemaker returned during my participation at the 2015 Workshop on Transforming Humiliation and Violent Conflict at Columbia University. The workshop represented one of a series of events sponsored by Human Dignity and Humiliation Studies, which is comprised of a network of academics, professionals, and practitioners. At the workshop, I was struck by the creativity of participants, all of whom are committed to the redress of practices that seek to dehumanize individuals, especially members of marginalized population groups. I am deeply indebted to Evelin Lindner and Linda Harling, who are founding president and director, respectively, of this network. I am grateful for the wonderful conversations I had with members of this network, especially Michael Britton, Connie Dawson, Tony Gaskew, David Ho, and Michael Perlin.

The ideas for this volume also intersect deeply with the mission of my home institution at the School for Conflict Analysis and Resolution at George Mason University. As the school's name indicates, we examine the causal drivers of protracted conflict globally, seeking to intervene where possible in conflict settings to reverse the downward spiral of conflict and promote long-term peace. My colleagues offer great inspiration for such work. I am particularly indebted to Mark Gopin, Karina Korostelina, Richard Rubenstein, Solon Simmons, and Tehama Lopez-Bunyasi, whose gifts over the years of kindness, generosity, and insight seem endless. Special thanks go to the dean of my school, Kevin Avruch, for offering a semester-long study leave (sabbatical) that provided the opportunity to complete this project. I also thank him for his unfailing encouragement and wisdom on this and other projects.

While my name appears on the book's cover, the chapter authors provided the substance to this volume. The chapters are organized around two major themes. First, certain population groups in this country are vulnerable to psycho-political violence in which they are targeted for systemic degradation, leading to feelings of inferiority. In such cases, the shame that such groups feel is systemically orchestrated by powerful social-political forces for disciplinary controls. The chapter authors provide the depth and breadth of the systemic humiliation in the United States today, demonstrating how deep-seated feelings of indignity can be generated by large-scale social-political institutions. Second, instruments of such systemic humiliation can be suppressed through policies and practices that foster a respect for the dignity of each person. The chapter authors of this volume examine corrective measures in which humanitarian norms are elevated as cardinal principles of social institutions. I am so grateful for their wisdom and professionalism displayed throughout this project. It has been a pleasure working with each author.

Additionally, I want to thank Alexis Nelson, who is the editor of the Sociology and Anthropology division of Palgrave Macmillan, for her encouragement and assistance from the beginning of this project. Finally, I thank the anonymous reviewer of the manuscript for the valuable recommendations and insights given on earlier drafts.

Arlington, VA, USA   Daniel Rothbart

CONTENTS

CHAPTER 1

Power and Humiliation

Daniel Rothbart

WHY HUMILIATION?

Almost everyone has been humiliated at some point in life. Sometimes the pain from humiliation is minor and can be shrugged off. Consider, for example, being verbally insulted for sitting during the playing of the national anthem. While the agent of the insult seeks to cast the seated person as unpatriotic, that person may dismiss the insult as silly. The insulted person may even retaliate with a counterinsult, as if to reverse the moral arrow toward the initial accuser. Of course, not all humiliations are innocuous. Bullying is a form of humiliation in which someone seeks to degrade another person, to lord over them, frighten them into submission, and establish dominance over their mind or body. Serious physical or psychological harm can result from such actions.

Not all instances of humiliation involve a person-to-person interaction. Consider the humiliations that many people go through in their experiences with large-scale social-political institutions. For example, employees who receive dismissal notices from their superiors may feel humiliated. Also, one can feel disgraced by receiving an eviction notice for failing to meet financial obligations to a lending institution. In another setting,

D. Rothbart (✉)
School for Conflict Analysis and Resolution, George Mason University, Arlington, VA, USA

© The Author(s) 2018
D. Rothbart (ed.), *Systemic Humiliation in America*,
https://doi.org/10.1007/978-3-319-70679-5_1

1

someone can feel humiliated by being verbally insulted by a police officer in the presence of one's children. In such cases, the employer, lending official or police officer is typically acting within their professional responsibilities without necessarily attending to the emotional impact of their actions. Unlike bullying, the agents of these social institutions need not harbor malice toward those affected.

But what if the emotional sensitivities of certain groups of people were strategically exploited by a large-scale social-political institution? Is it possible that some institutional practices function in part to disgrace a population group, exploiting their emotional vulnerabilities as a means of population control? If and where such exploitations occur, can measures be crafted to minimize or possibly prevent the pernicious impact of such institutional practices in ways that respect the dignity of those affected?

This volume offers insight into the power of social-political institutions to instill in certain people a sense of inferiority as a strategy for population control. Such power relies on the cunning of getting in the heads of targeted group members, invading their consciousness, distorting the sense of themselves, and diminishing their self-esteem, all for the purpose of rendering the group members compliant and possibly complicit in the prevailing social-political order. Power can be enhanced by making a targeted group feel inferior to society's "pure," "chosen," or "superior" people. These are the controls of political power.

Each chapter in this volume focuses on the power of a social or political institution to undermine a group's sense of self-worth for the purposes of disciplinary control. I am referring to a power that weaves through a system's routine operations, rules or decisions. Lacking a fixed point of origin, such power can be crafted in pristine offices, boardrooms, and legislative chambers. Such power is exhibited when directors, officials, agents, operators, or bureaucrats are simply doing their job. This is a power that lies beneath the pronouncements of the system's administrators' "reasonable decisions," "essential directives," and "common sense policies." Within the institution's operations, no one person is solely responsible for the humiliation, so culpability cannot be localized to a single individual. The hidden story situated beneath such power is its strategic function, which is to weaken the will of marginalized people to resist, rebel, and retaliate against the members of the high-power group, rendering them docile to the norms of society. The deployment of such power can be conjoined with conscious acts of denigration when, for example, a government bureaucrat insults members of a marginalized group for being "uppity" by stepping out of line from his or her assigned place. But unlike bullying, such power does not necessitate interpersonal insults. In fact, the system's operators, agents, or leaders may not be driven by personal malice toward a targeted group.

This volume advances a theme about modern American society that instruments of systemic humiliation deployed by certain social-political institutions are, in effect, politicized as a means for disciplinary control. These are politicized instruments of emotion-controls. It may seem odd to discuss the politics of an emotion. But why not? Many people have examined the politics of hate of propagandists of ethnic-based violence. This is a topic of serious social scientific research since the horrors of World War II. Currently, in the United States, the politics of fear seem to dominate the rhetoric of political candidates from a wide range of political persuasions. From right-wing conservatives we are told to fear Muslim terrorists, Mexican immigrants, urban thugs, and liberal elites, among many other groups. Left-leaning candidates also stoke fear among the electorate, railing against the threats from Wall Street bankers, "home grown" terrorists, Russian hackers, and the Koch Brothers. Just as both right-wing and left-leaning candidates exploit the emotional sentiments of the electorate, certain social-political institutions target population groups for their emotional weaknesses through measures that are buried under the patina of promoting public safety, well-being, or comfort.

In the following chapters, the authors examine the politics of humiliation as practiced by such institutions. Three questions are answered in these chapters: (1) What exactly is a humiliating experience? (2) How exactly do social-political institutions control population groups through instruments of collective humiliation? (3) What are the countermeasures to such instruments that show promise in fostering respect for the dignity of all?

1. According to nineteenth-century psychologists, emotions are inherently irrational, inhibitors of logical thought, and symptoms of fantasy, delusion, and madness. In this view, emotions are vestiges of human evolution from the "lower species," more like animalistic appetites than "higher" human capacities such as intelligence. Yet, recent experimental studies have revealed that social emotions are effused with cognitive function. With a social emotion one interprets, manages, responds to, and navigates through experience. Consider, for example, a parent's grief from the death of a child. Such understanding is not reducible to animalistic urges.

On the contrary, grief rests upon one's sense of self, one's relation to others, and possibly one's purpose for living. This emotion draws upon the parent's understanding of their relationship, special bonds with each other, and interdependency. Such an understanding includes a memory of experiences with the child, a sense of protracted interactions, and an anticipation of a future without the child (Nussbaum 2001: 1). Moreover, an experience of grief is not fleeting; it's not like a pinprick that comes and quickly goes. Grieving is a prolonged process of various degrees of intensity, as if ebbing and flowing with one's experiences.

Humiliation is an emotion of pain, but it's not like embarrassment. Where an embarrassment centers on a perceived inappropriate behavior, gesture, or appearance, a humiliation represents a threat to one's character, a rupture to one's value, worth or esteem. Some humiliating experiences come with a sense of threat to the sense of oneself as a whole person. For example, I once observed an event that caused a waiter's embarrassment after he indelicately dropped a large tray of food next to some customers. He apologized profusely to nearby customers. But his embarrassment quickly turned to humiliation when an irate customer hurled the insult, "You stupid klutz!" More than an attack on the waiter's skills, the insult targeted the whole person, diminishing his character, status, and value. With an experience of humiliation, one feels oneself to be the target of others' degradation; one is cast as a socially inferior person, typically in the presence of others. This experience also produces a serious reflection of the demerits of the accusation and that the insult is unfair, since "I" do not serve such denigration.

This deeply pernicious sense of humiliation as a rupture to one's identity is conveyed in riveting testimony by leaders of the civil rights movement of the 1960s. In his *Letter from a Birmingham Jail*, Martin Luther King wrote about the routine humiliations that invaded the soul, creating a debilitating "sense of nobodiness" among Negros. He wrote:

> [When] your first name becomes "nigger," your middle name becomes "boy" (however old you are) and your last name becomes "John," and your wife and mother are never given the respected title "Mrs."; when you are harried by day and haunted by night by the fact that you are a Negro, living constantly at tiptoe stance, never quite knowing what to expect next, and are plagued with inner fears and outer resentments; when you are forever

fighting a degenerating sense of 'nobodiness'—then you will understand why we find it difficult to wait. (King 1986)

Such disgraces represent dehumanizing indignities and are experienced routinely by Negros, according to King.

In like measure, James Baldwin wrote of the disgraces he endured at age ten from the abuse of police officers:

> When I was ten, and didn't look, certainly, any older, two policemen amused themselves with me by frisking me, making comic (and terrifying) speculations concerning my ancestry and probably sexual prowess, and for good measure, leaving me flat on my back in one of Harlem's empty lots. (Baldwin 1952)

Baldwin's humiliations came with a sense of powerlessness from living precariously at the whim of the police: "I was being spat on and defined and described and limited, and could have been polished off with no effort whatever" (Baldwin 1952). Has American society progressed by overthrowing the destructive forces of racial divisions of the Jim Crow era? Not according to many commentators on racial relations in this country, who, for example, write about systemically embedded racism (West 2014), the vulnerability of blacks' bodies (Coates 2015), and the extreme pain felt by blacks leading to the "tears we cannot stop" (Dyson 2017).

If we delve into the thought patterns associated with humiliation, we find three dominant narratives that spin around in one's head shifting the stories about oneself, the humiliating acts, and the agents of such acts. (1) Denigration—the humiliated person senses the slings and arrows of an insult through the messages of verbal abuse, bullying, or a threat to one's social status. This humiliated person assesses the gestures, speeches, or physical actions of others for their symbolic meaning, acts of contempt, belittlement, disgrace, or scorn. (2) Disbelief—with this comprehension of a humiliator's actions comes a sense of threat to one's value, rank, status, or power in a social order. This is a threat to one's relational positioning, that is, to one's sense of place, as if the pattern of one's social geography has shifted. Yet, the threat is perceived as unfair in cycles of thought that "I" am not worthy of such debasement since "I" am a person that deserves the esteem of others. (3) Indignation—with such disbelief comes a sense of indignation against the humiliating agent. The pain of being disgraced in the eyes of others is interlinked with anger, possibly indignation, at being such a target. This person may experience anger at the thought that the humiliator is seeking to degrade "me." The humiliated person reverses the moral arrow, as it were, by targeting the agent of the insult, with thoughts of the unfairness of the insult spinning in one's head.

2. Many modern social institutions have the power to transform individuals, converting them to regimented beings, or treating them like robots devoid of feelings, emotions, and sentiments. Such power has been a primary theme explore the instruments of the social sciences and humanities. The chapters below extend this theme to the power of systemic humiliation through instruments of disciplinary control. Four kinds of instruments can be identified. First, some of these instruments of systemic humiliation are revealed in directives of governing bodies, such as a presidential decision, judicial ruling, administrative regulations, or bureaucratic norms for proper procedures. Such directives are systemically humiliating to groups that are targets for specific constraints, burdens, or hardships. Examples are common in repressive societies: the directives by the Russian Tsar that Jews must live in designated regions of Eastern Europe, South Africa's Group Areas Act of 1950 that required residents to live in racially defined areas, the Reich Citizenship Law that stripped German Jews of their citizenship, and the laws of the Jim Crow south that imposed racial segregations in all public facilities.

The second sort of instrument centers on socially prevailing notions of rank-ordering around religion, nationality, ethnicity, or race, notions that imply the inferiority of certain people. Of course, such notions did not disappear with the demise of European colonialists and their denigration of "primitives," "savages," or "slaves." For example, protagonists of religious-based violence rationalize their militancy by invoking notions of their adornment by their God, so that "our" actions are virtuous, glorious, and inspired, presumably by their God's messages. The enemy's demonic nature follows in lockstep from such a rationalization.

A third instrument of systemic humiliation centers on a power of categorical erasure, where references to the targeted group are, or have been, removed from the general sites of recognition of legitimate members of the nation. Simply put, an entire population group can be expunged from the national consciousness even when these group members live side by side with others. The history of race in America includes a plethora of devices that are strategically designed to remove the presence of blacks from the national consciousness of whites. For example, many history textbooks are crafted to underreport the brutality experienced by blacks in the nineteenth and twentieth centuries. Their suffering during slavery is minimized, their terror at the hands of white vigilante groups is ignored, and their "re-enslavement" from the Jim Crow laws of the South is glossed over. Of course, such erasure has pernicious consequences. A group of people who are displaced from the prevailing political order do not deserve the riches of society, nor do they merit the protections of its law enforcement institutions.

A fourth sort of instrument centers on symbolic power. Examples are ubiquitous in the propaganda campaigns of protagonists of racial-ethnic conflict. Their tactics are well known. The group targeted for attacks are stigmatized through images of dirt and rhetoric about their filth, decay, or uncleanliness. Other stigmatizing images center on disease—"they" are dangerously sick, contaminated, or contagious. In addition, another form of degradation centers on bestial imagery, depicting the targeted groups as, for example, snakes, insects, cockroaches, and vermin. For example, in the prelude to Rwanda's genocidal violence in 1994, Hutu extremists launched a demonization campaign through the public media, in which the Tutsis were subjected to vile verbal assaults that illustrated all three images: Tutsis were seen as dirty, contaminated with contagious diseases, and essentialized as snakes and cockroaches.

3. We should recognize the counter-measures to these instruments, which represents a third theme of the volume. Systems of humiliation are not permanent fixtures in the American landscape. Such systems can be transformed in ways that elevate the respect for the inherent worth of all people to the status of a cardinal principle, serving as a driving normative force of social policies and institutional practices. As the chapter authors demonstrate, the principle of universal dignity can guide, for example, the work of police officers in their interactions with civilians, religious leaders in their attempts to reconcile racial conflicts, political leaders in the construction of poverty-relief programs, or, on a smaller scale, the parents regarding their relationship to their children. Such a principle is idealistic but it's not utopian. Systemic dignity typically represents a moralistic response to realistic understanding of dire life conditions, such as extreme poverty, preventable disease, perennial violence, and collective oppression.

The response calls for a commitment to mitigate their effects, terminate their outbreak, or prevent their occurrence. As a prototype for such deployment, consider how realist notions of international relations were challenged in the wake of World War II by the architects of the United Nations. Its charter of 1945 affirms a faith "in fundamental human rights, in the dignity and worth of the human person, in the equal rights of men and women and of nations large and small." Drawing from the norms of this charter, in 1948 the UN adopted the Universal Declaration of Human Rights [UDHR]. Although the architects of the UDHR failed to include a clear conception of a human rights norm, the UDHR clearly advances an equity model of human rights (Steiner and Alston 2000: 142). Each person—whether one is president or pauper, slave or slavemaster—has human rights regardless of their power, life condition, social status, or financial resources. Human rights are acquired at birth, inseparable from one's humanity, and unaltered by one's hardships, impoverishments, suffering, or powerlessness. With such endowment, the actual violation of a human right represents a nullification of one's humanity.

SUMMARY OF CHAPTERS

This volume comprises three parts. Part I—Chaps. 2, 3, and 4—introduces the notion of systems of humiliation and systems of dignity with clear applications to current practices. Chapter 2, "Can Systemic Humiliation Be Transformed into Systemic Dignity?" by Linda Hartling and Evelyn Lindner, serves as an excellent point of departure for subsequent chapters. This is quite appropriate given the two authors' leadership in the global movement called Human Dignity and Humiliation Studies. They offer the following provocative thesis: the crisis of American society today has reached a boiling point thanks to the impact of mutually reinforcing systems of humiliation. Hartling and Lindner probe beneath the surface of particular acts of physical violence to reveal how perpetrators of such violence are motivated by reactions to certain social practices of divisiveness and hatred. The authors begin with a riveting question: What social forces drove the perpetrator of the violence at the Pulse Night club in Orlando, Florida, leading to the highest number of fatalities at that time from a mass shooting at that time by a single person in this nation's history? The authors go beyond, and beneath, the narrow psychological explanations offered to date by many social commentators, that, for example, the shooter was bullied as a child, mentally unstable, or obsessively confused about his sexual identity. Hartling and Lindner examine the social forces that give rise to such violence, focusing on the patterns of collective denigration over differences in ethnicity, gender, and nationality. The instruments of such forces include narratives of ingroup purity and outgroup danger, advanced by claims that "our" survival demands "their" disciplinary control. These are forces that create competing systems of humiliation, leading to a "combustible social climate" according to Lindner and Hartling. They define systemic humiliation as those "policies, practices, traditions, attitudes, beliefs, or social arrangements that damage, deny, neglect, obstruct, or fail to support the equal dignity of all humans, thus preventing their full development and participation in society" (Chap. 2). Consider, for example, the practices of racial profiling by police officers, the excessive scrutiny by agents of the TSA of Muslim Americans in airports, and the deportation of undocumented immigrations by ICE officers. Such practices are rationalized by social conservatives as normal and necessary for the protection of the good people at home.

In the end, Lindner and Hartling offer American society that undermines the pernicious impact of systemic humiliation, replacing this with measures that foster systemic dignity. The notion of systemic dignity is normative but it is not other worldly; it is idealistic without being utopian. The authors define systemic dignity as those "policies, practices, traditions, attitudes, beliefs, or social arrangements that affirm and nurture the equal dignity of all humans, providing for their full development and participation in society" (Chap. 2). A case in point is the UDHR, which requires its member states to respect the humanity of each of its citizens, recognizing their inherent worth—their dignity—as beings who deserve the esteem of others, especially state governments. The normative vision associated with the UDHR serves as a prototype for American society, based on the imperatives that interlink the nation's security with the human security of all dignity systems.

In Chap. 3, "Insults as Tools of Systemic Humiliation," Karina Korostelina offers insight into the many expressions of systemic humiliation. Not limited to the one-on-one interaction of individuals, Korostelina explores the use of insult as a tool of protagonists of violent social conflicts to gain strategic advantage. She offers a taxonomy of the kinds of insults exhibited by such protagonists as follows:

Identity insult—"They" are inherently depraved, immoral or flawed beings.

Projection insult—"We" do not have a particular character flaw; "they" do.

Divergent insult—"We" are fundamentally different from "them."

Relative insult—"We" are unfairly deprived of power, status or resources because of "their" excessive greed.

Power insult—"We" are more worthy of access to power—political, social, or economic—than "they are."

Legitimacy insult—"They" have no right to access to power, status or resources; but "we" do.

Korostelina goes on to apply these six forms of insult to conflict settings.

She examines the social response to the 1957 desegregation of the public school system in Little Rock, Arkansas, revealing a lesser-known power imbalance between segments of the white community. In their control of the city's school board, the wealthy whites of Little Rock established policies designed to desegregate schools in the districts of poor whites while preserving de facto segregation in the districts of rich whites. Underpinning such policies were divergent insults that aggravated the boundary division between wealthy and poor whites. A second case that Korostelina presents centers on the 2014 shooting of Michael Brown in Ferguson, Missouri, by a white police officer. This case illustrated the police officer's projection insult of Michael Brown, the officer's legitimacy insult of African Americans, and the identity insult by Michael Brown's parents against the police officer. Korostelina's third case centers on the political controversy surrounding the 2014 nuclear deal between the United States and Iran—this contention between the administration and congregational Republicans illustrated three kinds of insults: power, legitimacy, and projection.

In Chap. 4 Solon Simmons examines the highly contentious and at times bizarre presidential campaign of 2016. He begins with the following provocative question: Why did Hillary Clinton lose a race in which she garnered strong support by a vast majority of members of the Democratic Party, including her former rival Bernie Sanders, while Donald Trump lacked experience in government, knowledge of international affairs, and civility in his relations with critics and the press? At one level, we could focus on the various insults hurled by Clinton and Trump, which often centered on appearances. Such insults included references to her "unsexy" appearance, his "goofy" hat, her "fake" smile, his "prowling" stance on stage, and his and her hair. Simmons probes beneath these silly jabs to reveal powerful narratives of intense humiliation among segments of the electorate. His methodology is quite revealing. By examining the transcripts of the Sunday morning interview show *Meet the Press* during the weeks leading up to election day, he shows how the stories of humiliation functioned as master narratives in these campaigns.

For example, Trump embellished a theme that Bernie Sanders had stressed earlier, that the system was rigged against working-class voters. This theme tapped into the rage felt by many working-class voters who witnessed excessive unemployment, persistent poverty, and diminished professional opportunities. Trump bombarded his audiences with stories about how "real Americans" were "getting screwed" by the Obama Administration, Washington bureaucrats, and Wall Street bankers. By accusing the Obama Administration of giving special favors to foreigners, including immigrants and with references to Mexican rapists, Trump combined the nativist notions that real Americans were losing jobs to foreigners with racist sentiments that white Americans were the real victims of this foreign invasion. Of course, Sanders vehemently railed against such sentiments, stressing that blacks and women were being exploited by Wall Street bankers and Washington political leaders. For her part, Hillary Clinton gave voice to the victims of bigotry by validating their humiliating experiences and the need to redress injustices of various forms. She cast her candidacy as the inevitable stage in the long march toward justice for all, as if walking in the footsteps of Martin Luther King and Barack Obama. She declared that it's time to redress social injustices of various sorts. Trump twisted her message by recasting her identity politics as weakening America, accusing "crooked Hillary" of imperiling the nation's security and undermining its global supremacy. He promised, if elected, a return to a golden age of greatness. All of which illustrates the competing systems of humiliation that drove the 2016 presidential campaign.

The authors of Chaps. 5, 6, and 7, which comprise Part II of this volume, extend a theme developed in Part I that clashing systems of humiliation underpin the protracted racial conflicts in America. In Chap. 5, "The Civil War at 150 Years: Deep Wounds Yet to Heal," Joseph Montville draws upon findings of political psychology to explain racially charged public insults, physical brutality, and rampant bigotry. Montville focuses on the divergent systems of humiliation experienced historically by both blacks and whites historically. For Southern whites, such humiliation is evident in the disgraceful defeat in the "war between the states," the shame of experiencing huge economic losses, and the indignity of witnessing former slaves being elevated to positions of political power as state legislators. These humiliations came with a sense of white victimhood, which in turn served as a prelude to the violent rage unleashed by militant terrorists of the late nineteenth and early twentieth centuries. The spectacle of lynching blacks was conjoined with declarations to "take back" the South from the Northern aggressors and to preserve the Southern way of life. As Montville shows, we live today with the reactions to the past and present white humiliations. This is evident in the chambers of the nation's political institutions exhibited by the vitriol of some Republican lawmakers in the elevation of a black man to the highest political office in the land, in Representative Jose Wilson's emotional outburst "You lie?" directed at President Obama in his 2010 State of the Union speech, and in the tactic of Senator Mitch McConnell never to support legislation coming from this president. Montville's theme is clearly borne out in the demonstrations by white nationalists, including the neo-Nazis and members of the Ku Klux Klan, in Charlottesville, Virginia, on August 11, 2017. In an eerie reversal of the cries of civil rights activists, the demonstrators in Charlottesville brandished signs reading "White Power" and "Proud to be White," implying their refusal to be humiliated by non-whites and their champions.

To overcome systems of humiliation, Montville advances a provocative proposal: this nation must reconcile with its past, heal the wounds of broken relationships, openly acknowledge past crimes, and seek an apology from the agents of systemic humiliation. He joins others in calling for a truth and reconciliation commission that is designed to break cycles of racial hatred, violence, and revenge. While the political obstacles to the actual formation of a national truth and reconciliation commission are imposing, it's unlikely to happen soon.

In Chap. 6, "Transforming the Systemic Humiliation of Crime and Justice: Reawakening Black Consciousness," Tony Gaskew extends Montville's themes regarding patterns of racism in this country to the current practices of the criminal justice system. Gaskew focuses on racial profiling, racially disproportionate sentencing, and excessive imprisonment of blacks, all of which represent institutional assaults, like lynching, on black bodies. Writing in the tradition of towering figures on race in America—Martin Luther King, Malcolm X, James Baldwin, Ralph Ellison, and, currently, Cornell West—Gaskew reminds us that such violence is advanced by an image of blacks as born criminals whose existence represents a serious threat to whites. Such perverse images comes with the radical historical erasure of, what Gaskew calls, Black Cultural Privilege. He is referring to the many riches that blacks have bestowed on humanity, providing the first language, civilization, and wisdom of moral virtues such as humiliation, forgiveness, pride, empathy, and compassion. In the nineteenth and twentieth centuries, these gifts were hijacked by white supremacists. Addressing a theme developed by Hartling and Lindner that systemic humiliation can be converted to systemic dignity, Gaskew proposes a complete overhaul of the criminal justice system. He implores blacks to oppose any attempt to participate in police-community dialogue, in police-sponsored programs for public safety and employment in the criminal justice system. Echoing a theme developed by Montville in Chap. 3, Gaskew calls for a nationwide commission for racial reconciliation to reveal the truth about police brutality, the trauma experienced by blacks, the stigma of black criminality, and the corruption of the privatization of criminal justice. Only through a national dialogue of racial injustice can the systems of humiliation be transformed to systems of dignity, grounded in an understanding of the deeper social and political forces that generated such violence.

Without the fanfare of a national dialogue, a quasi-commission designed to reveal the truth and promote reconciliation over racial conflicts did actually occur in Ferguson, Missouri, albeit on a small scale. In Chap. 7, Arthur Romano and David Ragland examine the case of a local community project called the Truth Telling Project [TTP] that took place in Ferguson in the aftermath of the killing of Michael Brown by police officers. Organized by people of color in the St. Louis area, this event created a social space for citizens to testify about their experiences with police-induced violence in that city and nationwide. TTP comprised two events in Ferguson: first, a summit meeting called Truth Telling Weekend, March 13–15, 2015, and, second, a Truth Initiative event of November 13–14, 2015. These events offered residents a safe space for telling their stories, engaging them in role-playing exercises to dramatize their encounters with police officers, and creating an educational theater to inform others of the assault on black bodies that occurs nationwide. One primary objective of TTP is individual transformation, converting one's self-image from being victims of police violence to agents of change. Such a transformation brings with it conversion from the malaise of a paralyzing oppression to a witness of injustice and from the silence of individual trauma to the cries that "we" are in pain and "our" suffering must be addressed.

Chapters 8, 9, and 10, which comprise Part III, extend the volume's primary themes to the field of mental health. In Chap. 8, "'To Wander Off in Shame': Deconstructing the Shaming and Shameful Arrest Policies of Urban Police Departments in Their Treatment of Persons with Mental Disabilities," Michael Perlin and Allison Lynch explore the systemically degrading treatment of individuals with mental illness by agents of the criminal justice system. The authors show that the cycle of arrest-institutionalize-release-repeat intensifies the emotional pain of the targeted individuals, producing effects that are counterproductive to their mental health. This cycle often begins with the police officer's perception that the behavior of these individuals is irrational and dangerous. In many cases, this sort of profiling can represent an initial stage to their subsequent imprisonment. In addition to the disgrace of losing personal liberties, incarceration comes with the danger of inadequate mental health facilities. To counter the stigma of criminalization given to individuals with mental illness, Perlin and Lynch recommend expansion of programs that train police officers in crisis intervention that are designed to treat these individuals as complex and valued beings. The authors identify such training as therapeutic jurisprudence, which privileges the ethics of care as a cardinal norm of criminal justice, establishing the inherent moral worth of every citizen as a legal imperative. By situating the ethics of care as a cardinal norm of criminal justice, therapeutic jurisprudence represents a paradigm shift in criminal justice generally and the treatment of persons with mental health in particular, all of which represent policies that foster systems of dignity in the treatment of mentally ill individuals.

The conversion of systems of humiliation to those of dignity also finds a grounding in much smaller social units—the family. In Chap. 9, "Systemic Humiliation in Families," Connie Dawson examines certain parenting styles of dysfunctional families. In one form of dysfunction, a domineering parent imposes control over the family through rules of shaming. Though rarely written in bold print or displayed on the family refrigerator, such rules are encultured as norms of family interaction. These rules establish the "taken for granted" standards as ordinary and rationalizing them as essential for familial security, well-being, or the ability to flourish. Dawson offers the following rules that define a shaming model of parenting:

Rule One:	*Be morally, intellectually, and socially right.*
Rule Two:	*When you make a mistake or get blamed for something, pass the blame elsewhere.*
Rule Three:	*Do not acknowledge your feelings about what's going on.*
Rule Four:	*Deep secrets: Do not raise the issue or ask questions about whatever might jeopardize the status quo.*
Rules Five:	*Don't communicate clearly. Be wary of commitments, promises, and agreements.*
Rule Six:	*Manipulate, threaten, coerce, and use whatever works to get what you need.*
Rule Seven:	*Deny reality. What's going on is not really going on. Accept discrepant behaviors and occurrences as normal.*

With such rules come rewards for their compliance and punishment for their violation. The psychological impact of this system of shaming includes emotional pain, chronic illness, fits of anger, and self-loathing. Yet, for Dawson, the shaming model of parenting can be converted to nurturing practices that foster trust-building, cohesion, and a sense of mutual support. With such practices, rules of shaming can be replaced by rules for promoting the inherent worth of family members.

The volume concludes with a searching and provocative exploration of pernicious notions of madness with Chap. 10, "Madness, Violence, and Human Dignity: Transforming Madness for Dignified," by David Ho. By madness, Ho refers to forms of mental disorder, such as psychosis, that are often associated with antisocial behavior. He rejects the familiar notion that madness fosters many forms of violence, arguing that this notion represents a distortion of the actual behavior of people with mental disorders. In addition to their nonviolent behavior, a majority of mental health patients exhibit signs of passivity, resignation, and despair for their plight, all of which is intensified by the resignation of the dehumanizing conditions of institutional living. David Ho then carries the reader from the taint of mental illness to the realm of spirituality. He develops the provocative thesis that the spiritual quest regarding life's meaning, purpose, and place in the universe is sometimes advanced through the creative inspiration among certain individuals that society casts as mad. He argues that the truly enlightened experience is one that fosters goodness and avoids the pernicious aspects of humiliation.

References

Baldwin, J. 1952. *Go Tell It on the Mountain.* New York: Dell Publishing.

Coates, Ta-Nehisis. 2015. *Between the World and Me.* New York: Spiegal & Grua.

Dyson, M.E. 2017. *Tears We Cannot Stop.* New York: St. Martin's Press.

King, M.L. 1986. Letter from a Birmingham Jail. In *The Essential Writings and Speeches of Martin Luther King, Jr.*, ed. M. James, 289–302. Washington, DC: Harper Collins Publishers.

Nussbaum, M. 2001. *The Upheavals of Thought: The Intelligence of Emotions.* Cambridge, UK: Cambridge University Press.

Steiner, H., and P. Alston. 2000. *International Human Rights in Context: Law, Politics and Morals.* 2nd ed. Oxford: Oxford University Press.

West, C. 2014. *Black Prophetic Fire.* Boston: Beacon Press.

PART I

Social Conflicts and the Politics of Emotions

CHAPTER 2

Can Systemic Humiliation Be Transformed into Systemic Dignity?

Linda M. Hartling and Evelin G. Lindner

The United States has reached a boiling point. We are not only awakening to a growing environmental climate crisis (EPA 2016; IPCC 2014), we are facing a *social-climate crisis* inflamed by a glaring economic gap between the rich and the poor (Wilkinson and Pickett 2009), a criminal justice system struggling to address unwarranted race-related shootings by police (Leadership Conference on Civil Rights 2016), retaliatory attacks on police (Fernandez et al. 2016), mass incarceration of marginalized populations (Gaskew 2014), a proliferation of gun violence (Gunviolencearchive.org 2016), the relentless drumbeat of terror, terrorism, and intractable conflict (Lindner 2006, 2009a, b, c), and a global refugee crisis (IDMC 2015a, b, c, d; UNHCR 2015). These contentious conditions are shaping social relations in the United States and are also evident in the atmosphere of heated interactions surging throughout the world.

The shooting in Orlando, Florida, considered at that time to be the "deadliest mass shooting by one person in United States history" (Barry et al. 2016), illustrates an urgent need to reflect on the complex social factors that precipitate violent crises. Was the shooter primarily a self-radicalized

L. M. Hartling (✉) • E. G. Lindner
Human Dignity and Humiliation Studies (HumanDHS),
Lake Oswego, OR, USA

© The Author(s) 2018
D. Rothbart (ed.), *Systemic Humiliation in America*,
https://doi.org/10.1007/978-3-319-70679-5_2

19

terrorist, a religious extremist, a child of first-generation immigrants caught in a "clash of cultures," a bullied and troubled adolescent who failed to receive urgently needed mental health services, a homophobic young man in the midst of his own sexual identity crisis, a disappointed security guard who was unable to realize his career goal of becoming a police officer, a misogynist who suffered from "toxic masculinity," or all of the above (Marcotte 2016; Sullivan and Wan 2016)? If one looks deeply, the disparate descriptions of the Orlando shooter challenge us to look beyond an individual actor and take a panoramic view. Understanding tragedies, such as this one, requires investigating the complex conditions contributing to a contentious and combustible social-global climate, raising our risk of acts of violence at home and around the world.

This chapter is an initial exploration of a deeply embedded social dynamic that we suggest plays a powerful role in fomenting and intensifying contentious conditions: *systemic humiliation*. This dynamic is a force that degrades our social infrastructure and disrupts our immediate and long-term communal cohesiveness. Public policies and practices poisoned by unacknowledged cycles of humiliation generate hot embers in our society, resulting in potentially explosive conditions that frequently go unrecognized until it is too late. More than ever before, the elements that constitute systemic humiliation should be recognized as fundamental mechanisms in the formation of modern society. We will describe how the meaning of humiliation has changed as our sense of human dignity has grown. Then we will explore relational ways to transform and replace systemic humiliation with the proliferation of systemic dignity. We suggest that cultivating dignity—at home and around the globe—can deescalate the contentious conditions poisoning our social climate and simultaneously create space for mutually beneficial arrangements of relationships to emerge, relationships that protect and provide for the full participation, growth, and development of all members of society.

How Human History Shapes the Meaning of Humiliation

For most of human existence, *Homo sapiens* likely thought they lived in a world of limitless land and abundant resources. When crises occurred during this time, humans could migrate to a new location and create new living arrangements. As long as the human population on planet Earth was small, there was always untouched land available. However, starting around 12,000 years ago, the situation began to change. Human experience began to be affected by what anthropologist Robert Carneiro (1970, 1988, 2012) calls *circumscription*, which means humankind started to become aware that the next valley could be "occupied" by others, limiting the space to roam freely in search of food and resources. From then on, circumscription began to indirectly "inform" humanity of the fact that resources and planet Earth are finite.

Within the context of circumscription, humans began adapting by developing complex agricultural systems that would intensify the yield of resources through innovations that made it possible to produce more food in a confined territory (Boserup 1965; Cohen 1977, 2009; see also Ury 1999). This was the beginning of the strategy of not only taking control over land and resources, but also taking control over people and animals to work the land in this new system (Gepts et al. 2012). Some groups discovered they could acquire resources through more brutal means, such as raiding and conquering others' lands. The introduction of this strategy triggered what political scientists call the *security dilemma* (Herz 1951, 1957). The security dilemma arises when in-groups are caught in fear of potentially hostile out-groups, who, if not killed, may kill. It may be summarized as: "We *have to* amass weapons, because we are scared. When we amass weapons, they get scared. They amass weapons, we get more scared." It is predicated on the horizontal differentiation of inside versus outside relationships, making it an honorable duty to kill outsiders in defense of insiders (Lindner 2017).

The security dilemma pushes also for the vertical differentiation of up versus down, organizing human activity around dominant/subordinate interactions. For the past thousands of years, this evolved into a male-dominant collectivist and ranked-honor societies with "strongman" elites at the top. Ranked honor is not a code of law, but a normative paradigm, a set of informal values that keeps people bound to remain within its confines. In ranked-honor hierarchies, elites have a duty to defend their honor not only by killing enemies who attack from outside, but also by keeping their peers in check with duel-like combat if their status is challenged and by holding down their inferiors (e.g., women, servants, slaves). Overtime, the horizontal in-group/out-group fears became wedded to powerful, up-down, honor-based social arrangements (e.g., empires, monarchies, dictatorial regimes, military powers, etc.). Thus, the appearance of the security dilemma marks the dawn of what Riane Eisler (1987) calls the *dominator model* in which superiors are served by underlings, and this is accepted and enforced by stringent "codes of honor."

Psychiatrist Jean Baker Miller (1976/1986) would call the dominator model a system of relationships organized around "permanent inequality" (6). There are many political sociologists (Bourdieu 1996, 1998), neo-Marxists (Marcuse 1969), and critical social scientists (Foucault 1977, 1991) who describe similar notions. Miller's formulation bridges the gap between personal-private systems of relationships (i.e., in the home, in the family) and the political-public systems of relationships (i.e., in politics, in the culture, in society). Like others, Miller suggests that once a subordinate group is defined as inferior, the superiors tend to label them as substandard and even defective by virtue of their birth. Furthermore, superiors relegate the least desirable roles to subordinates while saving the more desirable activities for themselves. In dominator systems of permanent inequality, "all human beings are born unequal in worthiness and rights—people are born into their rank and they are meant to stay there, only some might move up or down due to their own doing or undoing—and, as an unavoidable consequence, there will always be some who are more free than others, there will always be elites who preside over their subordinate collectives" (Lindner 2017, xxxix).

Beyond being socialized to stay in their place, underlings are enlisted in perpetuating the vertical arrangements of the dominator model. This involves not only coopting subordinates to voluntarily accept and maintain their own bondage; it also involves teaching them to misrecognize these arrangements as "honorable" behavior. This is the ultimate refinement of what Lindner (2009a) calls the *art of domination*; it results in subordinates participating in voluntary self-humiliation. Through the art of domination, whole societies can be held in collective capture, a collective Stockholm syndrome (when hostages identify with their captors) (Lindner 2009a; Ochberg 2005). These practices are invisibly woven into the fabric of societies in ways that make these social arrangements appear unquestionable, normal, and necessary. Thus, the dominator model becomes a self-perpetuating system of permanent inequality.

Despite the expansion of dominator arrangements over millennia, alternative ways of organizing human relationships and activity continued to evolve. In the middle of the eighteenth century, individuals began moving away from collective hierarchies. Travelers, for instance, began to insert themselves as subjects with a personal perspective, and eventually individuals began to envision the possibility of overcoming rigid hierarchies. In other words, at first, space opened up for human relationships to be organized around individual honor, then around equal dignity. This transformation closely preceded the American Declaration of Independence (July 4th, 1776)—"We hold these truths to be self-evident, that all men are created equal" (Jefferson 1776)—and the French Revolution (August 4th, 1789).

As ideas about social arrangements began to shift, the year 1757 is of particular significance (Lindner 2016). This was the year of the earliest recorded use of the term "to humiliate" and its meaning "to mortify or to lower or to depress the dignity or self-respect of someone" (Miller 1993, 175). Prior to that time, what we would call humiliating methods were accepted as a prosocial practice necessary to humble underlings, to keep them in line, and to ensure their continued service to God and the elites in the hierarchy (e.g., public humiliation inflicted on individuals in medieval times by placing them in devices known as the stocks or the pillory). In a world organized around "dominate or be dominated," humiliation was seen as a *legitimate tool* for managing subordination. For example, early American Puritans believed they were justified in using extremely brutal forms of public humiliation to manage the behavior of servants and other lower-status members of the community (Cox 2016).

Lindner (2016) suggests that the word "humiliation" provides us with an important linguistic marker for this historical shift in human arrangements of relationships, the shift away from collectivist honor/dominator arrangements of society, first toward the honor of an individual, culminating in the ideal of equal dignity for all. In this new social framework, humiliation becomes an *illegitimate tool* of social control, a relational violation, a violation of one's inherent sense of worth as a human being. In the twentieth century, this momentous social shift was globally affirmed in Article 1 of the United Nations Universal Declaration of Human Rights (December 10th, 1948) "All human beings are born free and equal in dignity and rights" (UN 2007, 5).

Although vast swaths of human relationships continue under the specter of the dominator model today, we are seeing the rise of new ways of organizing life on this planet under the principles of equal dignity and human rights ideals, toward what Eisler (1987) would call a *partnership model*. This doesn't mean the end of hierarchy. Unlike structural hierarchies that are organized to maintain domination (North Korea comes to mind), functional hierarchies remain useful in providing an effective way to conduct some forms of human activity. The example is the pilot team (pilot and copilot, for instance) that flies a plane and provides leadership. This is not the kind of leadership that looks down on members of the crew or the passengers as lesser beings. Rather, functional hierarchies can be arrangements in which leaders take primary responsibility for organizing conditions and activities that lead people into effective partnership and cooperative action (Morrell and Capparell 2001). An orchestra conductor provides the leadership that energizes and guides individual musicians to perform great symphonies. Carrying this further, we would suggest that an atmosphere of equal dignity enhances outcomes in functional hierarchies because it strengthens collaboration.

Although a partnership model—cultivated in the spirit of equal dignity—may be a promising path forward, humanity has a long way to go to leave behind modes of domination, and this transformative journey is riddled with risks. Raising people's awareness that they are deserving of equal dignity brings conflict to the surface. It allows subordinated groups to reinterpret treatment they acquiesced to under the hands of more powerful others in the past as painful indignities and humiliations in the present stir their resentment and desire for retaliation. At the same time, elites begin to fear the indignities and humiliations they could suffer when losing their privileged positions, stirring up their efforts to retain systems of domination. Growing feelings of humiliation from the top-down *and* the bottom-up magnify social tensions, increase deadly aggression, and threaten world affairs. These cumulative feelings of humiliation can become a "nuclear bomb of emotions" (Lindner 2006, 32) that could even lead to the unleashing of real nuclear bombs. If humanity is to survive this journey toward equal dignity, we urgently need to understand the experience of humiliation and do everything we can to clear it out of our social systems.

WHAT IS HUMILIATION? WHAT IS SYSTEMIC HUMILIATION?

The field of psychology initially conceptualized humiliation as a variant or subset of shame (Lewis 1987; Stolorow 2010), but recent research affirms that humiliation is distinct (Collazzoni et al. 2014a, b; Elison and Harter 2007; Hartling and Luchetta 1999; Kendler et al. 2003; Klein 1991; Leask 2013; Otten and Jonas 2014). In the context of modern human rights ideals, "humiliation" can be understood as "the enforced lowering of any person or group by a process of subjugation that damages their dignity or sense of worth" (Lindner 2006, xiv). With this in mind, we see that humiliation manifests in countless ways that are highly influenced by the cultural context in which these experiences occur. To help us grasp the far-reaching nature of this phenomenon, Brazilian peace linguist Francisco Gomes de Matos (2012) offers this mnemonic list of humiliating experiences: degradation, dehumanization, demoralization, denigration, depersonalization, deprivation, discrimination, dislocation, domination, exploitation, incrimination, intimidation, objectification, subjugation, terrorization, and vilification.

Broadly speaking, humiliation can be studied as (1) an internal experience (e.g., a feeling, an emotion), (2) an external event (e.g., a degrading interpersonal interaction, bullying, abuse, violent conflict, or genocide), or (3) as systemic conditions (e.g., systemic discrimination and economic injustice) (Hartling and Lindner 2016). These overlapping and intersecting dimensions make the study of humiliation complex: systemic conditions can trigger external events that generate feelings of humiliation *and* feelings of humiliation can generate external events that trigger humiliating systemic conditions.

This chapter is primarily focused on systemic humiliation, the type of humiliation that can poison our lives through degrading social policies, practices, and arrangements. Philosopher Avishai Margalit (1996) explains why societies should be concerned about this powerful dynamic: "Humiliation is mental cruelty. A decent society must be committed not only to the eradication of physical cruelty in its institutions but also to the elimination of mental cruelty caused by these institutions" (85). He contends that the "psychological scars left by humiliation heal with greater difficulty than the physical scars of someone who has suffered only physical pain," (87), and "a decent society is one that eradicates abuse, where humiliation is a particular form of abuse" (88). Humiliation undermines the fabric of society, disrupting our social cohesion and human development as individuals, families, communities, and as an entire civilization.

Looking back on slavery in the United States (Wyatt-Brown 2006) and apartheid in South Africa (Lindner 2009c), most would agree that these are obvious examples of brutal systemic humiliation. Yet, it is only after the fact that the full extent of these events became painfully obvious. Therefore, it is helpful to remember that investigating systemic humiliation frequently begins with studying the "tip of the iceberg." The tip of the iceberg means observable patterns of mistreatment, for example, insults used as tools of humiliation, as astutely described by Karina Korostelina in Chap. 3 of this volume; individuals being repeatedly pulled over by police for "driving while black" (Birzer and Birzer 2006; Kowalski and Lundman 2007), or similar visible events. It also includes the largely invisible operations of institutional abuses of power, social neglect, and infrastructure failures, such as the lead contamination causing a widespread water crisis in Flint, Michigan (Hanna-Attisha et al. 2016). One can be systemically humiliated not only by active practices of cruel or unjust mistreatment, but also by passive institutionalized forms of social exclusion (Baumeister et al. 2002, 2005; Baumeister and Tice 1990; Eisenberger et al. 2003; MacDonald and Leary 2005; Twenge et al. 2002), by policies that obstruct access to services or resources (Silver et al. 2006), or by being systemically treated as insignificant or invisible (Griffin 1991).

Consequently, in this discussion let's propose a broad and ambitious definition of systemic humiliation: *policies, practices, traditions, attitudes, beliefs, or social arrangements that damage, deny, neglect, obstruct, or fail to support the equal dignity of all humans, thus preventing their full development and participation in society.* By this standard, systemic dignity would be *policies, practices, traditions, attitudes, beliefs, or social arrangements that affirm and nurture the equal dignity of all humans, providing for their full development and participation in society.* Although bold, these "working" definitions are a synthesis of decades of research on the dynamics of humiliation (Lindner 2006, 2007b, 2009a, 2010, 2012) and human dignity (Lindner 2007a) combined with a relational-cultural theory of psychological health and development (Hartling 2008; Hartling and Lindner 2016; Jordan 2010; Jordan and Hartling 2002; Jordan et al. 2004; Miller 1988, 2003). Naming and defining systemic humiliation/dignity clearly, even if these are unfinished definitions, provides a springboard for future research and practical action.

It is also helpful to be specific about what we mean by "equal dignity" in these definitions. Equal dignity should not be misconstrued as a strategy to equalize individuals through social conformity. Quite the opposite, equal dignity means appreciating that people are highly diverse in their abilities, backgrounds, and experiences, *and,* concomitantly, equal in worth. Meeting in equal dignity allows us to create relational space for human engagement that is mutually enriching, enriched precisely by differences (Surowiecki 2004). Therefore, fostering conditions of dignity is profoundly practical. It welcomes and encourages diversity of thought, creativity, and cooperation that can lead to a better future for humanity. Rather than uniformity, equal dignity generates a social biosphere that is enriched by *unity in diversity* (Bond 1999). Although current political events are tarnishing the realization of this ideal in the United States (Balz 2016), it remains present in the motto on the Great Seal of the United States: "E pluribus unum," Latin for "out of many, one" (Putnam 2007). On a global level, the adoption of the United Nation's Universal Declaration of Human Rights inspired many human rights conventions designed to uphold the dignity of diverse and vulnerable groups. This includes the International Convention on the Elimination of All Forms of Racial Discrimination (UN General Assembly 1965, December 21), the Convention on the Elimination of All Forms of Discrimination against Women (UN General Assembly 1979, December 18), the Convention on the Rights of the Child (UN General Assembly 1989, November 20), and the Convention on the Prevention of the Crime of Genocide (UN General Assembly 1948, December 9).

Systemic humiliation obstructs our ability to benefit from diversity by limiting possibilities for each person's full development. This is an inevitable outcome of systems that subscribe to the dominator model of permanent inequality. Not only do these systems deprive subordinates of the opportunity for full participation and growth, even the elite members of these systems are deprived of fully unfolding in important domains of human activity (Miller 1976/1986). For example, historically, women have been hindered from realizing opportunities to develop in ways that would allow them to participate in the economic life of their families and communities. Furthermore, women were inculcated with the inherently contradictory message that family care work was "priceless," yet, by economic measures, "worthless" (Grace 1998; Miller 2006). Simultaneously, men were deprived of the opportunity to develop in ways that would allow them to fully share in the social and emotional activities of caring in their families, this "priceless/worthless" work. As the United States and other countries move toward the ideals of equal dignity—not only in theory, but also in practice—*both* women and men can chose to develop skills that allow them to participate in all aspects of family and community life. Societies can create arrangements that move everyone in the direction of realizing the mutually enriching benefits of equal dignity!

SYSTEMIC HUMILIATION INFILTRATES OUR LIVES

Unearthing overt and covert forms of systemic humiliation may be one of the greatest challenges for our social-global infrastructure today. Systemic humiliation infiltrates all levels of society and continues to reproduce itself.

One way it invades social arrangements is when powerful elites make decisions without the participation of the less powerful who are affected by those decisions. Often these decisions are in the economic interests of the more powerful (Kasperkevic 2016; Parker-Pope and Peachman 2016; Pollack and Creswell 2015).

An illustration of this dynamic might be found in recent developments in the General Educational Development (GED) test in the United States, which is offered as a high school equivalency examination for students who were not able to complete the requirements for a standard high school diploma. The GED program was originally implemented in 1942 as a way for soldiers returning from WWII to complete their high school requirements, creating a pathway for them to continue their education in college, attend a trade school, or find a better job (GED Testing Service 2016). Today, individuals who do not earn a standard diploma can choose to take the GED test to demonstrate they have met the requirements for a high school diploma. Many of these students have not been able to complete high school because of personal or social problems, including economic difficulties, behavioral problems, family dysfunction, and other hardships (Hahn et al. 2015; Lehr et al. 2003).

On January 1, 2014, the not-for-profit GED testing program was turned over to for-profit corporations. *The Washington Post* reporter Valerie Strauss describes this development as "what was once a program run by the non-profit American Council for Education is now a for-profit business that includes Pearson, the largest education company in the world" (Strauss 2016). This resulted in a new test that dramatically raised the requirements for passing. In an interview on National Public Radio, Anthony Carnevale, from the Center on Education and the Workforce at Georgetown University, claimed that the new GED test was designed to be in alignment with new demands required for a more modern workforce (Martin 2016). Yet, in effect, the consequences of this corporate takeover of a public program led to what should be called a *hurricane of humiliations* for students trying to improve their lives.

In the case of Oregon, students (often low-income) who take the new test have to pay double the amount they paid previously, from $60 to $120. In addition, they must pay for practice tests and retests; previously, they could take two free retests. Most dramatically, the rate of students passing the new formulations of this test drastically declined, not only in Oregon, but throughout the United States. In 2012, a total of 401,388 people passed the GED test (Kamenetz 2016). In 2013, people rushed to take the old test in its final year, creating a bump, with a total of 540,535 students passing. In 2014, 58,524 students passed the new test, essentially a 90 percent decline (Turner and Kamenetz 2016).

This case illustrates how systemic humiliation can infiltrate educational infrastructure and reproduce conditions of humiliation. A public program that one might say was designed to facilitate systemic dignity (in support of WWII soldiers) was hijacked. Powerful elites in government and in corporations allied to create an arrangement that rapidly led thousands of students to descend into a chain of humiliations: not being able to pay for the test; not being able pass the test; not being able to pay for the retests or practice test; having to pay test-prep companies for extra help; possibly still not being able to pass the test; then not being able to get into college, get financial aid, find a better job, or enter trade school; then not being able to find full employment, a living wage, or economic stability; and, quite likely, feeding into the "school to prison pipeline" (Gaskew 2014, 42).

Powerful corporate leaders are mastering the *art of domination-for-profit* by becoming what Lindner describes as "humiliation entrepreneurs" (2002, 128). They have sophisticated skills to coopt the actions of government elites. This makes it possible for them to take over public programs, capturing and expanding their territory for profit, regardless of the humiliating impact of their actions. In response to educator outcries, Pearson eventually lowered the passing score for their new GED test (Kamenetz 2016). This might have been a corporate admission of the injustice of their test, or it might have been a clever way to avoid losing lucrative revenue if critics insisted that the GED testing program be returned to a nonprofit provider. Whatever the case, this example illustrates how systemic humiliation—especially when driven by profit maximization—can infiltrate our social infrastructure, leading to what Saskia Sassen describes as "social and economic expulsions" (Sassen 2014). When humiliating arrangements like these are allowed to unfold, whole groups of individuals are denied the dignity of personal and educational development.

BLINDED BY FEAR AND EXTREME INDIVIDUALISM

Our blindness to the operations of systemic humiliation is a key obstacle to naming and replacing these deeply complex systems. Particularly when the security dilemma induces or intensifies fear, individuals and groups can develop a type of blindness in the form of mental and behavioral "tunnel vision" (Holbrook et al. 2015). Tunnel vision makes it all too easy to return to outdated dominator strategies of problem solving—"might makes right," "shock and awe"—triggering cycles of humiliation and conflict that can persist for generations. The 2003 US invasion of Iraq may be one of the most notable examples of our time (Fontan 2006).

In conditions of fear-driven tunnel vision, not only are we more likely to remain blind to forms of systemic humiliation, we are more likely be "blind to our own blindness" (Lindner 2012, 96). In other words, we become less likely to see the social arrangements that inflict humiliation, we are less likely to realize that we are becoming blind to these arrangements, and, on top of all this, we are less likely to see more dignifying possibilities for solving problems. Our blindness allows systemic humiliation to thrive.

The shooting of an unarmed teenager on April 9, 2014, in Ferguson, Missouri, followed by weeks of protests, was a reminder of the urgent need to overcome such blindness to humiliating practices and how catastrophic they can be (Buchanan et al. 2014). Waking up might begin with overcoming blindness to the *implicit bias* (Greenwald and Banaji 1995) that contributes to the brutal mistreatment of blacks and other marginalized groups (Spencer et al. 2016). We can also work to dissolve our blindness to structural humiliations embedded in our methods of offering support and services in communities, like those associated with the responses to Hurricane Katrina in 2005 (Elliott and Pais 2006) or the 2010 earthquake in Haiti (Katz 2013). Furthermore, we can work to dissolve our blindness to the millions of *microhumiliations* that wound people every day (e.g., words, attitudes, beliefs, and practices that devalue the dignity of others). All this may sound like "mission impossible," but it simply means doing what we can to enrich society with mutual dignity by cultivating systems that provide for the healthy development and participation of all people.

No one is immune to the problem of being blind to systemic humiliation, not the most intelligent, nor the most educated, the most psychologically minded, or the most politically powerful members of society. Indeed, many powerful, educated, and intelligent members of society may have built their wealth, status, or power by directly or indirectly profiting from their blindness to forms of systemic humiliation. Many are blind to how the Western political-military-industrial complex profits from, embodies, and perpetuates systemic humiliation around the world (Mehta 2012). Even charitable organizations are not exempt: those who dedicate their lives to working for the greater good may discover they are working in a system that unwittingly fans the flames of humiliation (Maren 1997).

How is this possible? There are likely many factors that make us blind to systemic humiliation, but let's examine one likely culprit, *extreme individualism*:

> In contexts that promote extreme individualism, the boundaries of the security dilemma have shrunk down to each individual's personal life. Through this shrinkage, every person is separated from her fellow beings. Everyone is forced into Machiavellian *hominus hominem lupus est* (man is a wolf to man, or, more colloquially, dog-eat-dog) relationships (Lindner 2017, 67–68).

Extreme individualism shrinks the boundaries of a security dilemma; threat is not just political or national, it is personal. Lindner suggests that the dog-eat-dog individualism we see gaining ground today in many parts of the world may be a perfect extension of the traditional ranked culture of the dominator model because it coopts people into thinking they are fighting for an honorable cause while they are participating in their own subjugation (Hardisty 1999). For example, extreme individualism may have been the blinding force that inspired the 41-day siege of Oregon's Malheur National Wildlife Refuge by an armed militia on January 2, 2016 (Zaitz 2016). The militia leaders claimed they wanted to liberate protected public lands from "government tyranny" and return it to "the people," even though "the people" already owned the land. A deeper analysis suggests that this group was guided by an ideology of extreme individualism that had seamlessly transformed them into useful tools in the long-term corporate initiative to privatize public lands (Gallaher 2016, 295). Associate Professor Carolyn Gallaher, who studies patterns of violence of militias, paramilitaries, and private military contractors, offers a perspective on this incident:

> because the occupiers framed their take-over as a fight *against* government tyranny instead of as a fight *for* privatization, they did not have to address the inequities that often attend privatization or to explain why those inequities would be preferable to government ownership. Indeed, though the occupiers claimed they wanted to give Malheur "back" to the region's ranchers, privatization is usually governed by neoliberal principles that favor corporate over producer interests (295).

The script of extreme individualism seems to have made the militia members blind to the possibility that they were being used as tools to serve corporate interests. Furthermore, it made them blind to the history of systemic humiliation of the original "owners" of the land, the Indigenous Paiute Tribe (House 2016). The US government seized 1.5 million acres of Paiute tribal lands in 1879 (for which the tribe was reimbursed nine decades later at a rate of $743.20 per tribal member).

Philip Cushman's book (1995), *Constructing the Self, Constructing America*, provides another view of how Western individualism idealizes self-sufficiency and independence and thus obstructs recognition of policies and practices that sustain or expand systemic humiliation. Hyperindividualism in a consumer economy leads people to believe they can—and should—liberate themselves from humiliating dependence through consumption and materialism. Thus, extreme individualism coopts people into participating in their own enslavement to an unsustainable economic system. Taking this further, Cushman describes how professional helpers may unwittingly perpetuate the ideals of extreme individualism:

> Psychotherapy is permeated by the philosophy of self-contained individualism, exists within the framework of consumerism, speaks the language of self-liberation, and thereby unknowing reproduces some of the ills it is responsible for healing (6).

There seems to be double blindness here. First, there is the macro-level blindness created by extreme individualism that generates feelings of deficiency that turn masses of people into servants of a consumer economy. Second, there is the meso-level blindness of a professional system that provides services that affirm individualism as a standard of healthy development. Fortunately, today there are signs in the field of psychology indicating that the script of extreme individualism is moving in the direction of more relational thinking (Hartling 2008; Jordan 2010; Lieberman 2015).

BLINDNESS AT THE HIGHEST LEVELS

But blindness to systemic humiliation can be even more abhorrent. Powerful professional organizations can present themselves as having the highest standards of scientific objectivity, political neutrality, and ethical standards, yet be agents of humiliating interventions that strengthen the security dilemma, trigger brutal dominator strategies, and spark cycles of humiliation that can even circle the world. Perhaps this can best be illustrated with the case of the American Psychological Association (APA) colluding with the US intelligence community. The APA is the world's largest professional association of psychologists. According to their website, the mission of the APA "is to advance the creation, communication and application of psychological knowledge to benefit society and improve people's lives" (APA 2016). Among other goals, this mission is to be accomplished by: "Improving the qualifications and usefulness of psychologists by establishing high standards of ethics, conduct, education and achievement" (Ibid.).

Despite espousing high ethical standards, in the years following the 9/11 terrorist attack in New York City, the APA secretly worked with representatives of the US Department of Defense (DoD), under the administration of President George W. Bush, to develop policies that would allow psychologists to "ethically" consult on brutal military interrogations of detainees (Hoffman 2015). Equally troubling, the APA launched a public relations strategy to give the impression that these new policies were concerned with the welfare of detainees and consistent with human rights standards (Soldz and Reisner 2015).

Finally, after allegations arose inside and outside of the organization, particularly the allegations made by *The New York Times* reporter James Risen (2014, 2015a, b), the APA initiated an independent investigation that resulted in what has become known as the "Hoffman Report" (Hoffman 2015):

> Our investigation determined that key APA officials, principally the APA Ethics Director joined and supported at times by other APA officials, colluded with important DoD officials to have APA issue loose, high-level ethical guidelines that did not constrain DoD in any greater fashion than existing DoD interrogation guidelines. We concluded that APA's principal motive in doing so was to align APA and curry favor with DoD. There were two other important motives: to create a good public-relations response, and to keep the growth of psychology unrestrained in this area (9).

The report notes that "[t]he DoD is one of the largest employers of psychologists and provides many millions of dollars in grants or contracts for psychologists around the country" (14). Perhaps this was one of the key reasons that the "APA remained deliberately ignorant" (11) about the damage to the organization and the field of psychology that would result from their secretive and coordinated efforts to appease and please the DoD. Even more troubling than the damage to the institution of psychology (Pope 2016), the APA's decisions provided systemic justifications for inflicting profoundly disturbing physical damage to human beings in the form of humiliating arrests, brutal captivity, renditions, torture, and, in some cases, horrific fatalities (Risen 2014).

How could some of the brightest minds in the APA hierarchy get caught up in an activity that is not unlike the dynamics that allowed sexual abuse to be kept secret in the Catholic Church (Terry 2008)? Psychologists Jennifer Freyd and Pamela Birrell (2013), in their book *Betrayal Blindness*, can help us understand some of the dynamics involved. They note that betrayers who hold a dominant position of power "help" those whom they betray remain incognizant of the betrayal by grooming unawareness and denial. For example, perhaps the DoD, in effect, groomed the leadership of the APA through decades of lucrative contracts and funding. Then, perhaps, the APA leadership groomed a cooperative committee, the Presidential Task Force on Psychological Ethics and National Security (PENS), to support the DoD's interests, starting with intentionally weighting the committee with members who had direct ties to the military (Hoffman 2015). If so, this grooming worked, accomplishing the mission of influencing the APA leadership to loosen ethics policies in service of the DoD's interests (Mayer 2008). All the while APA members and the general public were blinded to APA's link to the DoD's use of enhanced interrogations techniques, which we now acknowledge amounted to torture.

On the other hand, perhaps the leaders involved in this APA-DoD collusion suffered from another type of blindness, what law enforcement literature refers to as *noble cause corruption*: "corruption committed in the name of good ends" (Caldero and Crank 2011, 2). After the 9/11 attack, it is possible that APA leaders felt it was their patriotic duty to support the DoD's antiterrorism efforts by loosening ethical standards. If so, this type of blinding loyalty, even in the service of patriotism, would not be so unlike the devotion that evolves in ideological organizations and cults (Jemsek 2011). Loyalty, especially driven by fear, fuels conditions in which people will comply with harmful activities in support of a cause (Olsson 2005). Ironically, terrorism is implemented by many blinded by loyalty to what they define as *their* noble cause.

Although the APA is the example under discussion here, we are by no means using this example to disparage this particular organization or any others. Rather, we think this example illustrates the all-too-common vulnerability of many organizations (e.g., professional, governmental, educational, social, financial, etc.) to unwittingly or directly spread the virus of systemic humiliation. And let's not forget that a primary force behind this virus is the long history of the security dilemma along with its organizational handmaiden, the dominator model, which leads individuals and organizations to believe that if "you want peace, you must prepare for war" (IPublius Flavius Vegetius Renatus and Reeve 2004). The escalation of the security dilemma gives rise to ever more sophisticated variations of the dominator model that then generate and spread the contagion of systemic humiliation. What is the antidote to this contagion? We suggest that cultivating systemic dignity provides both a method of inoculation *and* an antidote to systemic humiliation.

ENVISIONING SYSTEMIC DIGNITY

What if social arrangements were organized around the motto, "If we want we want peace, prepare for dignity"? What kind of world would that be? Let's begin by asking an essential question, "What is dignity?" Western philosophers of many eras have explored the nature of dignity (Lebech 2009). Contemporary figures include Charles Taylor (1989, 1992; Taylor and Gutman 1994), Martha Nussbaum (2004), Hannah Arendt (1951), and others. Discourse analyst Michael Karlberg (2013) observes that "human dignity—like all concepts—takes on different meanings within different interpretive frames" (1). He describes three contrasting deep interpretive frames for understanding the meaning of human dignity: the social command frame, the social contest frame, and the social body frame. The *social command frame* is a legacy of patriarchal and authoritarian modes of thought, fitting with Riane Eisler's (1987) dominator model of society. It also fits with what cognitive scientists George Lakoff and Mark Johnson (1999) call the pedagogical framework of the "strict father." Human dignity in the social command frame signifies the status or rank of "dignitaries."

The *social contest frame* emerged in response to the injustice and oppression that resulted from the social command frame (Karlberg 2013). It draws on the social Darwinist metaphor of the "survival of the fittest" and is characterized in metaphors of war, sports, fighting, and market competition. It assumes that society needs to harness everyone's self-interested and competitive energy into contests, which will then produce winners and losers. In the long run, it assumes that (surviving) populations will be better off (Ibid., 7). Human dignity within the social contest frame denotes self-determination or autonomy (to compete for survival).

The *social body frame* is an understanding that society can be viewed as an integrated organic body. The well-being of the entire body is achieved by enhancing the possibilities for every individual to realize their potential to contribute to the common good within empowering social relationships and institutional structures that foster the growth of human development. Although it has roots in diverse cultures, Karlberg observes, this concept "has been reemerging in a modern form over the past century, in response to the ever-increasing social and ecological interdependence humanity is now experiencing on a global scale" (Ibid., 4). Within the social body frame:

> dignity can be understood in terms of the intrinsic value or worth of every human being as a member of an interdependent community—or social body. Moreover, the social body frame suggests that this intrinsic value is realized as individuals develop those latent capacities upon which the well-being of the entire body depends (Ibid., 6).

The social body frame is consistent with our definition of systemic dignity: *policies, practices, traditions, attitudes, beliefs, or social arrangements that affirm and nurture the equal dignity of all humans, thus providing for their full development and participation in society.* If we want to generate systemic dignity and reduce systemic humiliation, especially in today's highly interconnected world, the social body frame of human dignity seems like a necessity. If we want to weaken the influence of the security dilemma along with the genocidal/suicidal risks of the dominator model, realizing the social body frame of human dignity presents itself as our very obligation. Most of all, if we want peace, the social body frame helps us understand that we must prepare for dignity.

Designing a Future of Dignity

This chapter began with the question: Can systemic humiliation be transformed into systemic dignity? In the United States and around the world, we are seeing signs that social relationships have reached a boiling point.

Present-day Western culture seems to be fraught with risks, risks flowing from a blissful, even triumphant, overdoing of domination in all its forms, intensifying the security dilemma and creating cycles of systemic humiliation (e.g., extreme gaps in income, education, health, security, and alike). Despite the risks, competition for domination is rapidly globalizing. Cooperation between people is being weakened systemically. Increasingly, every individual is being sent into competition against everybody else, with the arena of cooperation shrinking until there is no other space left except the inner psyche of a person. Self-help books and business seminars teach better time management and efficiency training to "improve" people's ability to align their various inner parts so as to function more smoothly in the race, a race that ultimately does not serve them, but increases systemic humiliation. As a result, vulnerable individuals navigate "war zones" of insecurity fueled by systemic humiliation. The complex experience of Orlando shooter, mentioned at the beginning of this chapter, can be understood as an illustration of the risks of today's social war zones. We are in the midst of a social-climate crisis of systemic humiliation that heats up relations at home and around the world. But it doesn't have to be this way. We can replace systemic humiliation with systemic dignity. Now the question is, how?

Dignity Through Language

One secret to realizing systemic dignity comes right out of our mouths: words. We have inherited language (English in this case) that continues to carry messages of domination/subordination as a normative paradigm for arrangements in society. In 2006, Lindner wrote:

> Language was, perhaps, the first application of the idea that something can be put down; after all, we subject nature to our linguistic labels. The Latin root of the word *sub-ject* reveals it: *ject* stems from *jacere*, to throw, and *sub* means under (25).

The message of extreme individualism, discussed earlier, is easily evidenced by over 700 compound words in the *Oxford English Dictionary* that begin with the prefix "self" (OED 2016). This illustrates how language can carry the message of extreme individualism. Moreover, the plethora of self-focused words in the English language may underwrite what researcher and educator Jean Twenge describes as the US epidemic of narcissism (Twenge and Campbell 2009). Some would say that this narcissism was particularly evident in the language and actions of candidate Donald Trump (Nutt 2016), who was elected the 45th President of the United States.

In an interconnected world, more than ever before, we need a language of relationships, specifically a language that encourages mutually empathic, mutually beneficial relationships (Jordan and Hartling 2002). As Lindner suggests, we need to strengthen the language of *Homo amans*, the loving being (*amans* is the present participle of Latin *amare* or to love) (Scheler 1913/1923/1954). For a start, Oregon poet and writer Kim Stafford challenged Linda Hartling (2016) to compile a list of relational alternatives to the tyranny of "self" talk:

Self—> *Relational Being*

Self —> Beings-in-Relationship (Miller 1991)
Self-Actualization —> Mutual Actualization
Self-Development —> Mutual Development
Self-Esteem —> Social-Esteem (Jenkins 1993)
Self-Confidence —> Relational Confidence
Self-Defense —> Relational Safety —> Protective Connection
Self-Image —> Relational Images
Self-Made —> Co-Created
Self-Awareness —> Relational Awareness
Self-Care —> Mutual Care
Self-Responsibility —> Relational Responsibility —> Universal Responsibility
Self-Worth —> Mutual Worth —> Mutual Dignity
Self-Help —> Connected Caring
Self-Serving —> Community Serving
Self-Respect —> Relational Respect

Relational language provides the linguistic infrastructure for rethinking all human activity, opening the way to new cooperative engagement rooted in mutual dignity. Meeting in dignity is the seed to new possibilities. Francisco Gomes de Matos (2013, 36) sums this up in "A Dignity Acrostic":

*D*ignifying
*I*nteraction
*G*lobally
*N*urtures
*I*nterdependence
*T*ogetherness
*Y*es

Dignity Through Dialogue

Beyond the words that we use, we need to look at how we use words. Within academia and many other organizational frames, the verbal battle of win/lose debate has been the dominant model of engagement. S. Mike Miller (2012), former chair of Boston University's Department of Sociology and a cofounder of United for a Fair Economy, observes: "Debates might change your mind, but not very often" (18). Rather than debate, Miller urges the practice of *dialogue*, in which: "The aim is to build together rather than to block one another. We change others by changing ourselves in the course of dialogue" (4).

Based on more than a decade of global conferences and workshops, the Human Dignity and Humiliation Studies (HumanDHS) network has found that dignifying dialogue—what it calls *Dignilogue*—can lead to new paths of understanding and generate creative ideas to address real problems. In preparation for the 2015 Annual Workshop on Transforming Humiliation and Violent Conflict at Columbia University, working with S. Mike Miller's ideas, Linda Hartling and Philip Brown (Miller et al. 2015) compiled these quick dialogue tips:

Dignifying Dialogue

1. Presumes that every idea deserves a fair hearing.

   - Encourages us to do our best to understand the comment, assertion, or suggestion, rather than jumping to conclusions based on preconceived ideas or because of known or unconscious bias.
   - Refrains from verdict thinking; refrains from "yes" or "no" verdicts. Instead, it draws out the speaker or the discussion by asking clarifying questions and adding useful information that builds the outlook under discussion.

- Doesn't assume bad motivations on the part of the proponent (even people or ideas that you detest can be sometimes partially right).

2. Emphasizes appreciative enquiry, for example asking kindly, "How would that work?", or asking thoughtfully, "What are the best reasons for doing this in that way?", or exploring, "How might we build on, or add to, this idea?"

   - Encourages us to *ask ourselves* questions, for example, "What could make this person's idea workable or valid?" (Do mental experiments with the idea).
   - Involves exploring ideas/recommendations/suggestions before jumping to conclusions. Later, if you must, you can come to a conclusion.

3. Is a way to enjoy working with and building on others' ideas! Trying out a new idea can be exciting!

   - Is about *adding to*, rather than subtracting from, the discussion. Ask yourself, "What can I say that will be helpful to the dialogue?"
   - Is an opportunity to enjoy the challenge and the excitement of exploring a new idea or approach together with colleagues of diverse backgrounds and personal histories!

To reverse cycles of systemic humiliation, dignifying dialogue is a promising way to cultivate the conditions and plant the seeds for systemic dignity. As Miller (2015) notes, "Dialogue leads to dignity; dignity leads to dialogue."

LET'S SAY "YES" TO DIGNITY

Can we transform systemic humiliation into systemic dignity? Can we deescalate the dynamics of the security dilemma that incubates so much systemic humiliation in the world? Can we move away from kill-or-be-killed dominator models of organizing human activity toward dignity models of local and global cooperation? Not only do we emphatically answer "yes," we propose that we *must* transform systemic humiliation into systemic dignity if humanity is going to survive on this planet. Cognitive behavioral psychologist and Tibetan Buddhist practitioner Christina Clark (2016) points out, "If we learn to start with the assumption of equal dignity, people wouldn't have to grab at it through the back door" or fight for it in ways that will lead humankind into global suicide or ecocide (Lindner 2017). Working together, we can create global and local systems that generate dignity systemically, that provide for the development and participation of all people (Miller 1976/1986), and that build "decent" societies, as Margalit (1996) puts it.

There is no time to lose in this shared effort. We have reached a boiling point in social relations in the United States and around the world, intensified each day by the dynamics of humiliation. To turn this rising tide around, we can *make dignity our first thought*, not an afterthought. We have all the seeds of equal dignity we need. We can plant those seeds in every word we use, in every interaction, in every conversation, and then plant again. Together, we can make systemic dignity our new destiny.

References

APA. 2016. *About APA: Our Work*. American Psychological Association. http://www.apa.org/about/index.aspx. Accessed 22 Aug 2016.

Arendt, H. 1951. *The Origins of Totalitarianism*. New York: Schocken Books.

Balz, D. 2016. Killings and Racial Tensions Commingle with Divided and Divisive Politics. *The Washington Post*. https://www.washingtonpost.com/politics/killings-and-racial-tensions-commingle-with-divided-and-divisive-politics/2016/07/08/5a422e08-451e-11e6-88d0-6adee48be8bc_story.html. Accessed 25 Aug 2016.

Barry, D., S.F. Kovaleski, A. Blinder, and M. Mashal. 2016. "Always Agitated. Always Mad": Omar Mateen, According to Those Who Knew Him. http://www.nytimes.com/2016/06/19/us/omar-mateen-gunman-orlando-shooting.html. Accessed 27 Aug 2016.

Baumeister, R.F., and D.M. Tice. 1990. Anxiety and Social Exclusion. *Journal of Social and Clinical Psychology* 9: 165–195.

Baumeister, R.F., J.M. Twenge, and C.K. Nuss. 2002. Effects of Social Exclusion on Cognitive Processes: Anticipated Aloneness Reduces Intelligent Thought. *Journal of Personality and Social Psychology* 83 (4): 817–827.

Baumeister, R.F., C.N. DeWall, N.J. Ciarocco, and J.M. Twenge. 2005. Social Exclusion Impairs Self-Regulation. *Journal of Personality and Social Psychology* 88 (4): 589–604.

Birzer, M.L., and G.H. Birzer. 2006. Race Matters: A Critical Look at Racial Profiling, It's a Matter for the Courts. *Journal of Criminal Justice* 34 (6): 643–651. https://doi.org/10.1016/j.jcrimjus.2006.09.017.

Bond, M.H. 1999. Unity in Diversity: Orientations and Strategies for Building a Harmonious Multicultural Society. In *Social Psychology and Cultural Context*, ed. John Adamopoulos and Yoshihisa Kashima, 17–39. Thousand Oaks: Sage. See also http://bahai-library.com/bond_unity_diversity_strategies

Boserup, E. 1965. *The Conditions of Agricultural Growth: The Economics of Agrarian Change Under Population Pressure*. Chicago: Aldine.

Bourdieu, P. 1996. *The State Nobility: Elite Schools in the Field of Power*. Cambridge: Polity Press.

———. 1998. *Acts of Resistance: Against the New Myths of Our Time*. Cambridge: Polity Press.

Buchanan, L., F. Fessenden, K.K R. Lai, H. Park, A. Parlapiano, A. Tse, T. Wallace, D. Watkins, and K. Yourish. 2014. What Happened in Ferguson? *New York Times*. http://www.nytimes.com/interactive/2014/08/13/us/ferguson-mis-souri-town-under-siege-after-police-shooting.html. Accessed 13 Aug 2016.

Caldero, M.A., and J.P. Crank. 2011. *Police Ethics: The Corruption of Noble Cause*. 3rd revised ed. Amsterdam/Boston: Elsevier.

Carneiro, R.L. 1970. A Theory of the Origin of the State. *Science* 169: 733–738.

———. 1988. The Circumscription Theory: Challenge and Response. *American Behavioral Scientist* 31 (4): 497–511.

———. 2012. The Circumscription Theory: A Clarification, Amplification, and Reformulation. *Social Evolution and History* 11: 5–30. www.sociostudies.org/journal/articles/148694

Clark, C. 2016. Personal Communication. August 20.

Cohen, M.N. 1977. *The Food Crisis in Prehistory: Overpopulation and the Origins of Agriculture*. New Haven: Yale University Press.

———. 2009. Introduction: Rethinking the Origins of Agriculture. *Current Anthropology* 50 (5): 591–595. https://doi.org/10.1086/603548.

Collazzoni, A., C. Capanna, M. Bustini, P. Stratta, M. Ragusa, A. Marino, and A. Rossi. 2014a. Humiliation and Interpersonal Sensitivity in Depression. *Journal of Affect Disorders* 167C: 224–227. https://doi.org/10.1016/j.jad.2014.06.008.

Collazzoni, A., C. Capanna, C. Marucci, M. Bustini, I. Riccardi, P. Stratta, and A. Rossi. 2014b. Humiliation: An Excluded Emotion. *Journal of Psychopathology* 20: 252–257.

Cox, J.A. 2016. Bilboes, Brands, and Branks: Colonial Crimes and Punishments. *Colonial Williamsburg Journal*. http://www.history.org/foundation/journal/spring03/branks.cfm. Accessed 17 Aug 2016.

Cushman, P. 1995. *Constructing the Self, Constructing America: A Cultural History of Psychotherapy*. Garden City: Da Capo Press.

Eisenberger, N.I., M.D. Lieberman, and K.D. Williams. 2003. Does Rejection Hurt? An fMRI Study of Social Exclusion. *Science* 302: 290–292.

Eisler, R.T. 1987. *The Chalice and the Blade: Our History, Our Future.* 1st ed. Cambridge, MA: Harper & Row.

Elison, J., and S. Harter. 2007. Humiliation: Causes, Correlates, and Consequences. In *The Self-Conscious Emotions: Theory and Research*, ed. J.L. Tracy, R.W. Robins, and J.P. Tangney, 310–329. New York: Guilford Press.

Elliott, J.R., and J. Pais. 2006. Race, Class, and Hurricane Katrina: Social Differences in Human Responses to Disaster. *Social Science Research* 35 (2): 295–321. https://doi.org/10.1016/j.ssresearch.2006.02.003.

EPA. 2016. *Climate Change Indicators in the United States.* Washington, DC: United States Environmental Protection Agency.

Fernandez, M., R. Pérez-Peña, and J. Engel Bromwich. 2016. Five Dallas Officers Were Killed as Payback, Police Chief Says. *New York Times.* http://www.nytimes.com/2016/07/09/us/dallas-police-shooting.html. Accessed 16 Aug 2016.

Fontan, V. 2006. Hubris, History, and Humiliation: Quest for Utopia in Post-Saddam Iraq. *Social Alternatives* 25 (1): 56–60.

Foucault, M. 1977. *Discipline and Punish. The Birth of the Prison.* Harmondsworth: Allen Lane.

———. 1991. Governmentality. In *The Foucault Effect: Studies in Governmentality*, ed. Graham Burchell, Colin Gordon, and Peter Miller, 87–104. Chicago: University of Chicago Press.

Freyd, J.J., and P. Birrell. 2013. *Blind to Betrayal: Why We Fool Ourselves We Aren't Being Fooled.* Hoboken: Wiley.

Gallaher, C. 2016. Placing the Militia Occupation of the Malheur National Wildlife Refuge in Harney County, Oregon. *ACME: An International Journal for Critical Geographies* 25 (2): 293–308.

Gaskew, T. 2014. *Rethinking Prison Reentry: Transforming Humiliation into Humility.* Lanham: Lexington Books.

GED Testing Service. 2016. History of the Test. http://www.gedtestingservice.com/testers/history

Gepts, P.L., T.R. Famula, R.L. Bettinger, S.B. Brush, A.B. Damania, P.E. McGuire, and C.O. Qualset, eds. 2012. *Biodiversity in Agriculture: Domestication, Evolution, and Sustainability.* New York: Cambridge University Press.

Gomes de Matos, F. 2012. What Is Humiliation? A Mnemonically Made Checklist. Revised 28 Jan 2016.

———. 2013. *Dignity: A Multidimensional View.* Lake Oswego: Dignity Press.

Grace, M. 1998. The Work of Caring for Young Children: Priceless or Worthless. *Women's Studies International Forum* 21 (4): 401–413.

Greenwald, A.G., and M.R. Banaji. 1995. Implicit Social Cognition: Attitudes, Self-Esteem, and Stereotypes. *Psychological Review* 102 (1): 4–27.

Griffin, J.T. 1991. Racism and Humiliation in the African-American Community. *Journal of Primary Prevention* 12 (2): 149–167.

Gunviolencearchive.org. 2016. Gun Violence Archive. http://www.gunviolencearchive.org/. Accessed 21 Aug 2016.

Hahn, R.A., J.A. Knopf, S.J. Wilson, B.I. Truman, B. Milstein, R.L. Johnson, J.E. Fielding, C.J.M. Muntaner, C.P. Jones, M.T. Fullilove, R.D. Moss, E. Ueffing, and P.C. Hunt. 2015. Programs to Increase High School Completion. *American Journal of Preventive Medicine* 48 (5): 599–608. https://doi.org/10.1016/j.amepre.2014.12.005.

Hanna-Attisha, M., J. LaChance, R.C. Sadler, and A. Champney Schnepp. 2016. Elevated Blood Lead Levels in Children Associated with the Flint Drinking Water Crisis: A Spatial Analysis of Risk and Public Health Response. *American Journal of Public Health* 106 (2): 283–290. https://doi.org/10.2105/AJPH.2015.303003.

Hardisty, J.V. 1999. *Mobilizing Resentment: Conservative Resurgence from the John Birch Society to the Promise Keepers*. Boston: Beacon Press.

Hartling, L.M. 2008. Strengthening Resilience in a Risky World: It's All About Relationships. *Women & Therapy* 31 (2–4): 51–70. https://doi.org/10.1080/02703140802145870.

Hartling, L. 2016. "Self —> Relational Being," Field Notes: Observation and Reflections in the Natural World [Workshop]. Lewis and Clark College, Portland, 23–24 Apr 2016.

Hartling, L.M., and E.G. Lindner. 2016. Healing Humiliation: From Reaction to Creative Action. *Journal of Counseling and Development* 96: 383–390. https://doi.org/10.1002/j.1556-6676.2014.00000.x.

Hartling, L.M., and T. Luchetta. 1999. Humiliation: Assessing the Impact of Derision, Degradation, and Debasement. *Journal of Primary Prevention* 19 (5): 259–278.

Herz, J.H. 1951. *Political Realism and Political Idealism: A Study in Theories and Realities*. Chicago: Chicago University Press.

———. 1957. Rise and Demise of the Territorial State. *World Politics* 9: 473–493.

Hoffman, D.H. 2015. *Report to the Special Committee of the Board of Directors of the American Psychological Association: Independent Review Relating to APA Ethics Guidelines, National Security Interrogations, and Torture*. Chicago/Washington, DC: Sidley Austin LLP. July 2.

Holbrook, C., K. Izuma, C. Deblieck, D.M.T. Fessler, and M. Iacoboni. 2015. Neuromodulation of Group Prejudice and Religious Belief. *Social Cognitive and Affective Neuroscience*. https://doi.org/10.1093/scan/nsv107. First Published Online September 4, 2015.

House, K.M. 2016. Burns Paiutes to Ammon Bundy: You're Not the Victim. *The Oregonian*. http://www.oregonlive.com/oregon-standoff/2016/02/burns_paiutes_to_ammon_bundy_y.html. Accessed 15 Aug 2016.

IDMC. 2015a. *19.3 Million Displaced by Disasters but "Mother Nature Not to Blame" Says New Report.* January 5, 2016. http://www.internal-displacement.org/assets/library/Media/201507-globalEstimates-2015/20150706-GE-2015Press-release-FINAL-v1.pdf. Accessed 20 July 2016.

———. 2015b. *Global Estimates 2015: People Displaced by Disasters.* Geneva: Internal Displacement Monitoring Centre.

———. 2015c. *Global Overview 2015: People Internally Displaced by Conflict and Violence.* Geneva: Internal Displacement Monitoring Centre Norwegian Refugee Council.

———. 2015d. *A Record 38 Million Internally Displaced Worldwide as 30,000 People Fled Their Homes Each Day in 2014.* Geneva: Internal Displacement Monitoring Centre.

IPCC (2014) *Climate Change 2014: Synthesis Report Contribution of Working Groups I, II and III to the Fifth Assessment Report of the Intergovernmental Panel on Climate Change,* Geneva, Switzerland.

IPublius Flavius Vegetius Renatus, and M.D. Reeve. 2004. *Epitoma Rei Militaris.* Oxford: Clarendon Press, written possibly in the reign of Theodosius the Great, Roman Emperor from 379–395 Common Era, first printed edition Utrecht, 1473.

Jefferson, T. 1776. The Declaration of Independence. *Lit2Go Edition.* http://etc.usf.edu/lit2go/133/historic-american-documents/4957/the-declaration-of-independence/. Accessed 21 Aug 2016.

Jemsek, G. 2011. *Quiet Horizon: Releasing Ideology and Embracing Self-Knowledge.* Bloomington: Trafford.

Jenkins, Y.M. 1993. Diversity and Social Esteem. In *Diversity in Psychotherapy: The Politics of Race, Ethnicity, and Gender,* ed. J.L. Chin, V. De La Cancela, and Y.M. Jenkins, 45–63. Westport: Praeger.

Jordan, J.V. 2010. *The Power of Connection: Recent Developments in Relational-Cultural Theory.* London/New York: Routledge.

Jordan, J.V., and L.M. Hartling. 2002. New Developments in Relational-Cultural Theory. In *Rethinking Mental Health and Disorders: Feminist Perspectives,* ed. M. Ballou and L.S. Brown, 48–70. New York: Guilford Publications.

Jordan, J.V., M. Walker, and L.M. Hartling, eds. 2004. *The Complexity of Connection: Writings from the Stone Center's Jean Baker Miller Training Institute.* New York: Guilford Press.

Kamenetz, A. 2016. Lowering the Bar for the New GED Test. http://www.npr.org/sections/ed/2016/01/27/464418078/lowering-the-bar-for-the-new-ged-test. Accessed 18 Aug 2016.

Karlberg, M.R. 2013. Reframing the Concept of Human Dignity. Paper Originally Presented at the Conference "Reflections on Human Dignity" at the University of Maryland, 19 April 2013. www.humiliationstudies.org/documents/

KarlbergReframingtheConceptofHumanDignity.pdf. See also https://youtu. be/gvCFTUTkQ58

Kasperkevic, J. 2016. Mylan Ceo Sold $5m Worth of Stock While Epipen Price Drew Scrutiny. *The Guardian*. https://www.theguardian.com/business/2016/aug/27/mylan-ceo-sold-stock-epipen-price-hike-heather-bresch. Accessed 27 Aug 2016.

Katz, J.M. 2013. *The Big Truck That Went By: How the World Came to Save Haiti and Left Behind a Disaster*. Vol. 1. Basingstoke: Palgrave Macmillan.

Kendler, K.S., J.M. Hettema, F. Butera, C.O. Gardner, and C.A. Prescott. 2003. Life Event Dimensions of Loss, Humiliation, Entrapment, and Danger in the Prediction of Onsets of Major Depression and Generalized Anxiety. *Archives of General Psychiatry* 60 (8): 789–796.

Klein, D.C. 1991. The Humiliation Dynamic: An Overview. *Journal of Primary Prevention* 12 (2): 93–121.

Kowalski, B.R., and R.J. Lundman. 2007. Vehicle Stops by Police for Driving While Black: Common Problems and Some Tentative Solutions. *Journal of Criminal Justice* 35 (2): 165–181. https://doi.org/10.1016/j.jcrimjus.2007.01.004.

Lakoff, G., and M. Johnson. 1999. *Philosophy in the Flesh: The Embodied Mind and Its Challenge to Western Thought*. New York: Basic Books.

Leadership Conference on Civil Rights. 2016. Race and the Police. In *Justice on Trial: Racial Disparities in the American Criminal Justice System*. Washington, DC: The Leadership Conference on Civil and Human Rights. http://www.civilrights.org/publications/justice-on-trial/race.html. Accessed 20 Jan 2016.

Leask, P. 2013. Losing Trust in the World: Humiliation and Its Consequences. *Psychodynamic Practice: Individuals, Groups and Organization* 19 (2): 129–142. https://doi.org/10.1080/14753634.2013.778485.

Lebech, A.M.M. 2009. *On the Problem of Human Dignity: A Hermeneutical and Phenomenological Investigation*. Würzburg: Königshausen und Neumann.

Lehr, C.A., A. Hansen, M.F. Sinclair, and S.L. Christenson. 2003. Moving Beyond Dropout Towards School Completion: An Integrative Review of Data-Based Interventions. *School Psychology Review* 32 (3): 342–364.

Lewis, H.B., ed. 1987. *The Role of Shame in Symptom Formation*. Hillsdale: Lawrence Erlbaum Associates.

Lieberman, M.D. 2015. *Social: Why Our Brains Are Wired to Connect*. Oxford: Oxford University Press.

Lindner, E.G. 2002. Healing the Cycles of Humiliation: How to Attend to the Emotional Aspects of "Unsolvable" Conflicts and the Use of "Humiliation Entrepreneurship". *Peace and Conflict: Journal of Peace Psychology* 8 (2): 125–138.

———. 2006. *Making Enemies: Humiliation and International Conflict, Contemporary Psychology*. Westport: Praeger Security International.

———. 2007a. The Concept of Human Dignity. *Human Dignity and Humiliation Studies.* http://www.humiliationstudies.org/documents/evelin/TheConceptofHumanDignityforNoelleQuenivets.pdf

———. 2007b. In Times of Globalization and Human Rights: Does Humiliation Become the Most Disruptive Force? *Journal of Human Dignity and Humiliation Studies* 1 (1). www.humilliationstudies.upeace.org

———. 2009a. *Emotion and Conflict: How Human Rights Can Dignify Emotion and Help Us Wage Good Conflict.* Westport/London: Praeger.

———. 2009b. Humiliation and Global Terrorism: How to Overcome It Nonviolently. In *Nonviolent Alternatives for Social Change*, ed. Ralph Summy, 227–248. Oxford: Nonviolent Alternatives for Social Change.

———. 2009c. Why There Can Be No Conflict Resolution as Long as People Are Being Humiliated. *International Review of Education* 55: 157–181. https://doi.org/10.1007/s11159-008-9125-9.

———. 2010. *Gender, Humiliation, and Global Security: Dignifying Relationships from Love, Sex, and Parenthood to World Affairs, Contemporary Psychology.* Santa Barbara: Praeger.

———. 2012. *A Dignity Economy: Creating an Economy That Serves Human Dignity and Preserves Our Planet.* Lake Oswego: Dignity Press.

———. 2016. The Journey of Humiliation and Dignity, and the Significance of the Year 1757. http://www.humiliationstudies.org/documents/evelin/Significanceof1757.pdf

———. 2017. *Honor, Humiliation, and Terror: An Explosive Mix—And How We Can Defuse It with Dignity.* Lake Oswego: World Dignity University Press.

MacDonald, G., and M.R. Leary. 2005. Why Does Social Exclusion Hurt? The Relationship Between Social and Physical Pain. *Psychological Bulletin* 131 (2): 202–223.

Marcotte, A. 2016. Overcompensation Nation: It's Time to Admit That Toxic Masculinity Drives Gun Violence. *Salon.* http://www.salon.com/2016/06/13/overcompensation_nation_its_time_to_admit_that_toxic_masculinity_drives_gun_violence/

Marcuse, H. 1969. *An Essay on Liberation.* Boston: Beacon Press.

Maren, M. 1997. *The Road to Hell: The Ravaging Effects of Foreign Aid and International Charity.* New York: Free Press.

Margalit, A. 1996. *The Decent Society.* Cambridge, MA: Harvard University Press.

Martin, R. 2016. GED Gets a Makeover to Keep Pace with Changing Workforce. http://www.npr.org/2014/01/05/259886038/ged-gets-a-makeover-to-keep-pace-with-changing-workforce

Mayer, J. 2008. *The Dark Side: The Inside Story of How the War on Terror Turned into a War on American Ideals.* New York: Doubleday.

Mehta, V. 2012. *The Economics of Killing: How the West Fuels War and Poverty in the Developing World.* London: Pluto Press.

Miller, J.B. 1976/1986. *Toward a New Psychology of Women.* 2nd ed. Boston: Beacon Press.

———. 1988. *Connections, Disconnections, and Violations, Work in Progress.* Wellesley: Stone Center for Developmental Services and Studies, Wellesley College.

———. 1991. The Development of Women's Sense of Self. In *Women's Growth in Connection,* ed. Alexandra G. Kaplan, Judith V. Jordan, Jean Baker Miller, Irene P. Stiver, and Janet L. Surrey. New York: Guilford Press.

Miller, W.I. 1993. *Humiliation.* Ithaca: Cornell University Press.

Miller, J.B. 2003. Growth Through Relationships. In *Perspectives in Social Psychology,* ed. R. Ortiz and I. Rodriguez, 221–231. Boston: Pearson Custom Publishing.

———. 2006. Forced Choices, False Choices. *Research & Action Report: Wellesley Centers for Women* 27 (2): 16–17.

Miller, S.M. 2012. *Dignifying Dialogue: How to Dialogue and Why.* Boston: Center for Rebuilding Sustainable Communities after Disasters, University of Massachusetts. http://youtu.be/COnuz9mubnY

———. 2015. Personal Communication. October 10.

Miller, S.M., L.M. Hartling, and P.M. Brown. 2015. Dignilogue Tips. 2015 Workshop on Transforming Humiliation and Violent Conflict, Teachers College, Columbia University, December 3–4.

Morrell, M., and S. Capparell. 2001. *Shackleton's Way: Leadership Lessons from the Great Antarctic Explorer.* New York: Viking.

Nussbaum, M.C. 2004. *Hiding from Humanity: Disgust, Shame, and the Law.* Princeton: Princeton University Press.

Nutt, A.E. 2016. Is Donald Trump a Textbook Narcissist? *Washington Post.* https://www.washingtonpost.com/news/the-fix/wp/2016/07/22/is-donald-trump-a-textbook-narcissist/. Accessed 22 Aug 2016.

Ochberg, F.M. 2005. The Ties That Bind Captive to Captor. *Los Angeles Times.* http://articles.latimes.com/2005/apr/08/opinion/oe-ochberg8. Accessed 27 Aug 2016.

OED. 2016. Self-, *Prefix.* In *Oxford English Dictionary Online.* Oxford University Press. http://www.oed.com/search?searchType=dictionary&q=Self&_searchBtn=Search

Olsson, P.A. 2005. *Malignant Pied Pipers of Our Time: A Psychological Study of Destructive Cult Leaders from Rev. Jim Jones to Osama Bin Laden.* Baltimore: Publish America.

Otten, M., and K.J. Jonas. 2014. Humiliation as an Intense Emotional Experience: Evidence from the Electro-Encephalogram. *Social Neuroscience* 9 (1): 23–35. https://doi.org/10.1080/17470919.2013.855660.

Parker-Pope, T., and R.R. Peachman. 2016. Epipen Price Rise Sparks Concern for Allergy Sufferers. *New York Times.* http://well.blogs.nytimes.com/2016/

08/22/epipen-price-rise-sparks-concern-for-allergy-sufferers/?action=click&c ontentCollection=BusinessDay&module=RelatedCoverage&region=EndOfAr ticle&pgtype=article. Accessed 27 Aug 2016.

Pollack, A., and J. Creswell 2015. Martin Shkreli, the Mercurial Man Behind the Drug Price Increase That Went Viral. http://www.nytimes.com/2015/09/23/ business/big-price-increase-for-an-old-drug-will-be-rolled-back-turing-chief-says.html. Accessed 27 Aug 2016.

Pope, K.S. 2016. The Code Not Taken: The Path from Guild Ethics to Torture and Our Continuing Choices. *Canadian Psychology/Psychologie Canadienne* 57 (1): 51–59. https://doi.org/10.1037/cap0000043.

Putnam, R.D. 2007. *E Pluribus Unum*: Diversity and Community in the Twenty-First Century. *Scandinavian Political Studies* 30 (2): 137–174.

Risen, J. 2014. *Pay Any Price: Greed, Power, and Endless War*. Boston: Mariner Books.

———. 2015a. Psychologists Shielded U.S. Torture Program, Report Finds. *New York Times*. http://www.nytimes.com/2015/07/11/us/psychologists-shielded-us-torture-program-report-finds.html?hp&action=click&pgtype=Ho mepage&module=first-column-region&region=top-news&WT.nav=top-news&_r=0. Accessed 15 Aug 2016.

———. 2015b. Report Says American Psychological Association Collaborated on Torture Justification. *New York Times*. http://www.nytimes. com/2015/05/01/us/report-says-american-psychological-association-col-laborated-on-torture-justification.html?hp&action=click&pgtype=Homepage &module=first-column-region&region=top-news&WT.nav=top-news&_r=1. Accessed 15 Aug 2016.

Sassen, S. 2014. *Expulsions: Brutality and Complexity in the Global Economy*. Cambridge, MA: Belknap Press.

Scheler, M. 1913/1923/1954. *The Nature of Sympathy*. London: Routledge and Kegan Paul. German original *Wesen und Formen der Sympathie*. Bonn, Germany: F. Cohen, 1923, neu aufgelegt von *Zur Phänomenologie und Theorie der Sympathiegefühle und von Liebe und Hass*. Halle, Saale: Max Niemeyer, 1913, www.sdvigpress.org/dox/101173/101173.pdf

Silver, H., S.M. Miller, and C. Hartman. 2006. From Poverty to Social Exclusion: Lessons from Europe. In *Poverty and Race in America: The Emerging Agendas*, 57–70. Lexington: Lexington Books.

Soldz, S., and S. Reisner. 2015. Opening Comments to the American Psychological Association (APA) Board of Directors. *Counterpunch*. http://www.counter-punch.org/2015/07/13/opening-comments-to-the-american-psychological-association-apa-board-of-directors/. Accessed 15 Aug 2016.

Spencer, K.B., A.K. Charbonneau, and J. Glaser. 2016. Implicit Bias and Policing. *Social and Personality Psychology Compass* 10 (1): 50–63. https://doi.org/10.1111/spc3.12210.

Stolorow, R.D. 2010. The Shame Family: An Outline of the Phenomenology of Patterns of Emotional Experience That Have Shame at Their Core. *International Journal of Psychoanalytic Self Psychology* 5 (3): 367–368. https://doi.org/10.1 080/15551024.2010.485347.

Strauss, V. 2016. The Big Problems with Pearson's New GED High School Equivalency Test. *Washington Post.* https://www.washingtonpost.com/news/answer-sheet/wp/2015/07/09/the-big-problems-with-pearsons-new-ged-high-school-equivalency-test/. Accessed 15 Aug 2016.

Sullivan, K., and W. Wan. 2016. Troubled. Quiet. Macho. Angry. The Volatile Life of the Orlando Shooter. *Washington Post.* https://www.washingtonpost.com/national/troubled-quiet-macho-angry-the-volatile-life-of-omar-mateen/2016/06/17/15229250-34a6-11e6-8758-d58e76e11b12_story.html. Accessed 10 Aug 2016.

Surowiecki, J. 2004. *The Wisdom of Crowds: Why the Many Are Smarter Than the Few and How Collective Wisdom Shapes Business, Economies, Societies, and Nations.* New York: Doubleday.

Taylor, C. 1989. *Sources of the Self: The Making of the Modern Identity.* Cambridge: Cambridge University Press.

———. 1992. *The Ethics of Authenticity.* Cambridge, MA: Harvard University Press, originally published in Canada in 1991 under the title *The Malaise of Modernity,* an extended version of the 1991 Massey Lectures.

Taylor, C., and A. Gutman. 1994. The Politics of Recognition. In *Multiculturalism: Examining the Politics of Recognition.* Princeton: Princeton University Press.

Terry, K.J. 2008. Stained Glass: The Nature and Scope of Child Sexual Abuse in the Catholic Church. *Criminal Justice and Behavior* 35 (5): 549–569. https://doi.org/10.1177/0093854808314339.

Turner, C., and A. Kamenetz. 2016. A "Sizable Decrease" in Those Passing the GED. http://www.npr.org/sections/ed/2015/01/09/375440666/a-sizable-decrease-in-those-passing-the-ged. Accessed 13 Aug 2016.

Twenge, J.M., and W.K. Campbell. 2009. *The Narcissism Epidemic: Living in the Age of Entitlement.* New York: Free Press.

Twenge, J.M., K.R. Catanese, and R.F. Baumeister. 2002. Social Exclusion Causes Self-Defeating Behavior. *Journal of Personality and Social Psychology* 83 (3): 606–615.

UN. 2007. *1948 Universal Declaration of Human Rights.* New York: United Nations Department of Public Information.

UN General Assembly. 1948. Convention on the Prevention and Punishment of the Crime of Genocide. *United Nations, Treaty Series* 78: 277, December 9. http://www.refworld.org/docid/3ae6b3ac0.html. Accessed 27 Oct 2016.

———. 1965. International Convention on the Elimination of All Forms of Racial Discrimination. *United Nations, Treaty Series* 660: 195, December 21. http://www.refworld.org/docid/3ae6b3940.html. Accessed 27 Oct 2016.

————. 1979. Convention on the Elimination of All Forms of Discrimination Against Women. *United Nations, Treaty Series* 1249: 13, December 18. http://www.refworld.org/docid/3ae6b3970.html. Accessed 27 Oct 2016.

————. 1989. Convention on the Rights of the Child. *United Nations, Treaty Series* 1577: 3, November 20. http://www.refworld.org/docid/3ae6b38f0.html. Accessed 27 Oct 2016.

UNHCR. 2015. *Worldwide Displacement Hits All-Time High as War and Persecution Increase.* Geneva: United Nations High Commissioner for Refugees.

Ury, W. 1999. *Getting to Peace: Transforming Conflict at Home, at Work, and in the World.* New York: Viking.

Wilkinson, R.G., and K. Pickett. 2009. *The Spirit Level: Why Greater Equality Makes Societies Stronger.* New York: Bloomsbury Press.

Wyatt-Brown, B. 2006. Honour, Irony, and Humiliation in the Era of the American Civil War. *Social Alternatives* 25 (1): 22–27.

Zaitz, L. 2016. Militia Takes Over Malheur National Wildlife Refuge Headquarters. *The Oregonian.* http://www.oregonlive.com/pacific-northwest-news/index.ssf/2016/01/drama_in_burns_ends_with_quiet.html. Accessed 15 Aug 2016.

CHAPTER 3

Insults as Tools of Systemic Humiliation

Karina V. Korostelina

One common way of humiliating someone is through insults. Defined as a "behavior or discourse, oral or written, which is perceived, experienced, constructed and, at times, intended as slighting, humiliating or offensive" (Gabriel 1998, 1331), insults are perceived by the targets as both intentional and illegitimate (Felson 1982). Produced on all levels of society, they have the potential to challenge social relations, incite violence, and contribute to the deepest patterns of humiliation. Based on the analysis of three cases of interactions between racial groups, between a community and police, and between two political parties, this chapter shows how insults function socially as a powerful form of three types of humiliation—hierarchical, reverse, and reciprocal.

All insults are created and sustained through social interaction (Kashima et al. 2008). Commonly understood as a dialogic process (Maitra and McGowan 2012; Gabriel 1998; Eribon 2004), insults embroil both a recipient and insulting party and depend on the particular culture or society (Neu 2008). Many social insults are written into the fabric of our institutions and practices, thus contributing to the production and reproduction of humiliation. They also help produce or maintain power relations that promote one group over another, thus defining people's

K. V. Korostelina (✉)
School for Conflict Analysis and Resolution, George Mason University,
Arlington, VA, USA

© The Author(s) 2018
D. Rothbart (ed.), *Systemic Humiliation in America*,
https://doi.org/10.1007/978-3-319-70679-5_3

53

responses to shame, the development of stigma, and victimization in general (Gabriel 1998). As Linda M. Hartling and Evelin Lindner show in Chap. 2 "Can Systemic Humiliation Be Transformed into Systemic Dignity?" of this volume, permanent inequality creates superordinate groups as a result of the systemic humiliation toward subordinate groups. Through the use of insult, a dominant group can stigmatize a minority group (Eribon 2004) in the emphasis on cultural and historical differences (Enaharo 2003). A history of racism affects interpretations of insult and production of hate speech to minorities that could be accepted by the majority (Matsuda 1993). While society builds institutions and practices to protect from certain insults, these attempts, in an almost paradoxical way, contribute to the harmful impact of the prohibited words (Jones 2003; Maitra and McGowan 2012).

Rituals of shame and humiliation can be encoded into social encounters. Humiliation, as "the enforced lowering of a person or group, a process of subjugation that damages or strips away their pride, honor or dignity" (Lindner 2001), aims to make the insulted person or group feel inferior. Insults can also create social boundaries between people and redefinition of legitimacy. Based on culturally specific codes of honor, reactions to insults are as much about our care for the presentation of self as they are about the "right" interaction with the other (Miller 1995). Insults generate emotionally intense reactions in ways that are similar to humiliation, shame, guilt, and anger (Gabriel 1998).

Thus, insults contribute to the development and reformulation of self-image and identity of all parties, especially the insulted person or group. Humiliation and insult create an unfavorable situational identity by making a person or a group appear weak, incompetent, and cowardly (Weinstein and Deutschberger 1963). Other identity traits of degradation are ugly, ignorant, boorish, boring, dirty, to name a few.[1] Being insulted can lead to the imputed negative identity or, alternatively, to reprisal or retaliation in an attempt to dismiss this unfavorable self-image (Felson 1978).

This chapter concentrates on intergroup insult between social groups. It targets a social group as a whole entity, and the majority of members of these groups recognize and acknowledge its effects. The analysis below focuses on how insults between racial and political groups in the United States change the dynamics of intergroup relations and serve to intensify old tensions or to generate new conflicts. As this chapter shows, one intergroup insult can produce another, spiraling into destructive series of humiliations and potentially causing aggressive reactions.

TYPES OF INSULT

Depending on the nature of conflict, parties deploy insults for various purposes that go to core issues of conflict. People use insults because they want to strip the other party of positive identity, increase or emphasize differences between parties, blame others to justify their actions, deny rights of the other party to show their privileged or superior position, strengthen their power over others, or legitimize themselves and devalidate others. Based on theories of social identity and power, the author identifies six specific forms of intergroup insult (Korostelina 2014).

Identity Insult

People strive for positive identity. People have a need to feel good about themselves, in relation to other groups, often attributing to them negative characteristics and faults. This process called favorable comparison is motivated by the desire to increase self-esteem (Tajfel and Turner 1986). People with salient social identity tend to use comparison with other groups and emphasize differences between their group members and members of other groups (Turner et al. 1987, 50). Insults can be a very effective tool in increasing self-esteem through favorable comparison. Among the several categories of insults, the offence that puts us in a better light in comparison to others is called *identity insult*, which is deployed to attribute negative features, dishonest motivations, and warped values to others, leading to denigrations of their actions. Identity insults usually involve a comparison with the insulted party and a description of that party as having negative features or intentions.

Projection Insult

To maintain their self-confidence and self-respect, people often justify their behavior by projecting negative intentions on others (Volkan 1997). By stressing that other peoples' behavior provokes one's own actions, the insulting person seeks to preserve their positive self-image, as if to declare: "We committed violent acts not because we are aggressive, but because they threatened us and we had to defend ourselves." Similarly, if people become aware of their own negative behavior, they experience a discord between the positive views they hold of themselves and a negative assessment of their actions. With this discomfort, which is known as cognitive dissonance (Festinger 1957), people see a conflict between their expectations regarding how they should behave and their actual behavior. To reduce this cognitive dissonance, people prefer to maintain their positive self-image and consistent beliefs and thus usually change their assessment of the situation and blame others: "I was late not because I am not well organized, but because traffic was unpredictable." This validation process of negative behavior can be supported by *projection insults*. Insulters use *projection insults* to justify particular actions or deny their own negative features by attributing them to others or to a situation created by others. It is usually used when people face some consequences of their bad behavior and blame others for provoking it.

Divergence Insult

Social boundaries involve constructs of similarities and differences between people and, consequently, define the relationship between "them" and "us" (Barth 1981). Building and changing social relationships always involves changes to social boundaries, making them more permeable or impervious. To define whether a social boundary will be more or less inclusive, people stress the resemblances and disparities between them (Horowitz 1975). People and groups recognize clear boundaries in relation to the outgroup and often reject attempts to weaken such boundaries (Cohen 1985, 1986). If boundaries between groups are permeable, members of low-status groups are more likely to move across those boundaries with the view to try to create contact with a high-status group. Conversely, members of high-status groups strengthen their identification with their group and protect its existing boundaries (Ellemers et al. 1997). High-status groups will often create different policies and actions that close boundaries and prevent associations with groups of lower status (Hutnik 1991). Thus, people usually create social boundaries to help defend their own group from the perceived threat of outsiders, and, in doing so, further define reasons for exclusion (Tilly 2005). *Divergence insult* can help enhance differences and social boundaries between sides and highlight distance between them.

Relative Insult

Relative deprivation—the perception of being disadvantaged—often comes from comparisons with others (Davis 1959; Gurr 1993; Runciman 1966).

In many cases, people compare themselves with other people or social groups. This appraisal leads them to believe that people or members of other groups have more advantages in terms of societal positions, power, or resources. These perceptions of relative deprivation, whether real or imagined, lead to feelings of being victims of injustice, being disadvantaged and underprivileged. To reduce this feeling of deprivation and deficiency, some people tend to think of themselves as superior to others by using *relative* insults, which are frequently used when to restore a perceived imbalance relating to resources or social positions, or challenging a situation that is believed to be unjust. People deny certain rights of others and emphasize their own privileged position through inclusive rights to control, to make decisions, and to perform actions and define the connotations of events and situations.

Power Insult

With respect to these kinds of insult presented above, people seek to enhance their power over others. Power relations underlie all communications among people, thus shaping the ways in which we see others and ourselves. In every interaction, people behave according to established power balance with one of the persons having more power or an equal power position. The classic definition of "power" is the ability of a person or a group to influence the behavior of others or their ability to achieve objectives and goals (Cartwright 1959; Deutsch and Gerard 1955; Festinger 1954). A group or a person in power can create a situation that precludes other people from satisfying their needs or achieving their goals. Power also involves dependence and coercion against people's will, changing their will and beliefs through norms and social consensus (Moscovici 1976). Thus, people in power can create conditions in which the inferior people will feel inadequate to deal with a current situation to satisfy their needs. *Power insults* occur through attempts to redefine the power dynamics in social relationships, occurring typically in situations of competition over real or perceived power.

Legitimacy Insult

In comparison with coercive power, legitimacy of power rests on internalized acceptance that a person has legitimate rights to influence people, who in turn are then obligated presumably to comply. Such power becomes a product of dominant ideology, embedment of social norms and beliefs in the social order, and consensus about the social goals (Kelman 2001). People interpret and evaluate the use of power through the lens of their salient group membership: members of ingroup are considered of greater normative value than outgroup members (Turner 2005). To preserve their legitimacy of power, its agents need to employ constant process of legitimization of themselves and delegitimization of others. *Legitimacy insults* initiate and promote a process that legitimizes insulters and delegitimizes the other side. Thus, *legitimacy insults* help a person or a group to diminish the legality and rightfulness of the other side and increase his own or his group validity. Sometimes, both sides of a conflict can use the same dimension to portray other as illicit and illegitimate.

The following cases describe how different insults are used on an intergroup level to humiliate the outgroup.

DESEGREGATION PROCESS IN LITTLE ROCK, ARKANSAS

In the 1954 case *Brown v. Board of Education*, the Supreme Court ruled that school segregation was unconstitutional, signifying the breakdown of race-based *de jure* segregation. Later, in a 1955 decision to the Brown case (*Brown v. Board of Education II*), the Court directed all federal district courts to monitor compliance with the decision to integrate schools. Pursuant to Federal mandate, the school board in Arkansas developed a court-approved plan to integrate the schools. However, the governor was deeply opposed to integration and with the help of the State Legislature passed a new state law and state constitutional amendments forbidding integration. Nevertheless, nine black students enrolled in Central High School in the fall of 1957. The power struggle that ensued between segregationists and integrationists, the state and federal governments, and the governor of Arkansas and the president of the United States became known as the "Little Rock Crisis."

The city of Little Rock experienced a deep divide within the white population. The white elite, business, and civic leaders possessed unilateral power over the community, while these poor white people did not have access to instruments of governance and decision-making. Working-class whites typically held industrial, sales, and service jobs or owned small businesses. The elite business leaders maintained a monopoly of power to determine the public's best interests without being challenged by other groups (Anderson 2004). Despite their opposition to desegregation efforts, the elites offered "token" gestures toward the integration of schools. Knowing that many elites and working-class whites viewed desegregation as a threat to their social standing, the elites decided to put the pressure of desegregation strictly on the working class. This scheme helped them preserve their social status and way of life while creating an image of societal harmony in the city that would be now regarded as desegregated.

In compliance with the *Brown* decision, the superintendent of Little Rock Schools, Virgil T. Blossom, created a plan of gradual desegregation. This plan outlined the integration process of Little Rock Schools, which started with the high schools and would then trickle down to elementary schools. Those elites, who controlled the school board by assisting in the recruitment of candidates and financially supporting their campaigns, aimed to "protect" the rich white communities from perceived threats associated with desegregation. Thus, they lobbied the school board to select Central High School, located in the working-class white community, as a first test case in this desegregation effort. This plan created a boundary within the white population, cushioning the elite whites from the effects of integration while exposing the working-class whites to the problems associated with the process (Murphy 1997). The Blossom Plan deepened class divisions between whites. In order to protect their own group's self-esteem and supremacy in the social order, the elite whites distanced themselves from working-class whites and put them down, which was perceived as both divergence and identity insult by the working people.

Many working-class whites also supported segregation, linking their self-esteem to white privilege as part of the southern way of life. Even if they were in a disadvantaged position in comparison with the white elite, working-class whites still saw themselves as privileged and superior to African Americans (Kirk 2002). The desegregation plan created a boundary between whites, promoting the change in social standing for working-class whites on par with African Americans. This represented a case of divergence insult. Working-class whites felt threatened and deeply offended by their diminished social standing and consequently sought to preserve their prevailing social position over African Americans. As a response, the working-class whites used various tactics to preserve their higher status and elevate sense of moral worth. They generated a strong state and local political base, had support of the governor of Arkansas, and used many projection insults with strong negative characterizations as well as violence toward African Americans.

On September 4, 1957, the Arkansas governor gave an order to prevent the nine African American students from enrolling at Central High School. Despite the threat of violence, a local federal court ordered the school board to carry out the plan. The next day, the US government challenged Governor Faubus's order in the local federal court and President Dwight Eisenhower sent in National Guard troops to protect the nine students from mobs. Faubus first agreed to use the National Guard to shield the African American students, but on returning to Little Rock, he discharged the troops, leaving the nine teenagers unprotected from an angry white mob. Within hours, the out-of-control mob had beaten several reporters and thrown bricks at the school, smashing windows and damaging doors. By noon, local police were forced to evacuate the African American students. Only by the end of September were they finally able to return to school and attend classes safely. These actions of white working people created strong divergence insult for African American community as they show strong resistance to desegregation and unwillingness to see African Americans as equal citizens.

Although the elites privately supported arguments made by segregationists, publicly they maintained a moderate stance in local and statewide politics. Elites used projection insults to blame working-class whites for violence, negatively characterizing them as "extremist, rural, lunatic fringe, low-breeding and rednecks." Thus, the white elite created a favorable comparison, presenting themselves as supporters of desegregation and blaming working-class whites for social discord and intolerance. Therefore, the white elite created both projection and identity insults for working-class whites. First, the promotion of desegregation policies only in poor white areas stripped working-class whites of their positive identity that was based on a privileged position in comparison with African Americans. Second, the accusation of working-class whites as violent created for them a negative identity of intolerant and cruel people in comparison with the white elite. Finally, the aggressive actions of white working-class people that emphasized differences between them and African Americans and showed refusal to change racial boundaries created multiple divergence insults and systemic humiliation of African American communities.

Shooting of Michael Brown

Eighteen-year-old Michael Brown Jr. was shot in August 2014 by Darren Wilson, a white Ferguson police officer. The parents of Brown, Lesley McSpadden and Michael Brown Sr., started a campaign to bring Wilson to justice for killing their son allegedly in cold blood. They held several press conferences demanding that a grand jury should indict Wilson immediately. Reverend Al Sharpton said at one of the news conferences: "Whether they wear blue jeans or blue uniforms, criminals must be held accountable" (Rhodan 2014). Lending support to their position, Urban League President Marc Morial connected the history of lynching to the shooting of Michael Brown: "A hundred years ago, this country had a pandemic of lynching. This pandemic, to this day, is what that pandemic was to that day—the use of official power and excessive force to take the lives of innocent people" (Coleman and Toppo 2014). Furthermore, the Brown family lawyer, Benjamin Crump, described this case in the context of race discrimination by the police in United States today, where African American communities are "in the midst of a pandemic of police misconduct" (Coleman and Toppo 2014). While awaiting the decision of the grand jury, Brown's parents declared: "We are praying for an indictment. To me that would mean that (the police) did do their investigation fairly and it was unbiased" (Bacon and Alcindor 2014).

Brown's parents and friends portrayed him as an innocent boy with no criminal record as an adult, pending charges, or serious felony convictions as a juvenile. Brown had just graduated from an alternative education program and was to start attending Vatterott College, a technical school to become a heating and cooling engineer. Beliefs in Brown's innocence sparked heated protests in Ferguson, where peaceful protests were mixed with looting and violence on the streets.

Fueling the protests, witnesses to the shooting claimed that Wilson ordered Michael Brown and his friend, Dorian Johnson, to move off the street and onto the sidewalk. Johnson stated on CNN and other news outlets that the officer told them to either "Get the f*** on the sidewalk" or "Get the f*** out of the street." The officer's car almost hit Johnson and Brown: "We were so close, almost inches away, that when he tried to open his door aggressively, the door ricocheted off both me and Big Mike's body and closed back on the officer" (Clarke and Lett 2014). According to Johnson's statement, the officer grabbed Brown by his neck. Brown was trying to pull away but the officer continued to pull him to the car. Wilson shot Brown while he was still in the car, wounding him, and the two boys began to flee. Wilson pursued them, leaving his vehicle and firing at least six shots, fatally wounding Brown. Johnson described:

> I saw the officer proceeding after my friend Big Mike with his gun drawn, and he fired a second shot and that struck my friend Big Mike. And at that time, he turned around with his hands up, beginning to tell the officer that he was unarmed and to tell him to stop shooting. But at that time, the officer fired several more shots into my friend, and he hit the ground and died.

Piaget Crenshaw, another witness, said that Brown "was running for his life and just got shot and turned around and didn't try to reach for anything. He put his hands in the air being compliant and he still got shot down like a dog" (Clarke and Lett 2014).

The case has received nationwide attention. Senator Rand Paul of Kentucky took a stand blaming police for race-based prejudice and violence. He said that "the shooting of 18-year-old Michael Brown is an awful tragedy" and that "anyone who thinks race does not skew the application of criminal justice in this country is just not paying close enough attention" (Suderman 2014). Lacy Clay, the US congressman who represents Ferguson, also stated that he had "absolutely no confidence in the Ferguson police, the county prosecutor. We know we won't get a fair shake there" (Reilly 2014). Days later, he called for "a national conversation about how police forces should interact with the African-American community."[2]

Brown's parents and supporters conveyed to the public their sadness over the loss of a loved one. In explaining Brown's death as a result of blatant racist attitudes of police officers, they exhibited relative insult toward the police. The connection with the history of segregation and lynching created the generalization of insult: the actions of white policemen were viewed as racial violence based on their similarity to previous racial violence in the United States. The connection with other cases of racist conduct by police helped create a conglomeration of insults: the more often an action was repeated, the more it was perceived as offensive and abusive. This framework created identity insult, portraying Officer Wilson as evil and aggressive with blatant racist attitudes. On the other side, the absence of apology and acknowledgment of excessive action by the officer created projection insults for Brown's family. They felt that their son had been unfairly portrayed by the officer and the investigation overall demonized his character.

The official investigation revealed that just before the accident, Brown and Johnson were involved in a robbery at the Ferguson Market and Liquor. The surveillance video captured Michael Brown pushing a clerk before walking out of the store with a pack of Swisher Sweets, cheap cigars that are commonly used to roll blunts. Later, Johnson's attorney, Freeman Bosley, stated: "This is not a theft, it's more of a shoplifting situation." When Wilson saw Brown and Johnson "walking down the middle of the street, blocking traffic," he approached them and asked to get out of the street (Clarke and Lett 2014). Wilson tried to exit his vehicle but Brown pushed him back into the car, which led to a physical confrontation and struggle over the officer's gun. A shot was fired inside the police car. As the investigation found, the wound in Brown's hand was from close range and Brown's blood was found on Wilson's uniform could be consistent with a struggle in the police car. Brown's blood was also found on the gun and spattered on an inside door panel of the car, which confirms that he could have been reaching for a gun (Altman 2014). Wilson told investigators that he felt threatened by Brown fighting inside a police car. When Brown had pushed him back into his car, hit him, and grabbed at his drawn gun, Wilson felt "like a five-year-old holding on to [US wrestler] Hulk Hogan". He also said that after Brown fled the vehicle, "he turned around in a threatening manner, prompting Wilson to fire the fatal shots". Shawn Parcells, who assisted Dr. Baden in the autopsy, stated that the investigation revealed that at least some shots were fired "at a short range" (Halligan 2013). The toxicology report showing the presence of marijuana in Brown's system indicated that he could have been under the influence of drugs: "the levels in Brown's body may have been high enough to trigger hallucinations" (Altman 2014). After long deliberation, the grand jury decided that Wilson would not be charged with the killing of Brown.

However, Brown's parents claimed that they were completely offended by the decision of the grand jury and the portrayal of their son. Brown's father said that his son's character had been "crucified," and his mother said that Wilson had been "disrespectful". For them, when Wilson said he had a "clean conscience" and, in his statement, added, "I know I did my job right", his words sounded as legitimacy insults. Brown's parents and supporters did not trust the investigation and did not believe official descriptions of the events of that night. As Brown's mother stated: "I don't believe a word of it. I know my son far too well... Our son doesn't have a history of violence."

The case of Michael Brown's killing exposed long-standing structural problems and humiliation processes that have a long history in the United States. The memory of segregation and traumas of lynching create a background for the perception of the current events and actions. These perceptions are reinforced when discrimination and prejudice guide behavior of some policemen and officials. The feelings of relative deprivation and humiliation among African Americans created a foundation for insults and delegitimization of police actions and investigations. The mistrust between African American communities and police has led to multiple insults.

RESISTANCE TO NUCLEAR DEAL

The fractious debate over a nuclear deal with Iran in 2014 involves numerous power and legitimacy insults. While Obama's administration argued that the pact would be the best way to keep Iran from obtaining a nuclear bomb, the critics portrayed a deal as a dangerous act that would allow Iran to eventually build weapons that could be used against Israel or other countries.

In the midst of negotiation with Iran, the Republican House speaker, John A. Boehner, invited Prime Minister Benjamin Netanyahu of Israel to speak to a joint meeting of Congress about the danger of the developing deal. Omitting usual diplomatic protocol, Netanyahu did not meet with Mr. Obama. These actions were created to emphasize the power of the Senate Republicans and diminish the power of the office of president and were perceived by President Obama and his administration as a power insult.

After a week, 47 Republican senators signed a letter warning the Iranian political leadership about making an agreement with President Obama. Mr. Cotton who drafted the letter stressed that he and other congressmen were outraged that the president completely omitted the Congress in the process of negotiation. He stated: "The only thing unprecedented is an American president negotiating a nuclear deal with the world's leading state sponsor of terrorism without submitting it to Congress" (Baker 2015). The letter declared that any agreement without legislative approval could be reversed by the next president: "The next president could revoke such an executive agreement with the stroke of a pen, and future Congresses could modify the terms of the agreement at any time" (Baker 2015). This letter aimed at reducing the legitimacy of Secretary of State John Kerry's office that announced the expecting completing of the agreement before an end-of-March deadline. The White House and congressional Democrats perceived the letter as insulting, calling it an unprecedented violation of the tradition of leaving politics at the water's edge.

Discrediting the power of Republican Congressmen, President Obama stated: "It's somewhat ironic to see some members of Congress wanting to make common cause with the hard-liners in Iran. It's an unusual coalition" (Baker 2015). Vice President Joe Biden acknowledged the power insult by stressing that the letter was designed to weaken the president in the process of important negotiations: "The decision to undercut our President and circumvent our constitutional system offends me as a matter of principle." The vice president responded with another power insult, in which he diminished the capacity of Congress to impact the decision. He said:

> As a matter of policy, the letter and its authors have also offered no viable alternative to the diplomatic resolution with Iran that their letter seeks to undermine...In thirty-six years in the United States Senate, I cannot recall another instance in which Senators wrote directly to advise another country—much less a longtime foreign adversary—that the President does not have the constitutional authority to reach a meaningful understanding with them (Karl and Parkinson 2015).

Josh Earnest, the White House press secretary, called it "just the latest in an ongoing strategy, a partisan strategy, to undermine the President's ability to conduct foreign policy." Other Democrats emphasized that the letter illustrated attempts by Republicans to gain control over the outcomes of negotiation.

Democratic leader Harry Reid condemned the letter from the Senate floor, calling it Republican "gimmicks" on Iran (Everett 2015). He added that the "Republicans are undermining our commander in chief while empowering the ayatollahs. This letter represents a symbolic slap in the face of not only the United States, but our allies. This is not a time to undermine our commander in chief purely out of spite" (Baker 2015). Kerry also dismissed the letter, stating that it is "incorrect when it says that Congress could modify the terms of an agreement" (Diamond 2015). Hillary Clinton joined the attacks on Republicans who had signed the letter, discrediting their actions: "Either these senators were trying to be helpful to the Iranians or harmful to the commander in chief in the midst of high-stakes international diplomacy. Either answer does discredit to the letter's signatories" (Gaffe and Eilperin 2015). Thus, Democrats were denying the power of Republican Congressmen and diminishing their ability to influence the process of negotiation. Newspaper editorials were also critical of the letter, including one from the *Pittsburgh Post-Gazette*, which wrote that Senator Pat Toomey (R-Pa.) and his colleagues should be "ashamed" for signing the letter (Everett 2015).

In response, Republican leaders rejected the Democrats' criticism, portraying them as irresponsible and powerless. Senator Jim Risch stated: "This indignation and breast-beating over this letter is absolute nonsense" (Diamond 2015). Senator Tom Cotton confirmed his resolve and explained that Republicans wrote the letter "to make sure" that leaders in Iran realize a constitutional role of Congress in approving any potential agreement. He created a new power insult by reducing the power of the president and emphasizing his inability to secure the approval of the deal. Cotton declared: "It's the job of the President to negotiate but it's the job of Congress to approve. We're simply trying to say that Congress has a constitutional role to approve any deal, to make sure that Iran never gets a nuclear weapon. Not today, not tomorrow, not ten years from now" (Karl and Parkinson 2015). Toomey emphasized that Republicans are the only ones who are concerned with Iranian nuclear problem. He said, "That letter is just the most recent case of my doing all that I can to prevent Iran from having a nuclear bomb" (Everett 2015). National Republican Senatorial Committee Chairman Roger Wicker of Mississippi also dismissed the importance of Democratic attacks on the letter, describing them as "wailing and gnashing of teeth" (Everett 2015).

The reaction of Iran also included a legitimacy insult. Mohammad Javad Zarif, Iran's Foreign Minister, completely diminished the importance of the letter: "In our view, this letter has no legal value and is mostly a propaganda ploy" (Baker 2015). Ayatollah Ali Khamenei, Iran's supreme leader, emphasized that the letter is a sign of "disintegration" in Washington. He created a strong projection insult, describing America as deceiving and cunning. "Of course I am worried, because the other side is known for opacity, deceit and backstabbing...Every time we reach a stage where the end of the negotiations is in sight, the tone of the other side, specifically the Americans, becomes harsher, coarser and tougher. This is the nature of their tricks and deceptions" (Stanglin 2015).

The foreign leaders also criticized the letter. Germany's Foreign Minister Steinmeier described the letter as "not very helpful" as negotiations with Iran enter a "delicate phase." Later, at the meeting with meeting with U.S. Secretary of State John Kerry, Steinmeier said that calling the senators' March 9 letter unhelpful was "an understatement" (Stanglin 2015). The British foreign secretary Philip Hammond speaking to members of Parliament emphasized that the Republican letter could throw "a spanner in the works" at the negotiations and will have an "unpredictable effect" on the government in Tehran (Stanglin 2015).

The exchange of insults continued after the deal was signed. The White House was instrumental in securing the vote that supported the agreement. Democrats saved the deal and blocked all Republican Party's attempts of obstruction. The president declared it as a significant win: "This vote is a victory for diplomacy, for American national security, and for the safety and security of the world. I am heartened that so many senators judged this deal on the merits, and am gratified by the strong support of lawmakers and citizens alike" (Bouie 2015).

The Republican leaders reacted with fury. The presidential candidate and New Jersey Governor Chris Christie told Fox News: "I believe that the American people are going to look back on this and say this was the single worst thing this president's ever done. Every death that Iran causes is now on Barack Obama's head" (Mathes and Clark 2015). Senator Mitch McConnell, Republican of Kentucky and the majority leader, reinforced this power insult, stressing that

> Mr. Obama is likely to go down in history as a rare president whose single biggest foreign policy and domestic achievements were won with no Republican votes, a stark departure from his 2008 campaign that was fueled by the promise of bridging Washington's yawning partisan divide (Steinhauer 2015).

Both Republicans emphasized President's Obama's misuse of power and coercion of Republicans. House Speaker John Boehner was also extremely critical of the deal, declaring that:

> This deal is far worse than anything I could have imagined.... This is such a bad deal the Ayatollah won't even have to cheat to be steps away from a nuclear weapon...Never in our history has something with so many consequences for our national security been rammed through with such little

support…The regime may have bamboozled this administration, but the American people know that this is a rotten deal.

The White House responded with another power insult, stressing that Republicans lack the power and ability to veto the Iranian deal. White House spokesman Josh Earnest said, "[T]his obviously is not the first time we've seen Republicans who are unsuccessful in trying to prevent the President from doing something using their official duties as a member of Congress resort in desperation to a piece of litigation" (Duran 2015). House Minority Leader Nancy Pelosi went even further, calling the Republican strategy "cute": "You know what? That's cute. That's cuuute, as we say in Texas" (Schulberg and Bendery 2015).

In this exchange of power insults, both Republicans and Democrats were diminishing the power of each other, describing it as weak, corrupt, coercive, and exclusive. Both sides were emphasizing that other party does not have enough power to change the situation or overuse power for the wrong causes. They also exhibited the higher power of their own party. These three strategies of power insult helped both political parties to increase their feeling of power in situation of uncertainty or to cope with inability to change the situation. In addition, both parties used legitimacy insults to portray another party as invalid and unable to preserve the interests of the country. These power and legitimacy insults promoted humiliation of politicians from the oppositional party, portraying them as irresponsible, corrupt, and unfitting the office.

DISCUSSION

These three cases illustrate how insults were used as powerful tools of humiliation. The first case—desegregation in Little Rock—reveals the dynamics of humiliation of African Americans by both elite and blue-collar white people. Unwilling to equate themselves with the African American community, the city elite limited desegregation processes to poor parts of the town, creating identity and divergence insults toward both African Americans and blue-collar whites. These whites reacted with divergence insults toward African American teenagers and the community in whole. The city elite interpreted aggressive actions of blue-collar white people as bigoted and discriminatory while portraying themselves as supporters of desegregation. These actions of the city elite created projection insult for blue-collar white people, transforming the humiliation process toward them.

In the second case—Michael Brown's killing—the long history of humiliation and relative deprivation through discrimination, lynching, and unfair police practices created a foundation for relative insults. Parents of the killed teenager as well as African American community positioned the prejudice among police as a major reason for killing. They delegitimize the results of investigation and saw it as continuation of the practices of systemic humiliation.

In the third case of political debates around Iranian deal, congressional Democrats and Republicans used different actions and statement to humiliate each other through power and legitimacy insults. Both parties sought to diminish the power of the political opponents, presenting them as illegitimate, dishonest, and unfitted to have power. With such efforts, both sides portrayed actions of the other group as promoting parochial party interests that endanger the country.

All three cases show that the humiliation process can be represented in three forms: (1) hierarchical humiliation—asymmetric humiliation of marginalized groups by the group in power; (2) reverse humiliation—a process employed by minority in response to long-lasting systemic humiliation by powerful groups; and (3) reciprocal humiliation, vicious exchange of humiliation between two mostly equal parties. The hierarchical humiliation aims at striping other party of positive identity, strengthening social boundary, and justifying discriminative actions by projecting bigotry on the other side. To achieve these goals, the party in power is using identity, projection, and divergence insults. The reversal humiliation targets the outgroups that created a systemic humiliation for the ingroup for a long time. As a respond to relative deprivation, it intends to diminish rights and privileged positions of party in power. The mostly often insult used in this process is relative insult. Reciprocal humiliation aims at increasing the power and legitimacy of the ingroup completely delegalizing the outgroup. In this process, both groups use power and legitimacy insults to diminish validity of their opponent. In all three forms, insults served as powerful and effective tool of humiliation.

NOTES

1. It is worth noting that the perception of insult depends on a person or group's ego-syntonic self-identity: an identity of being weak could be accepted by some people (e.g. some women).
2. Ferguson's congressman Representative Clay on State of the Union with Candy Crowley: "Ferguson police were way too heavy-handed in the way they interacted with peaceful demonstrators." (2014, August 17). *CNN Press Blogs*, retrieved from: http://cnnpressroom.blogs.cnn.com/2014/08/17/fergusons-congressman-rep-clay-on-state-of-the-union-with-candy-crowley-ferguson-police-were-way-too-heavy-handed-in-the-way-they-interacted-with-peaceful-demonstrators/

REFERENCES

Altman, A. 2014. What the Ferguson Leaks Tell Us About Michael Brown's Death. *Time*, October 23. Retrieved from http://time.com/3534140/ferguson-michael-brown-grand-jury-leaks-investigation/

Anderson, Karen. 2004. The Little Rock School Desegregation Crisis: Moderation and Social Conflict. *The Journal of Southern History* 70: 603–636.

Bacon, J., and Y. Alcindor. 2014. Ferguson Decision Will Be 'Defining Moment' for Mo. *USA Today*, November 3. Retrieved from http://www.usatoday.com/story/news/2014/11/13/crump-ferguson-michael-brown/18961421/

Baker, P. 2015. G.O.P. Senators' Letter to Iran About Nuclear Deal Angers White House. *NY Times*, March 9. Retrieved from http://www.nytimes.com/2015/03/10/world/asia/white-house-faults-gop-senators-letter-to-irans-leaders.html?_r=0

Barth, F. 1981. *Process and Form in Social Life*. London: Routledge and Kegan Paul.

Bouie, J. 2015. Obama's Secret Weapon. *Slate*, September 11. Retrieved from http://www.slate.com/articles/news_and_politics/politics/2015/09/the_republican_party_helped_obama_win_on_the_iran_deal_the_gop_s_partisan.html

Cartwright, Dorwin. 1959. *Studies in Social Power*. Ann Arbor: Research Center for Group Dynamics, Institute for Social Research, University of Michigan.

Clarke, R., and C. Lett. 2014. What Happened When Michael Brown Met Officer Darren Wilson. *CNN*, November 11. Retrieved from http://www.cnn.com/interactive/2014/08/us/ferguson-brown-timeline/

Cohen, A.P. 1985. *The Symbolic Construction of Community*. London: Tavistock.

———. 1986. Belonging: The Experience of Culture. In *Symbolising Boundaries: Identity and Diversity in British Cultures*, ed. A.P. Cohen. Manchester: Manchester University Press.

Coleman, C., and G. Toppo. 2014. Ferguson Police Chief Issues Apology to Brown Family. *USA Today*, September 25. Retrieved from http://www.usatoday.com/story/news/nation/2014/09/25/michael-brown-case/16199575/

Davis, J.A. 1959. A Formal Interpretation of the Theory of Relative Deprivation. *Sociometry* 22: 280–296.

Deutsch, Morton, and Harold B. Gerard. 1955. A Study of Normative and Informational Social Influences Upon Individual Judgment. *The Journal of Abnormal and Social Psychology* 51 (3): 629–636. https://doi.org/10.1037/h0046408.

Diamond, J. 2015. Kerry, Ayatollah Denounce GOP Letter to Iran. *CNN*, March 12. Retrieved from http://www.cnn.com/2015/03/11/politics/john-kerry-iran-letter-hearing/

Duran, N. 2015. White House Dismisses GOP, Says Iran Deal in Effect Next Week. *Washington Examiner*, September 10. Retrieved from http://www.washingtonexaminer.com/white-house-dismisses-gop-says-iran-deal-in-effect-next-week/article/2571788

Ellemers, N., R. Spears, and B. Doosje. 1997. Sticking Together or Falling Apart: Ingroup Identification as a Psychological Determinant of Group Commitment Versus Individual Mobility. *Journal of Personality and Social Psychology* 72: 617–626.

Enaharo, Khari. 2003. *Race Code War*. Chicago: African American Images.

Eribon, Didier. 2004. *Insult and the Making of the Gay Self*. Trans. Michael Lucey. Durham: Duke University Press Books.

Everett, B. 2015. Iran Letter Blowback Startles GOP. *Politico*, March 11. Retrieved from http://www.politico.com/story/2015/03/republicans-surprised-by-iran-letter-blowback-116003.html

Felson, Richard B. 1978. Aggression as Impression Management. *Social Psychology* 41 (3): 205–213.

———. 1982. Impression Management and the Escalation of Aggression and Violence. *Social Psychology Quarterly* 45 (4): 245–254. https://doi.org/10.2307/3033920.

Festinger, Leon. 1954. A Theory of Social Comparison Processes. *Human Relations* 7 (2): 117–140. https://doi.org/10.1177/001872675400700202.

Festinger, L. 1957. *A Theory of Cognitive Dissonance*. Stanford: Stanford University Press.

Gabriel, Yannis. 1998. An Introduction to the Social Psychology of Insults in Organizations. *Human Relations* 51 (11): 1329–1354.

Gaffe, G., and J. Eilperin. 2015. In Wake of GOP Letter to Iran, Battle Erupts Over Blame for Dysfunction. *The Washington Post*, March 10. Retrieved from http://www.washingtonpost.com/politics/in-wake-of-gop-letter-to-iran-battle-erupts-over-blame-for-dysfunction/2015/03/10/91411d08-c755-11e4-a199-6cb5e63819d2_story.html

Gurr, T.R. 1993. *Minorities at Risk: A Global View of Ethnopolitical Conflict.* Washington, DC: United States Institute of Peace.

Halligan, S. 2013. Local Expert Explains New Autopsy Finding for Ferguson Teen Michael Brown. *KHSB.com*, November 13. Retrieved from http://www.kshb.com/news/local-news/local-expert-explains-new-autopsy-finding-for-ferguson-teen-michael-brown

Horowitz, D.L. 1975. Ethnic Identity. In *Ethnicity, Theory and Experience*, ed. N. Glazer and D. Moynihan. Cambridge: Harvard University Press.

Hutnik, N. 1991. *Ethnic Minority Identity.* Oxford: Clarendon Press.

Jones, William K. 2003. *Insult to Injury: Libel, Slander, and Invasions of Privacy.* Boulder: University Press of Colorado.

Karl, J., and J. Parkinson. 2015. Tom Cotton Denies GOP Letter Undermines Iran Nuclear Talks. *ABC News*, March 9. Retrieved from http://abcnews.go.com/Politics/tom-cotton-denies-gop-letter-undermines-iran-nuclear/story?id=29513847

Kashima, Yoshihisa, Klaus Fiedler, and Peter Freytag. 2008. *Stereotype Dynamics: Language-Based Approaches to the Formation, Maintenance, and Transformation of Stereotypes.* New York/London: Lawrence Erlbaum Associates.

Kelman, Herbert C. 2001. Reflections on the Social and Psychological Processes of Legitimization and Delegitimization. In *The Psychology of Legitimacy: Emerging Perspectives on Ideology, Justice, and Intergroup Relations*, ed. J.T. Jost and B. Major, 54–73. New York: Cambridge University Press.

Kirk, John. 2002. *Redefining the Color Line: Black Activism in Little Rock, Arkansas 1940–1970.* Gainesville: Florida UP.

Korostelina, K.V. 2014. *Political Insults: How Offenses Escalates Conflict.* University of Oxford Press.

Lindner, Evelyn G. 2001. Humiliation as the Source of Terrorism: A New Paradigm. *Peace Research* 33 (2): 59–68.

Maitra, Ishani, and Mary Kate McGowan, eds. 2012. *Speech and Harm: Controversies Over Free Speech.* Oxford: Oxford University Press.

Mathes, M., and D. Clark. 2015. White House Clinches Support for Iran Nuclear Deal. *Yahoo News*, September 2. Retrieved from http://news.yahoo.com/white-house-wins-enough-senate-support-iran-deal-152239372.html

Matsuda, Mari. 1993. *Words That Wound.* Boulder: Westview Press.

Miller, William I. 1995. *Humiliation: And Other Essays on Honor, Social Discomfort, and Violence.* Ithaca: Cornell University Press.

Moscovici, Serge. 1976. *Social Influence and Social Change.* London/New York: Published in cooperation with European Association of Experimental Social Psychology by Academic Press.

Murphy, Sara. 1997. In *Breaking the Silence: Little Rock's Women's Emergency Committee to Open Our Schools, 1958–1963*, ed. Patrick C. Murphy. Fayetteville: Arkansas UP.

Neu, Jerome. 2008. *Sticks and Stones: The Philosophy of Insults.* Oxford/New York: Oxford University Press.

Reilly, M. 2014. Ferguson's Congressman Has 'No Confidence' in Local Cops to Give Brown Family 'A Fair Shake'. *Huffington Post*, August 17. Retrieved from http://www.huffingtonpost.com/2014/08/17/lacy-clay-michael-brown_n_5685892.html

Rhodan, M. 2014. Civil Rights Leaders Want Feds to Intervene in Time. *Ferguson Probe*, September 25. Retrieved from http://time.com/3430523/ferguson-michael-brown-civil-rights/

Runciman, W.G. 1966. *Relative Deprivation and Social Justice: A Study of Attitudes to Social Inequality in Twentieth Century England.* Berkeley: University of California Press.

Schulberg, J., and J. Bendery. 2015. House GOP Comes Up with New Meaningless Way to Oppose Iran Deal. *The Huffington Post*, September 10. Retrieved from http://www.huffingtonpost.com/entry/iran-deal-vote-delay_55f066bfe4b093be51bd1201

Stanglin, D. 2015. Ayatollah, German Foreign Minister Slam GOP Letter on Iran. *USA Today*, March 12. Retrieved from http://www.usatoday.com/story/news/world/2015/03/12/ayatollah-ali-khamenei-iran-gop-letter-nuclear-talks/70197140/

Steinhauer, J. 2015. Democrats Hand Victory to Obama on Iran Nuclear Deal. *NY Times*, September 10. Retrieved from http://www.nytimes.com/2015/09/11/us/politics/iran-nuclear-deal-senate.html

Suderman, P. 2014. Rand Paul: Scene in Ferguson Resembles 'War More Than Traditional Police Action.' *Reason.com*, August 14. Retrieved from http://reason.com/blog/2014/08/14/rand-paul-scene-in-ferguson-resembles-wa

Tajfel, H., and J.C. Turner. 1986. The Social Identity Theory of Intergroup Behavior. *Psychology of Intergroup Relations* 5: 7–24.

Tilly, C. 2005. *Identities, Boundaries and Social Ties.* Boulder: Paradigm.

Turner, John C. 2005. Explaining the Nature of Power: A Three-Process Theory. *European Journal of Social Psychology* 35 (1): 1–22. https://doi.org/10.1002/ejsp.244.

Turner, J.C., M.A. Hogg, P.J. Oakes, S.D. Reicher, and M.S. Wetherell. 1987. *Rediscovering the Social Group: A Self-Categorization Theory.* Cambridge, MA: Basil Blackwell.

Volkan, V. 1997. *Bloodlines: From Ethnic Pride to Ethnic Terrorism.* New York: Farrar, Straus and Giroux.

Weinstein, Eugene, and Paul Deutschberger. 1963. Some Dimensions of Altercasting. *Sociometry* 26: 454–466.

CHAPTER 4

Systemic Humiliation and Practical Politics: Class Thematic Reasoning and the Rise of Donald Trump

Solon Simmons

For decades, we will wonder, why did it happen? How could the 2016 election have upended in so remarkable a fashion? What forces animated the populist surge and nurtured the disruptions that tore through all the checks and balances that the private party systems have put in place to prevent an unqualified outsider from seizing control? Why was the opposition in the Democratic Party so ineffective in mounting effective resistance? Finally, what does this mean for conflict behavior and conflict resolution efforts in the United States moving forward? Definitive answers to these questions will be hard to find, but one thing that is certain is that the conventional view of politics and political dynamics—the climate of common sense that animates the leadership cadre of the country—was out of step with the voting public. How the leadership class came to be so out of touch with the fire of indignation in the mass public, how ideas that seemed so secure were cast aside, and how a mode of thinking that seemed so natural to elites, especially those on the left, became a minority view that helped to create a unified Republican government is a story that social scientists

S. Simmons (✉)
School for Conflict Analysis and Resolution, George Mason University,
Arlington, VA, USA

D. Rothbart (ed.), *Systemic Humiliation in America*,
https://doi.org/10.1007/978-3-319-70679-5_4

and historians will puzzle over for decades. At the heart of these developments is the problem of society-wide conflict and the role that systemic humiliation—both of those in the cultural/representational majority and of those outside it—plays in conflict dynamics. The asymmetry of cultural power is critical for any explanation of how an appeal to identity works, and power needs to be recognized in its various and separable forms, but the very surprise of an event like this demands a new explanation, albeit one that builds on older ideas about how economic and cultural forces combine and interact in surprising and often unpredictable ways.

In order to learn more about how elite opinion came to be so disconnected with the tenor of the times, we should track its development, which demands that we look to a data source that tracks elite opinion. We know of many ways to track public opinion, but much less about how to track elite opinion, especially of those elites who are in a current position to make decisions about government policy. Fortunately, there is no better source to gauge how the operative American elite thinks about its politics than on the Sunday morning talk shows and among these, the oldest, *Meet the Press* (MTP), is the leading representative. Whatever developments may be under way in the broader field of public opinion, if you want to know what the Washington establishment thinks is relevant to discuss at any time, the Sunday morning talk shows are the place to look. It is here that we can learn what points of emphasis are in play and which arguments are seen to be persuasive and timely. I'll exploit the conversation preserved in the transcripts of *Meet the Press* throughout the 2016 elections season to illustrate how the conventional wisdom missed the biggest story of our times, the return of the conceptual rhetoric of class politics and the polarizing entanglements of cultural division and status politics. I will argue that Donald Trump took advantage of an opening in the political culture, a discursive vacuum around the concept of class that was empty because of the way that American elites managed the legacy of systemic humiliation of marginalized groups in American political culture. In this sense, humiliation is the cause of our current predicament and explains the rise of Donald Trump. Although the story is a complicated one, I should state at the outset that although Trump, like Nixon and Reagan before him, was the beneficiary of the complex soup of symbolic politics that emerged out of what I might call post-humiliation politics, he provided no clear solutions to it. For those who resented the claims of those who demanded full inclusion in the American way of life (often white men), Trump offered a loose security agenda and an inchoate class populism, but more than anything else he promised his people that they need not be concerned about the legacy of systemic humiliation. It was all in the past, as was American greatness.

If humiliation, organized and structured forms of humiliation, is the cause of our current predicament, we need to understand what kind of humiliation we are talking about and around what sorts of problems it is organized. In anticipation of election day, the historian Rick Perlstein was quoted in a story for the *New York Times' The Upshot* as he looked back over the long-term trends in political division in Chicago in the twentieth century and concluded: "This story could be written in one word; the one word would be race" (Badger and Bui 2016), and Perlstein was right. But if source of the malady was clear, the full story is a good deal more complicated. It involves centuries of racial oppression, the epic quest for civil rights to resist it, the emergence of a broader coalition of cognate groups (based in gender, ethnicity, sexuality, etc.) organized around that coalition's victories, the eclipse of an older system on the left that placed a priority on the moral category of universalistic social equality in opposition to economic or material inequality, the proliferation of customizable communication technology, and the unyielding momentum of demography. The results of these developments split the country in two, opening discursive ground for someone like a Donald Trump to occupy. One might summarize all of this as the rise of the ideology of indignation, a populist conflation of class thematic reasoning and multicultural incompetence, culminating in a culture rich with insulting interpretations of those positioned somehow outside of the dominant image of the American community, a topic addressed at length in Chap. 3 of this volume (Korostelina 2018). This is another way to frame the story of the rebellion of the "white working class," a term that finally came into vogue after the election. Trump's rise to the presidency in 2016 was like Dr. Strangelove's Major Kong riding the ICBM to oblivion: vague class rhetoric was the rocket and racial/identity indignation was the fuel. As the popular critic, Michael Moore had predicted, the Trump effect was itself a kind of symbolic insult directed from what he called "the former middle class" of the upper Midwest toward some conception of a Washington elite, and as Moore predicted, it felt good.

Donald Trump was only able to rise, flawed as his candidacy was, because he occupied discursive ground that neither party was comfortable occupying in a meaningful and authentic way: the rhetoric of class politics and market abuses. The argument presented here builds on a theoretical perspective that I first introduced in my book *The Eclipse of Equality* (Simmons 2013), in which I proposed a way to sort political arguments into broad categories that are defined by their opposition to a specific form of violence. Some arguments are defined by their opposition to physical violence; we might call these Hobbesian after Thomas Hobbes (Hobbes 1994). Others are defined by their opposition to government coercion; we might call these Lockean, after John Locke (Locke 1980). Other arguments are defined in their opposition to economic power even as it is expressed in systems of free exchange. We might call these Marxian after Karl Marx (Marx 1994). Finally, another group of arguments are defined by their opposition to cultural privilege and the internalized insults that result from it, which we might call Fanonian after the Martiniquean psychoanalyst, Frantz Fanon (Fanon 2008). Each of these four theorists is remembered because he focused on a form of social power that could and would be abused if left unchecked. Those of us who interpret conflict today travel in the channels that these great interpreters carved for us, even if our arguments stray from many of the assumptions and the logic of the four virtuosi.

Taking this approach as background, let's consider the problem of racial difference in the United States. The civil rights era produced two great heroes: one for the left, Martin Luther King, and one for the right, Ronald Reagan (Simmons 2013). Each represented a dominant interpretation of the events of the era. Martin Luther King became the celebrated hero and political interpreter who explained how cultural power—read identity—was being systematically abused in his time. Ronald Reagan emerged as a folk hero and politician in reaction to MLK-like interpretations. His focus was on freedom from government coercion, in his case a government that was attempting to transform the American way of life. As he would say in his inaugural address, "In this present crisis, government is not the solution to our problem; government is the problem." What did not emerge in the wake of the civil rights movement was a champion of Marxian arguments, even in its liberal and democratic forms. True, many critics of laissez-faire economics developed in the 1970s, 1980s, and 1990s, but none of the deep critics of Anglo-American forms of capitalism became national leaders on the scale of a King or Reagan. As markets followed their natural course of equilibration toward a global standard of wages and working conditions, the American middle class of the postwar period, predicated on high-paying and often unionized jobs in the manufacturing sector, was put under severe stress. And because no

American leader was confident enough to wage a national campaign based on a social critique of unregulated capitalism as Bernie Sanders would eventually do, the Democratic Party became less confident in traditional message of support for "the little guy."

Marx has long been a four-letter word in the American political lexicon, and the ideological turmoil of the Cold War further stigmatized class ideologies (Bell 1960), undermining support for the little guy narrative that was never altogether secure, even when Franklin Delano Roosevelt proved it could be supported by concrete policies that benefitted the "one-third of a nation ill-housed, ill-clad, ill-nourished" (Gerring 1998). The combination of declining confidence of Democratic leaders in their attacks on market failures and abuse with the racial and cultural disruptions of the 1960s (including challenges to culture in all its forms: religious, sexual, musical, lifestyle, etc.) gave elites on the right, like Reagan and his followers, an opening to recast Democrats and the progressive Roosevelt agenda itself in Lockean terms, the dominant narrative of American politics (Edsall 1991; Hartz 1955). After Reagan (and others like him), any movement to use tax dollars for the purpose of checking the power of private enterprise was positioned as a threat to community integrity and an abuse of government power. Movement conservatives came to recognize the truth of racism, sexism, and other forms of abuse of cultural privilege, but tarnished their adversaries as defenders of disorder when they fought for forms of political redress for past abuses (Nash 1976). This style of argument had an appeal for Lockean liberal America, and, in this way, cultural indignation slowly displaced class thematic reasoning as a popular form of critique in critical voting populations (Lipset 2001; Scammon and Wattenberg 1971).

The grand irony of the 1970s and after was that Democrats were quick to embrace the new revolutionary idea of a postcolonial society in its various forms, fighting for identity, just as quickly as Republicans recognized the power of Reagan's defense of freedom from government coercion, but no party defined itself by its fight against economic inequality precisely at the moment that economic inequality was becoming a central challenge as a result of a variety of developments that would later be called globalization (Mishel et al. 2012). This irony, as the world passed into a phase of unparalleled global trade with its corresponding industrial dislocation and concentration of wealth, demonstrates the extraordinary discursive gulf in American and global politics (Teixeira and Rogers 2000). The major political parties and their leaders simply forgot how to care about the potential for abusive power in business, markets, and fiscal and monetary systems. When they did make arguments in this mold, there were formulaic, stale, and unsupported by technical economic theory and the policies that draw upon it. The arguments of economic progressives had lost their moral warrant in the hearts and minds of the people. Class thematic reasoning itself soon blended indistinguishably with identity critiques to the point that few people today can explain what makes a class critique distinct from an identity critique (Wright 1997; Fraser 1997; Michaels 2006). Neoliberal economics came to dominate the field of economics and power was not a consideration in generating assumptions for the mathematical models that led the leading lights of that field to Nobel Prizes. Not until Thomas Piketty and Emmanuel Saez initiated an empirical and statistical rather than theoretical and mathematical investigation of wealth and income inequality did the conversation begin to change (Piketty 2014). These economists introduced the world to the category of the 99% and thereby provided the intellectual cover for nascent political movements like Occupy Wall Street and the Bernie Sanders campaign to survive ("Sanders Proposes Wealth Tax; Piketty,... – U.S. Senator Bernie Sanders | Facebook" 2017).

Even so, these new movements are less than convincing in the way they link their moral critique of the problems in the political economy with plausible solutions. They are thin on policy. Therefore, even though the Trump phenomenon of 2016 and the success of his vague popular appeals has demonstrated that class politics is finally back, in most cases it is little more than a primal urge unsupported by popular, evidence-based, and rational arguments. If leaders on the left are unable to finally accept the challenges that arise from this fact, they will find it increasingly difficult to support a progressive identity politics as well. Whatever lessons one draws from this political earthquake, one of them must surely be that we need to develop better and more widely recognized tools for the analysis and resolution of class conflicts.

METHOD OF ANALYSIS

The discipline of conflict analysis and resolution and the field of peace and conflict studies, of which it is a part, is still in formation, even if its origins can be traced to the various wars of the twentieth century, going back to World War I. The combination of conflict analysis and conflict resolution into a single package was a novel coinage that can be traced to the formation of the George Mason School in the early 1980s, a very recent innovation in the development of a scientific field. What marks the majority of scholars at The School for Conflict Analysis and Resolution (SCAR) is their interest in examining the qualitative data of discourse about conflict insofar as it reveals important insights on the development of social identity and a critique of power. These data are gathered in many ways, through intervention recordings, interviews, media analysis, historical materials, focus groups, and so on, and are subjected to analysis that borrows from the categories of analysis that derive their origins from the traditional disciplines. What is true of SCAR scholars, in general, will be true of this chapter as well, and I propose a critical approach to the analysis of discourse that I will apply to a data source that was chosen for its unique capacity to represent the opinions and arguments of the top-level political leaders and decision-makers in the United States—the television program called *Meet the Press*. I will also use a category that is traditional in my home discipline of sociology, especially its use by scholars active before the Marxist turn in the 1970s like Reinhard Bendix, who used it to refer to interpretative interventions—thoughts, beliefs, emotional appeals, and arguments—of leaders as they attempt to steer those available to led to accomplish practical ends (Bendix 2001).

To tell this story, I am going to draw on my own expertise in analyzing the discourse of politics, especially as it plays out in elite circles, proximate to power. In fact, I will use a technique that I pioneered in my book *The Eclipse of Equality*, in which I drew upon a data source that I consider to be a unique window into the mind of American leaders. Most people who care about American politics around the world don't watch this show, but all the leaders who will ever hold national positions in American politics have appeared there, and they take seriously what their peers say when they appear. There are dozens of examples of this going back to the show's origin in 1945, but the most salient recent case was when Joe Biden launched the push for gay marriage in the Obama administration by floating his perspective on *Meet the Press* (Becker 2015). The media environment is more fragmented and channeled by social media than ever before, but *Meet the Press* has never changed in its substantive role since World War II; it challenges national leaders to defend their opinions in a public setting that all their peers will hear. In fact, the Sunday shows (those programs that air on Sunday mornings in the United States, of which *Meet the Press* is only the leading example) may be the only setting in which a true national dialogue still takes place.

For a full discussion of what makes *Meet the Press* a unique and pertinent data source for the analysis of ideological data in the U.S. case, I refer the reader to my book. What is important to state here is that the transcripts and recordings of *Meet the Press* provide an analyst with a bounded, internally consistent, and regularly available data source on the ideological practice of American elites. Because it is the business of the show's producers to capture the most important news story in any given week in a way that is accepted by the leadership cadre as an unbiased representation of that news week, the data produced by analysis of the transcripts and recordings represent as unbiased a sample of the conventional wisdom in Washington as can be found by far more exhaustive searches through media data. At the very least, the *Meet the Press* archive allows for the analysis of historical change in elite conversations in that whatever biases it does contain are constrained by its business model that attempts to maintain a consistent approach to news coverage that reaches back to its origins in the 1940s.

My approach to the use of these data for this chapter was to focus on race and the cultural changes that have been advocated by the broader civil rights coalition that took its inspiration from the struggle for racial justice in the 1960s. It is the cultural political agenda of this broader collation and the resistance to it of a substantial and nontrivial portion of the white majority that I'll posit as the defining political cleavage of the political contest that was channeled into the 2016 election season and the dramatic Trump victory. Based on this assumption, I'll hone in on arguments about race and look for tensions in these arguments in relation to class.

In order to find a reliable way to navigate the 400,000+ words of transcribed text that are present in the MTP Sunday morning interviews for the calendar year 2016 leading up to and just after election day, I adopted a keyword search phrase approach to hone in on those passages of the program in which racial issues were discussed. Issues are signaled in popular discourse with pat phrases and the use of those phrases signals a particular nuance of how the issue is being discussed. So, for example, when white people are discussed in a program like MTP, there are different ways to refer to them that signal different attitudes and assumptions about them. For example, the word "Caucasian" is never used and is not contained in the transcripts. However, "white people," "white voter," and white working class are contained. Similarly, a word once dominant in the older transcripts, "negro," is never used, but "African American" is typical even if "black" no longer is. Because I wanted to capture all those

Table 4.1 Search terms for passages on race and class in *Meet the Press* data

	Pressure framing	Neutral framing
Out-group	"Black Lives Matter" 23 matches	"African American/African-American" 92 matches
In-group	"Working class/working-class" 25 matches	"White Voter" 19 matches

conversations in which not only the racial group but the activities of its pressure groups were discussed, I settled on the analysis of passages captured in a search on the four phrases as depicted in Table 4.1. This approach captured presentations of people of both European and African descent in a neutral frame, "African American" and "white voter," and also in terms of the more divisive terms of pressure groups associated with them, "black lives matter" and "working class." Although I began looking for "white working class," it quickly became clear that working class had become a shorthand for the downwardly mobile white voter, if not for the white person in general, who was not involved in liberal causes and who worked in cutting-edge service industries. As Joan Williams has recently argued, the category really refers more to a kind of middle-class experience than to any close connection to poverty (Williams 2017). Working class, in popular discourse, is much like how "middle American" once was (which was only referenced once in the transcripts).

In order to represent this conversation fairly, I read through every passage that contained a phrase match and I watched all 43 episodes to provide context for any given passage. I also experimented with dozens of other search phrases and combinations. These four seemed to provide the best coverage of discussions about race and class and their intersection in the data.

THE ANGER AND INDIFFERENCE OF THE AMERICAN ELECTORATE

As the exhausting election season of 2016 wound to a close, it became increasingly common for people to question what would happen after it was all over. Trump, himself, began speaking of the system in terms that Sanders had used before, "This is a rigged system, folks." There were even questions if Trump would accept the outcome of the election if he were to lose. These concerns all pointed to the fact the election was only an expression of much deeper and unresolved problems in the body politic. The concerns were present from the beginning of the formal campaign season, as we see in an episode from January 3, 2016, in which two reporters reflect on the general tone of the conversation.

RICHARD DORMENT:
But what's different about this moment in time is that...is rather than anger just being, you know, in discrete pockets across the political and ideological spectrum, we're seeing it everywhere. We're seeing it explain Donald Trump and Bernie Sanders. We're seeing it explain Black Lives Matters and the immigration movement. It's everywhere right now.
...
SARA FAGEN:
It's not just political institutions, it's the courts. It's religion, it's the news media. It's everything.

And from the start it was clear that the firebrand socialist Bernie Sanders was channeling the anger in the electorate in a shocking way. Sanders was running as a Socialist, something that even Ralph Nader had not been confident enough to do. Most importantly, he resurrected an older tradition of placing centrality on class thematic reasoning in every argument that he made. This was so shocking because since the Kennedy era Democratic leaders had placed more narrative emphasis on social status or cultural identity to set the master theme for their investigations of injustice. Most Democrats placed the fight against humiliation at the center of their worldview, but Sanders saw how the explosion of economic inequality had become to driving issue of the day. His message was strident, confident, and consistent throughout the campaign as this example from a January 24, 2016, demonstrates:

BERNIE SANDERS: You know what, in the last election, 63 percent of the American people didn't vote. 80 percent of young people didn't vote in the midterm election. That is why the rich get richer. And that is why billionaires are able to buy elections... So Chuck, what I am trying to do now, is change the dynamics of American politics. Bring millions of young people, working-class people, in to stand up and fight for their rights.

And Sanders message was not a comfortable one; it struck at the foundation of the system of political economy in the country. The language of a rigged system that Trump would later invoke was first prominent in Sanders' narration. In a February 21 appearance in the heat of the Democratic Primary, he made the case for the class bias of the primary process in response to skeptical questions from the show's host.

CHUCK TODD:

Let me start with something you said on Friday. You said on Friday, "It could be that 10, 20, 30 years from now, people will look back at what happened in Nevada and say, 'This was the beginning of the political revolution.'" Obviously the results didn't turn out the way you thought. What happened, sir?

SEN. BERNIE SANDERS:

Well, what happened is over the last five weeks, Chuck, we came from 25 points down to five points down. As I understand it, we actually won the Latino vote yesterday, which is a big breakthrough for us. But the voter turnout was not as high as I had wanted. And what I've said over and over again, we will do well when young people, when working-class people come out. We do not do well when the voter turnout is not large. We did not do as good a job as I had wanted to bring out a large turnout.

CHUCK TODD:

You know that at the last minute, there were reports that Harry Reid and the Culinary Union were working to try to beef up turnout in places where Hillary Clinton was going to do well, including right there on the Strip in Las Vegas. Do you think that made a difference?

SEN. BERNIE SANDERS:

It's hard to say. But what I do know is, Chuck, that our message of a rigged economy in which people in Nevada and around this country are working longer hours for low wages, why almost all new income and wealth is going to the top one percent. And I'll tell you something else, there's issue of a corrupt campaign finance system, where big money interests and Wall Street are trying to buy elections. Those are the issues that are resonating. Again, I wish we had had a larger voter turnout. But by the way, we did phenomenally well with young people. I think we did well with working class people. But remember, we were taking on a candidate who ran in 2008. She knew Nevada a lot better than we did, she had the names of a lot of her supporters.

As it turned out, the revolution Sanders was dreaming of was not triggered in Nevada, but perhaps Donald Trump's was, a revolution that combined vague economic promises and business friendliness with a fear of the outsider and the threat of otherness. Both Trump and Sanders were able to capitalize on their outsider status, occupying the fallow terrain of class politics as the popular host of NBC's *Morning Joy* noted.

JOY-ANN REID: And not only that, but Donald Trump is actually doing what Bernie Sanders was billed as doing. He's doing new voters into the process.

The anger and indignation of the electorate was always present and seemed to confound establishment figures like David Brooks of the *New York Times*. This exchange, recorded after the primary season on July 31, between Brooks and the Republican strategist Alex Castellanos shows that Trump's tactics were both tantalizing to those who sensed a change in the atmosphere and ridiculous from the perspective of those who knew how the political map behaved in the modern political era.

DAVID BROOKS: Yeah, and it's about national mood. That's why Trump is here, that's why Bernie Sanders was here. And frankly, if you're trying to win Pennsylvania, like, these are long shots. These are like-, Steph Curry doesn't take these shots...
    ALEX CASTELLANOS: Not so much. Pennsylvania is like Ohio this year. Trump has rearranged the map. You know, this is the angry working class guy election. And one of the questions we've had is, Is the angry white guy, is that a stronger component of this election?

Castellanos recognized how important the energy of the "angry white guy" was, even as the headlines were tracking racial tension and unrest on the other side of the racial divide in the form of the black lives matter movement and the salience of the police violence in African-American communities. What is most striking is how the Meet the Press conversation demonstrates how little credence Washington elites gave to the populist threat of the white working class even as African-American racial tension was taken quite seriously. It had become clear that Trump believed that he had a chance to run the table in the industrial Midwest and to bring out white working class voters in a way that no Republican since Reagan had done before him. On October 2, as the election approached, Chuck Todd used a segment called Data Download, which is meant to provide a broad overview of the empirical facts at play in the political data to dismiss the threat of the white working class as implausible.

CHUCK TODD: Welcome back to this week's Data Download. There's been the belief by some that in 2016, a working class white army is going to emerge for Donald Trump and swing key states for him... in these places where Trump has the most votes to gain – the voters who could potentially win him this election – there's no evidence that people are registering to vote in droves. In fact, there's no evidence that anybody's in these counties registering people to vote. Many of the folks in these counties stayed home in 2012, and it's quite possible we'll see the same thing this November.

But the political experts who served as guests on the panel could feel that something was different this time, even if the data all seemed to point to the safety of conventional interpretation. As this exchange between Amy Walter and Rich Lowry demonstrate:

AMY WALTER: The surprise would be those people that Chuck pointed out who don't vote, who aren't normally part of the process. If they come out, that would be the surprise.

RICH LOWRY: Even though you don't see it in the registration data, and they don't have any ground operation to speak of, because I still would not be shocked if he can change the electorate somewhat by turning out these working class white voters who were missing in 2012. And his core message is built for those people.

But whatever the experts were beginning to suspect about the stability of the Midwest and the pliability of the white working class, the Clinton campaign appeared to be less motivated by a gambit to capture this segment than on winning the general election the way it had won the Democratic Primary, by energizing the African-American vote. Just two days before the election, we see this report from Kristen Walker on Clinton's closing strategy:

KRISTEN WELKER: Well, Chuck, look, Pennsylvania is a part of Secretary Clinton's firewall, and in order to win here, in order to win the White House, she has to get large margins of African-American voters in urban areas like right here in Philadelphia, that was on display during that Katy Perry concert here last night. Clinton has made 16 stops to Pennsylvania since the DNC. A lot of those stops aimed at energizing African-American voters. And Chuck, consider this, President Obama got 93% of the black vote here in Pennsylvania in 2012. Now Clinton doesn't need to match that, but she's gotta get comparable numbers. It's not just here. It's in other battlegrounds, like North Carolina and Ohio, where she'll be joined by

LeBron James a little bit later on today. And to help her make her case, she has a million volunteers stretched all across the country helping to get out the vote. Chuck.

As things happen, this election was one in which Trump appeared to benefit from the class-tinged anger of the white working class, but Clinton could not capitalize on the anger of the African-American community that was beleaguered by police violence. The reasons for this have to do with how each side relied on the moral emotions at play in the conflicted setting. The Democrats relied in the energizing force of humiliation and a critique of the abusive power of majoritarian status (white, straight, married, male, etc.). Most of the powerful attack ads and news stories that the Clinton campaign pushed carried an aura of identity. The Republicans countered with the indignation of white voters and their allies that comes from a sense of having been displaced in history and the insecurities that arise from it, a kind of renaissance of Hobbesian ideas. The mechanism of that displacement was global economic change, but once the Sanders argument that could channel that critique into practical politics had been defeated and co-opted into the anti-humiliation story, Trump could fill the space with his own culturally inflected, right-wing version.

FIGHTING HUMILIATION ON THE AMERICAN LEFT

It is important to remember that if the Meet the Press record can be trusted, Sanders lost the Democratic primary because he was opposed by forces that feared his attempt to change the topic of the national conversation from culture to class, and African-Americans, and classic civil rights causes like police violence were the most prominent weapons used against him. Sanders was attempting to shift the focus from outrage in the face of cultural humiliation to outrage in the face of economic exploitation and opportunity hoarding. The Sanders opposition was often friendly and sympathetic, but the tone was clearly set more against the Sanders narrative than against Sanders himself. He was stigmatized as insensitive to racial injustice in his quest for class equity. This is clear throughout the MTP data series in 2016. We can see it clearly in the February 14 episode in the run-up the South Carolina primary.

CHUCK TODD: But a recent NBC News/Wall Street Journal/ Marist poll gave Hillary Clinton a 57 point lead among African Americans in South

Carolina. No surprise then that the morning after New Hampshire, Sanders travelled to Harlem for breakfast with my next guest, civil rights leader and MSNBC host Al Sharpton. Reverend Sharpton, welcome back to Meet the Press.

REV. AL SHARPTON: Thank you.

CHUCK TODD: I want to play for you an interaction that Bernie Sanders had on Friday with an African American voter in Minnesota and get your response on the other side. Here it is.

(BEGIN TAPE)

FEMALE VOICE: So the question specifically, my black son, okay, I know you're scared to say black, I know you're scared to say reparations, because it seems like every time...

BERNIE SANDERS: Hold on, ma'am, I don't think that's the fairest...

FEMALE VOICE: I'd like to finish.

BERNIE SANDERS: We have the highest rate of childhood poverty of any major country on earth, especially within the African American community.

SHOUT FROM CROWD: Say black!

BERNIE SANDERS: But I, I've said "black" 50 times, all right? That's the 51st time.

(END TAPE)

CHUCK TODD: Is that a fair criticism from the crowd of him?

REV. AL SHARPTON: Well, I think that what it is, is that people have felt, in our communities, ignored and marginalized in that people have kind of, like, generally discussed things. And we supposed to assume we're part of that, when we have some very specific needs. And all of us don't agree, nobody can deliver the black vote. ... Part of the problem that I think that is coming to the surface in this is that we have experienced both in the liberal north and the south, hostility. Let's not forget Howard Beach, where Bernie Sanders was born in New York, Howard Beach was in the north. People like me emerged in the north. I never lived in the south. We're dealing with Hollywood, progressive Hollywood, with an Oscar whiteout right now. So I think what a lot of people are beginning to see is, "Wait a minute, we do not want to be marginalized, and we don't want to be thrown into a situation where specific needs are not dealt with."

The problem as Sharpton told it was that black people were being "ignored and marginalized" and made to feel subject to hostility by being overlooked for their accomplishments; in short, they were feeling humiliated by the election and by developments in culture more generally. The concern was how the class narrative might crowd out the status narrative that had been so helpful throughout the era of civil rights. It was also clear to expert observers that Clinton was trouncing Sanders and his class story because of the power of African-American leaders and the status narrative that animated them that Sharpton alluded to as "specific needs." This passage from Joy-Ann Reid on February 21, captures the sentiment concisely.

> JOY-ANN REID: It makes me uncomfortable. But I do have to say that Hillary Clinton understands fundamentally that her candidacy is in the hands of African Americans, full stop. In Nevada, it was a 72 percent route with African Americans that carried her over the top. South Carolina, she will be saved by African Americans over age 50. And not even just all African Americans, but African Americans of a certain age, right, over 50. And she knows that that is what she needs.

Much as Al Gore had before her, Hillary Clinton was reluctant to use Bill Clinton as a surrogate. This was a problem because Bill had been so adept in triangulating the competing forces of the class and status narratives in the 1990s. This Clintonian ambivalence led to complications in the narrative space 20 years after the fact, especially with respect to his crime bill. The only clear example of Bill's role in the campaign came in an April 10 episode after he had been publicly castigated for what was discussed as his insensitivity in the face of African-American protestors of his crime bill of the 1990s. This exchange captures the general reception of Bill Clinton in the conversation that year.

> JOY-ANN REID: Bill Clinton, I think, is living emotionally through the repudiation of much of his legacy, whether it's on L.G.B.T. rights or whether it's on this crime bill or on criminal justice.
> CHUCK TODD: You're right.
> JOY-ANN REID: His legacy is being relitigated in the negative. And I think it's hard for him to deal with it. But what he didn't understand is in the role of surrogate, it is not your job to defend yourself. And this complicated bill, that has no clean hands, by the way, no clean hands.

Reid's reference to dirty hands shows how the Clintonian synthesis had slid over into stigma in the Democratic ranks. Democratic leaders and their supporting activists were possessed of a clean vision of politics defined by opposition to the politics of humiliation. Clinton's clever appeals to the indignation of a white middle class in the 1990s that blended deep stories of equality and security was portrayed on the left as a relic, like something a crazy uncle might bring up at Thanksgiving dinner. But the conservative editor of the *National Review*, Rich Lowry, an avowed conservative, seemed to sense the rhetorical bind in which the Democrats found themselves as racial issues buried the old synthesis.

> RICH LOWRY: I found Bill's performance quite invigorating, which is a sure sign it was a disaster in the context of democratic primary politics. But he's right. I mean, the bill came in a context of a three-decade crime wave that was devastating to American cities. And even if you think we've gone too far in incarceration, and I think there's a very good case we have, the increase is primarily driven by violent offenders and people who have committed serious property crimes. So this was not a policy that was born of racism or pointless matter.

By September of the general election, Sanders was vanquished and Trump had been thoroughly tarnished with the stigma of racism, ethnocentrism, sexism, and other examples of how unclean his hands were as defined by the anti-humiliation root narrative. It was at that point that Hillary Clinton finally committed what Chuck Todd took to be an example of dangerous overreach in her identity arguments when she deployed her line about how half of Trump's supporters could be put in the "basket of deplorables" for their commitment to discrimination and harassment. On the episode from September 11, Todd gave a leading Clinton supporter, and Obama staffer, Stephanie Cutter, a chance to walk back the line that condemned so large a portion of the American people as racist and beyond redemption, but her response demonstrated how confident the Democratic Party establishment was that the anti-humiliation narrative had enough power to carry the median voter and win the November election.

> CHUCK TODD: Stephanie, it's tough to defend the remark, is it? Or no? Do you think it's tough to defend the remark "deplorables" to stereotype a group of people, or no?
> STEPHANIE CUTTER: Absolutely not. I think that her only mistake is that she said half of his supporters were deplorable. But does anybody around this table, have they not seen Trump's rallies? Have they not seen Trump's own remarks? He is attracting a certain type of voter. She gave a whole speech on describing them, they're called the alt-right. And they Tweet racist things, he retweets them, he says it from the stump. From research in this election we know that his own words, calling Mexicans

rapists, criticizing a Gold Star family, these are the most potent things against him with Independent voters. So what she said was not wrong, her only mistake was that she described half of his supporters that way.

The data are clear in the way they demonstrate the confidence of Democratic leaders in the general appeal and power of the anti-humiliation master narrative and the centrality of racial injustice to it. This line from Clinton's running mate, Tim Kaine, on September 18, is a good example:

> SENATOR TIM KAINE: I think the fidelity to our values is at stake, Chuck. …And Chuck, it's really important to know how painful that is to so many people. Because, as you know, from the time African-Americans came here to Jamestown in 1619, through the Dred Scott decision in the 1850s, if you were African-American in this country, you could not be a citizen. Whether you were slave or free or born here or born elsewhere, you could not be a citizen. And we had to fight a civil war and change the constitution to change that. So when Donald Trump, for five years, has been promoting the notion that an African-American president is not a citizen, that is extremely powerful and painful to African-Americans and to others who know this painful chapter in America's history.

Clinton ran her general election in a way not dissimilar to the way she won the primary. She invoked the power of the fight against systemic humiliation. The rhetorical paradigm from which she drew inspiration was a status master narrative from which an infinite variety of novel stories could be spun. Because of the tragic history of the United States on matters of race, the major narrative focus was on African-American voters. For whatever reason, turnout in this group seems not to have been strong enough to carry her to victory. One reason for this is the animating power of her story was not a racial narrative but a gender variation on the anti-humiliation theme. As her own tweets after news of the loss on November 8 make clear, her campaign was predicated on the possibility of removing the humiliation that came from being a woman in a world dominated by white men. Her most moving postelection day tweet spoke to the plight of women of the future in a world dominated by men and the challenge of believing in gender equality now that her own campaign had come to an end.

Hillary Clinton: To all the little girls watching...never doubt that you are valuable and powerful & deserving of every chance & opportunity in the world.

The tweet was comforting to those of us who had daughters of our own to whom we had to break the devastating news the next morning, but the emerging and breakout story of the election was not about girls, but instead about the once-forgotten power of the white working class. Indignation, the humiliation of the in-group, would prove to be the most powerful moral emotion of the season.

ENLISTING THE INDIGNATION OF THE WHITE WORKING CLASS

Although the Obama Democrats never forgot about the plight of working people, because of who he was, his regime was easy to frame in terms of his race and the cultural tides of change. And because the field of class politics was left largely abandoned after Bernie Sanders had exited the race in July, Trump was able to use the arguments that Bernie had developed as an empty vehicle for his own ambitions. He fueled his efforts with the sense of threat to the cultural entitlement of the majority group. In so doing, he effectively pivoted from the class root narrative to the security root narrative by stressing the linkage between purportedly dangerous minorities and economic distress. His class argument was one specifically tailored to appeal to the character structure of the middle-class American voter that leaders would soon frame with the label white working class.

Questions about the electoral power of the white voters who lived in nonmetro areas and who had less than a college degree were nothing new. What was new was that Trump was willing to use his position in the Republican Party to craft an appeal to these voters that Republican leaders had long feared because of the disruptive power of the message. Renascent class politics always had the potential to validate social programs and redistribution programs that Republicans had long opposed. This demanded a delicate balance of arguments that toyed with racial prejudice but one that assiduously avoided any arguments that validated the role of government in the economy. But Trumpian indignation, which blended concerns about factional violence from minorities with the threat to the economic interests of workers, crossed the populist line with gusto and incorporated the chauvinistic self-conception of Americans that they are and should be number one in the world. He invoked a deep story of economic national-ism that neither the Republicans nor the Democrats were willing to, mak-ing a big gamble that he could turn the lower middle-class white voter to his agenda by decrying the elitism of his opponent and by portraying her as out of touch and corrupted by foreign wealth. Critical to his approach was how he used status anxiety to fuel class resentment. Hints of this opportunity were in the air from early 2016 as this segment from March 13 demonstrates.

CHUCK TODD: Trump has been running in states where the unemploy-ment rate is above the national average of five percent. And two, he's win-ning in states where the African American population is above eight percent. Now to be sure, this doesn't apply to every state Trump has won. However, he is nine for nine in states where both of those factors are in place. So, what does that tell us about where Trump might win in the future? Of the 24 remaining contests on the GOP side, four have unemployment above five percent and black population above eight percent. And guess what? Three of those four states are voting on Tuesday: Illinois, North Carolina, and Florida. And guess what? Polls are showing that he is ahead in all of those three states. There is after fourth, Connecticut, also fits this. They don't vote until April 26th. So what does this all mean? People vote for many dif-ferent reasons. But what Trump has tapped into, this issue of race and eco-nomic struggle, they're closely tied and he's taking advantage of it.

Canny observers were always aware that the Trumpian synthesis offered something new where the Clinton argument fell flat. Joy Ann Reid on May 22 put this in terms "the dream" and noted that Clinton lacked it.

JOY ANN REID: I think what Donald Trump sort of hit upon with his "make America great again" message is this sense of nostalgia that a certain kind of white, particularly white voter, has for a bygone era. And it gets right to it. I think that it's good that the Clinton campaign are strategizing. But it's interesting that, in your interview, she seemed so much like a strategist. And so many of her answers felt like this is Hillary, the smart political strate-gist telling you what she intends to do, and it's still not giving her campaign sort of a driving dream

In a preelection discussion about what might happen in the election, Richard Rubenstein and I hosted a discussion with members of the conflict resolution community. As it turns out, this was the only setting in which I privately admitted to a colleague that I thought Trump would win, and it is where Dr. Rubenstein dropped a line that has stuck with me since. He said that all politicians lie as part of the job. The problem he saw for Clinton was that Trump lied like a politician, whereas Clinton lied like a lawyer. What he meant by this was that she was always technically correct and supported with a sense of plausible deniability, but her winning arguments always also left behind a sense of unease and corruption. This might help to explain why, when the late in the campaign October FBI revelations broke, Clinton was so vulnerable.

Worse for her, the Clinton campaign did have a driving dream and it was to bring the country together across the divides of status, identity, and humiliation that were such a vexing part of the American story. Any narrative needs heroes and villains and Clinton's villains were the "deplorables." But by taking such a clear side in this culture war between mainstream Americana—full of cultural insensitivity bias and bigotry as it was—and the brighter and more inclusive future she was striving to create, Clinton managed to lose just enough of those who identified with the cultural mainstream to tip the electoral vote against her popular vote victory. The power of the backlash against the vision of deplorable Americana was clear in this segment on October 2, demonstrating how Trump was using attack ads to build on this theme and how Clinton spokesman, Robby Mook, embraced it in the days when it seemed clear that a Clinton victory was a surety.

CHUCK TODD: I want to play a new ad that the Trump campaign is hitting on Hillary Clinton and get you to respond to it on the other side.
(BEGIN TAPE)
HILLARY CLINTON: Why aren't I fifty points ahead, you might ask.
MALE NARRATOR: Maybe it's because the director of the F.B.I. said you lied about your e-mail.
JAMES COMEY: There was classified material e-mailed.
MALE NARRATOR: Or maybe it's because your policies have allowed ISIS and terrorism to spread. Or maybe it's because you call Americans deplorable.
(END TAPE)
CHUCK TODD: So it's that last part, the "deplorable," and, and everything they put together in that ad, anything in that ad that tells you it's not an effective hit on Secretary Clinton?
ROBBY MOOK: Well, a lot of it simply isn't true. You know, the, the F.B.I. said that there was no wrongdoing that they would bring against

Secretary Clinton. I think a lot of the people that stand by Donald Trump are deplorable. And the things that they say are deplorable.

In a prescient article in the Atlantic about the media relationship with Donald Trump, Salena Zito drew a distinction between reading messages literally and taking them seriously. Her claim was that the media took Trump literally but not seriously, whereas his supporters took him seriously but not literally. What is true of a Trump voter is true in narrative more generally. The points Trump made did not always make literal sense, but they did have figural integrity. The Trump ad in the segment above works because it blends three distinct images into a coherent picture that I call the ideology of indignation: the Clinton statement portrays an elitist arrogance in that it suggests that she believes that she is entitled to win; the clip about her lying to the FBI both speaks to her character and to the vague idea that she had compromised national security, somehow, by using a private e-mail server, an idea reinforced by the fact that she is said to have let ISIS and terrorism spread; and to top it off, her focus on deplorables proves that she places culture change above security and is willing to condemn large swaths of the electorate as morally polluted simply because they want to defend the American way of life. The narrative is tight and appeals beyond Trump and his message. Ted Cruz had vetted this narrative in support of his own primary campaign as in this March 13 episode that explains the source of the anger (what I would here call indignation) in the campaign.

CHUCK TODD: I want you to react to something here that President Obama said at a fundraiser, responding to the tone of Donald Trump rallies. Here it is, sir.
(BEGIN TAPE)
PRESIDENT OBAMA:
And what's been happening in our politics lately is not an accident. For years, we've been told we should be angry about America and that the economy's a disaster. And that we're weak. And that compromise is weakness. And that you can ignore science and you could ignore facts and say whatever you want about the president. And feed suspicion about immigrants and Muslims and poor people and people who aren't like us.
(END TAPE)
CHUCK TODD:
That's the president essentially saying, "This has been happening for years," before most of his term.

SEN. TED CRUZ:

You know, Chuck, Barack Obama's a world class demagogue. That language there is designed to divide us. No, Mr. President, we're not angry at that. We're angry at politicians in Washington, including you, who ignore the men and women who elected you. Who have been presiding over our jobs going overseas for seven years. Who have been cutting deals that are enriching the rich and powerful, the special interests and the big corporations, while working men and women are seeing their wages stagnating. And [Obama] talks about immigrants and Muslims. Mr. President, we're mad at a president who wants to bring in Syrian refugees who may be infiltrated by ISIS. And you're unwilling to be commander in chief and keep us safe.

Although class was the moral concern that was to dominate this campaign, security supported by a vague and implausible cultural populism with hints of class thematic reasoning would win it in the end. The Sanders message has been turned against itself in a shocking pivot.

THE PROMISE AND LIMITS OF THE CONCEPT OF SYSTEMIC HUMILIATION

How Trump pulled off his surprise attack should have been no surprise. It has everything to do with how arguments framed in the spirit and idiom of one root narrative can be used to pivot to another. In this case, how the social category of racially charged cultural indignation experienced by many white Americans, itself a reaction to the politics opposed to systemic humiliation, could be used as a kind of fuel to power the vehicle of populist politics to anti-progressive ends in an era in which economic inequality is fast becoming the driver of the political dynamic. As the marginalized and excluded finally asserted control over a major political party and used it to redress the wrongs of legacies of systemic humiliation, the marginalizers and excluders had been weaned from that same party and recommitted to a project of neoliberal economics. The irony of this conversion is that many of the white working-class voters, and those white voters of other occupational and educational backgrounds as well, were having their lives disrupted less by the actions of their government and more by developments in global markets.

In another era, these white voters would have been animated by leaders like Bernie Sanders or Harry Truman, placing the blame on economic elites and Wall Street bigwigs more than the so-called cultural elites who advocated for social justice, but the symbolic terrain of conflict discourse has shifted from class to identity. The most powerful stories on the left invoke atrocities of structured humiliation more than impersonal exploitation, thought of as "just business." As Richard Rubenstein has written, class struggle is the conflict that "dare not speak its name" (Rubenstein 2017). When leading leftist intellectuals and political leaders ruminate on injustice, they are more eloquent when confronting the legacies of systemic humiliation than they are the legacies of economic exploitation.

One example that stands out to me in the Meet the Press archive comes from a July 10 episode, which was aired in reaction to the tragic assassinations of police officers in Dallas that were part of a series of escalations in response to police shootings of black men. In that episode, the Georgetown sociologist, Michael Eric Dyson played the role of cultural critic, one who held the mirror up to white America to insist that the problem of race was not a problem with blackness, but rather with whiteness.

MICHAEL ERIC DYSON: Well, hold on. So it is about race. So when you say, "Hold on, hold on, it's not about race," of course it is, it's just not about blackness. It's also about whiteness. And we don't have a conversation in this country with race and whiteness. Whiteness is at stake; Donald Trump has, I think, in a beguiling way seduced many working-class white people into believing that he will be their defender when, indeed, he is not.

With his phase, "whiteness is at stake," Dyson was bravely articulating a point that many of us who fight for racial justice recognize. It is not enough to speak about the challenges faced by the out-group on which generations of humiliating baggage has been placed. It is also important to look at the dynamic of cultural exclusion, controlled as much by the in-group as the out-group and how the dominant party protects its privilege. This is a powerful plotline in the status-identity root narrative. But what Trump knew was that the driving dream to move the majority of Americans to action in this year had been identified by Bernie Sanders. America had not yet recovered from the Great Recession of the 2008. White people (only among others) were still suffering from the loss of homes, jobs, and lifestyles that they had assumed were their birthright. Moreover, and critically, these white voters were challenged at the same time by cultural change that could be made to appear more salient: Latin immigration, black political insurgence, transgendered bathrooms, gay marriage, the rise of China, Muslim terrorist attacks in the country, and so on. And all of this had occurred under the oversight of the first African-American president. This opened an opportunity for a crazy political entrepreneur to play with the ideology of indignation to mount a class populist challenge to first the Republican and then the Democratic establishment.

The effects of this narrative transition were immediately clear upon the Trump victory. Not only did older academic arguments like Seymour Martin Lipset's working-class authoritarianism argument reappear (Lipset 1959), prominent examples were a piece in the *New York Times* by the intellectual historian Mark Lilla and a forgotten book by the philosopher Richard Rorty (Lilla 2016; Rorty 1999), but the Democratic politicians who had promoted the interpretive use of the class narrative in the past but had been overlooked ("I'm a broken record on this") began to speak up. One of these was Joe Biden, who appeared on Meet the Press on October 16, in the final weeks leading up to the November 8 election.

> VICE PRESIDENT JOE BIDEN: The truth is, I don't think we ... and I'm a broken record in the Democratic Party on this... I don't think we speak enough to the plight of ... of family, husband and wife makin '80, 90, $100,000 a year, two kids and they're struggling'...
>
> CHUCK TODD: You know what they say? I talk to these voters. They sit there and they say, "You know what? Obama and Biden, they worry about this minority group. They worry about that minority group. They worry about these voters over here. They worry about this state. What about me?"
>
> VICE PRESIDENT JOE BIDEN: "They don't talk to me."
>
> CHUCK TODD: That's what I hear. I hear this more often when I'm in Waterloo, Iowa, Scranton, Pennsylvania.
>
> VICE PRESIDENT JOE BIDEN: And by the way, and I do, too. What happened is, we had to spend so much time dragging the car outta the ditch, worrying about going over the cliff, dealing with people who didn't have enough to eat, making sure that people were able to just hang on, that it's only now that we got the economy back and wages are starting to raise ... rise, that we can begin to focus on what is a large portion of the middle class who's felt like they've been left behind and we don't talk to their needs.

This analysis of the role played by the structures of social status and cultural identity in the elevation of Donald Trump to the American presidency provides us with a lesson in the limits of the concept of systemic humiliation. On the one hand, it is clear that the legacies of systemic humiliation were critical in setting the discourse for the campaign and are unavoidable for any serious discussion of current problems. Evidence from elite conversations in the Sunday morning weekly news programs are unambiguous, demonstrating the extent to which leaders of the Democratic Party support the theme. If we can believe what they say, Democratic Party elites in 2016 were convinced that the legacies of systemic humiliation of marginalized citizens, in particular the legacies of institutionalized racism and sexism, were a major factor in the election. The Democratic Party and its nominee, Hillary Clinton, placed the repair of these past and present abuses in the center of their message. Clinton's campaign slogan, "stronger together," is a perfect capsule of the sentiments of a political movement organized in opposition to systemic humiliation. It seems safe to say that the problem, or perhaps the problematic, of systemic humiliation is the most salient theme in leftist politics in the United States and perhaps the world, and the wounds of these abusive legacies are only now beginning to be sorted out. Nevertheless, from the perspective of practical politics, the utility of the broader theme of systemic humiliation may have its limits. Few leaders could serve as such a gross embodiment of the various legacies of systemic humiliation in the country as does Donald Trump; by most measures, he reminds us of the worst of the histories of racism, ethnocentrism, sexism, and bullying in general, and yet he won the presidential election and governed. If such a figure can win an election against so qualified an opponent as Hillary Clinton, and one who stands so unabashedly in opposition to the legacies of systemic humiliation, and if the party Trump joined, the Republican Party, can enjoy such unchallenged dominance in the country's congressional offices and statehouses, then from a practical standpoint, it seems clear that the anti-humiliation agenda, and its supporting dignitarian imagination, with its emphasis on status concerns, has practical limits, whatever its ethical virtues.

In summary, the study of elite discourse in the US presidential election of 2016 demonstrates that the broader theme of systemic humiliation has finally come of age in the field of practical politics as it had long been in the analysis of conflict dynamics. Even as populations reel under pressure from sources of social power other than the insults and microaggressions that animate the dignitarian imagination, such as market forces and corporate interests, government intrusion and violations of human rights, and physical threats from terrorists, criminals, and military rivals, leaders can narrate the course of human events with stories drawn from a rich field of anti-humiliation arguments, however awkward the fit between events and interpretation. These identity arguments now have incredible ideological power. Given the prevalence and intensity of identity conflicts around the world, the thickening of the dignitarian imagination that animates opposition to identity-based injustices is a welcome development, but as populations with large majorities of citizens of European ancestry pass into this new era in which the viability of middle class livelihoods can no longer be taken for granted, attention must be paid to alternative interpretations of the same events and troubles. Insofar as these troubles arise from the kinds of impersonal economic contests in the global economy that tend to leave many people behind, there is reason to pay more attention to what we might call class thematic reasoning—the capacity to tell compelling stories about economic abuses in universalistic terms and with the backing of empirical evidence. If the trouble is impersonal, economic exploitation, treating only the psychological effects of that exploitation—what Sennet and Cobb called the hidden injuries of class—can only help so much (Sennet and Cobb 1973). If poverty is the primary disruptive social force, opposing insults from the comfortable will only redirect the disruption. If class is the problem, identity can only be the answer for so long.

References

Badger, Emily, and Quoctrung Bui. 2016. Why Republicans Don't Even Try to Win Cities Anymore. *The New York Times*, November 2, sec. The Upshot. https://www.nytimes.com/2016/11/03/upshot/why-republicans-dont-even-try-to-win-cities-anymore.html

Becker, Jo. 2015. *Forcing the Spring: Inside the Fight for Marriage Equality*. New York: Penguin Books.

Bell, Daniel. 1960. *The End of Ideology: On the Exhaustion of Political Ideas in the Fifties*. Cambridge, MA: Harvard University Press.

Bendix, Reinhard. 2001. *Work and Authority in Industry: Managerial Ideologies in the Course of Industrialization*. New Brunswick: Transaction Publishers.

Edsall, Thomas. 1991. *Chain Reaction*. New York: Norton.

Fanon, Frantz. 2008. *Black Skin, White Masks*. Trans. Richard Philcox. Revised edition. New York/Berkeley: Grove Press.

Fraser, Nancy. 1997. *Justice Interruptus*. London: Routledge.

Gerring, John. 1998. *Party Ideologies in America 1828–1996*. Cambridge: Cambridge University Press.

Hartz, Louis. 1955. *The Liberal Tradition in America*. New York: Harvest.

Hobbes, Thomas. 1994. *Leviathan: With Selected Variants from the Latin Edition of 1668*, ed. Edwin Curley. Indianapolis: Hackett Publishing Company.

Korostelina, Karina. 2018. Insults as Tools of Systemic Humiliation. In *Systemic Humiliation: Finding Dignity Within Systems of Degradation*, ed. Daniel Rothbart. London: Palgrave Macmillan.

Lilla, Mark. 2016. Opinion | The End of Identity Liberalism. *The New York Times*, November 18, sec. Opinion. https://www.nytimes.com/2016/11/20/opinion/sunday/the-end-of-identity-liberalism.html

Lipset, Seymour Martin. 1959. Democracy and Working-Class Authoritarianism. *American Sociological Review* 24: 482–501.

———. 2001. The Decline of Class Ideologies: The End of Political Exceptionalism. In *The Breakdown of Class Politics*, ed. Terry Nichols Clark and Seymour Martin Lipset. Washington, DC: Woodrow Wilson Center Press.

Locke, John. 1980. *Second Treatise of Government*. 1st ed. Indianapolis/Cambridge: Hackett Pub Co.

Marx, Karl. 1994. *Selected Writings*, ed. Lawrence H. Simon. Indianapolis: Hackett Pub Co.

Michaels, Walter Benn. 2006. *The Trouble with Diversity: How We Learned to Love Identity and Ignore Inequality*. New York: Metropolitan Books.

Mishel, Lawrence, Josh Bivens, Elise Gould, and Heidi Shierholz. 2012. *The State of Working America*. 12th ed. Ithaca: ILR Press.

Nash, George H. 1976. *The Conservative Intellectual Movement in America: Since 1945*. New York: Basic Books Inc..

Piketty, Thomas. 2014. *Capital in the Twenty First Century*. Trans. Arthur Goldhammer. Cambridge, MA: Belknap Press: An Imprint of Harvard University Press.

Rorty, Richard. 1999. *Achieving Our Country: Leftist Thought in Twentieth-Century America*. Cambridge, MA: Harvard University Press.

Rubenstein, Richard E. 2017. *Resolving Structural Conflicts: How Violent Systems Can Be Transformed*. 1st ed. London: Routledge.

"Sanders Proposes Wealth Tax; Piketty,... – U.S. Senator Bernie Sanders | Facebook." 2017. https://www.facebook.com/senatorsanders/photos/a.91485152907.84764.9124187907/10152656769767908/. Accessed July 31.

Scammon, Richard M., and Ben J. Wattenberg. 1971. *The Real Majority*. New York: Coward, McCann & Geoghegan, Inc..

Sennet, Richard, and Jonathan Cobb. 1973. *The Hidden Injuries of Class*. New York: Vintage Books.

Simmons, Solon. 2013. *The Eclipse of Equality: Arguing America on Meet the Press*. Stanford: Stanford University Press.

Teixeira, Ruy, and Joel Rogers. 2000. *America's Forgotten Majority: Why the White Working Class Still Matters*. New York: Basic Books.

Williams, Joan C. 2017. *White Working Class: Overcoming Class Cluelessness in America*. 1st ed. Boston: Harvard Business Review Press.

Wright, Erik Olin. 1997. *Class Counts: Comparative Studies in Class Analysis*. Cambridge: Cambridge University Press.

PART II

Race, Violence and the Road to Justice

CHAPTER 5

The Civil War at 150 Years: Deep Wounds Yet to Heal

Joseph V. Montville

THEORY AND ANALYSIS

The editors of this volume draw on a variety of approaches, for example, social identity theory, moral philosophy, sociological theory, and clinical psychology. This chapter uses a variation of the latter, political psychology, that reflects my experience in practical analysis and conflict resolution efforts over 30 years as a diplomat and subsequently. While most of that time was focused on international ethnic and sectarian conflicts, the insights gained thereby are fully applicable to the question of unhealed wounds in American history.

The psychology of victimhood is an automatic product of aggression and resultant traumatic loss in individuals and peoples. The refusal of aggressors to acknowledge the pain of the hurts inflicted on victims, and therefore the absence of remorse by the aggressors, creates an overwhelming sense of injustice in the victims. A society, a leadership, a world, and, indeed, a universe the victims had heretofore assumed would shield them from harm have all let them down. Their new psychology would henceforth keep the victimized people highly suspicious and on permanent alert for future acts of aggression and violence. It would also make them

J. V. Montville (✉)
School for Conflict Analysis and Resolution, George Mason University,
Arlington, VA, USA

© The Author(s) 2018
D. Rothbart (ed.), *Systemic Humiliation in America*,
https://doi.org/10.1007/978-3-319-70679-5_5

strongly resistant to pressures to make peace before the aggressors acknowledge the victims' losses and ask forgiveness for their violence. The victims' collective sense of security in their identity, their self-concept, their basic dignity, and a future for their children has been dealt a devastating blow.

This concept of victimhood psychology is derived from dynamic or depth psychology, especially the subfield called ego psychology or psychology of the self. But it is interesting, and gratifying, to note that some specialists in philosophy and law have come to similar conclusions about the harm to the victim's sense of self resulting from criminal acts. Thus, in *Forgiveness and Mercy* (1988) Jeffrie Murphy, dealing with the issues of forgiveness, mercy, and justice, sees the resentment in victims of crime, and their consequent demand for retributive justice, as defense, above all, of the self. Murphy writes, "In my view, resentment (in its range from righteous anger to righteous hatred) functions primarily in defense, not of all moral values and norms, but rather of certain values of the self....I am...suggesting that the primary value defended by the passion of resentment is self-respect, that proper self-respect is essentially tied to the passion of resentment"(p. 16). Gregory Rochlin (1978), emeritus professor of psychiatry at the Harvard Medical School, wrote from the perspective of a clinician at a community-based psychiatry department at Cambridge Hospital. In *Man's Aggression: The Defense of the Self*, Rochlin reported on his experience in treating patients in addition to his scholarly research. He found that insults to or aggression against the self-concept produced an automatic reactive aggression in defense of the self. His thesis is that narcissism, which he defined as love of the self, is a fundamental part of the human being's psychological security system. Narcissism is critical to the defense of the self. Thus when the love of the self is jolted either through threat, insult, or, especially, physical assault, there is an automatic, fear-based psychophysiological reaction. Everett Worthington (1998) has described the fear-based stress response system of the victim as elevations in epinephrine, corticosteroids, and other stress hormones. This stress-response system can be mobilized by the sight of the aggressor, or hearing sounds associated with him or them, or simply through recalling from memory the original threat or attack.

Thus, in victimhood psychology, the individual or group, which by definition has sustained traumatic loss, is overwhelmed with a sense of existential injustice, and yet, in the absence of acknowledgment and remorse from the aggressor, still fears further attacks. Memory sustains fear, which activates stress-related hormones, which overall mobilize individuals or groups into militancy in defense of the self. In this high state of narcissistic rage, sense of injustice, basic distrust, and continual fear, it is little wonder that ethnic and sectarian conflict has always been and continues to be so resistant to traditional diplomacy and negotiating processes. As with individual victims of trauma, peoples and nations require complex healing processes to get beyond their psychological and physiological symptoms to become full partners in reconciliation and peacebuilding.

As an example of this psychology in an individual—there will be more below—I quote from a book review by Sarah Boxer in the October 27, 2016, *New York Review of Books*. The two-volume book's title is *The Arab of the Future*, by Riad Sattouf. Boxer describes Abdel-Razak, a principal character, as a victim of systemic humiliation by the decades-old history of European colonialism and episodic military violence:

> Abdel-Razak is not evil. He never beats his wife. He's usually nice to his son. He's just a man full of pent-up humiliation trying to get somewhere in the world, looking up to those with power or money, looking down on those he views weak or beneath him—particularly, women, blacks, Jews, and animals.

INTRODUCTION

The impetus for this chapter was the widely shared concern about the paralysis of the federal government under our first African-American president. A minority of Americans had through the instrumentality of the Republican Party in Congress devoted itself to making President Obama's administration a failure at apparently any cost. Senate Minority Leader Mitch McConnell (R-KY) had said in *The National Journal* on November 4, 2010, "The single most important thing we want to achieve is for President Obama to be a one-term president." While I have heard that McConnell told fellow Republicans in Congress that the party should not permit any legislation that make the first African-American look good, I cannot verify this independently. But we can look at the voting data from the 2012 presidential election to see that, empirically, most states of the former Confederacy plus West Virginia had the lowest totals for President Obama. Thus, it's fair to assume that these numbers laid the basis for the Republican majority in the House and Senate, which has been judged to be the least productive in modern times.

The unprecedented use—or abuse—of the filibuster by the Senate Republicans to achieve McConnell's goal meant that the Democratic majority had to have 60 votes for any bill of substance. The late Common Cause president Bob Edgar announced on May 15 that the organization had gone to federal court to challenge the constitutionality of the Senate's filibuster rules. "Once used to extend debate," Edgar said, "the filibuster has become a partisan weapon that now is routinely used to block action—and even debate—on hundreds of bills and nominations." The Republican majority in the House of Representatives had voted 33 times in what might be called a compulsive legislative tantrum to repeal President Obama's Affordable Health Care Act. (On February 2, 2016, Republicans voted for the 62nd time to repeal all or part of Obamacare.)

In November, 2014, Representative Pete Olson (R-TX) introduced a motion to impeach the country's first black chief law enforcement officer, Attorney General Eric Holder, for a variety of alleged offenses. Seven months later in 2014, the motion had 26 cosponsors.

The Brookings Institution's Thomas Mann and the American Enterprise Institute's Norman Ornstein, arguably the two most respected scholars of the Congress in the country and scrupulously nonpartisan, said in their book, *It's Even Worse Than it Looks: How the American Constitutional System Collided With the New Politics of Extremism* (2012), "The GOP has become an insurgent outlier in American politics. It is ideologically extreme; scornful of compromise; unmoved by conventional understanding of facts, evidence, and science, and dismissive of the legitimacy of its political opposition" (p. 4).

This goal of this chapter is to try to uncover the historical basis for the intensity of red state antagonism toward President Obama particularly in some southern and border states of the former Confederacy. The analytical approach is political-psychological and is meant to lay out a number of questions that call for answers. It is not meant to be an indictment of the historical actors to be discussed. Rather, it aims to describe some of political, economic, and psychological environments rooted in the pre-Civil War, the War itself, Reconstruction, and post-Reconstruction eras that may shed some light on the sources of destructive behaviors and also historical wounds unhealed to this day that have contributed to the near paralysis of the federal government's ability to function. At the end, the chapter also examines the phenomenon of unacknowledged moral debts to the white South and African slaves of Northern slaveholders, particularly of New England. The hope is that acknowledgment of the harm inflicted by Northern and Southern whites on each other and on black slaves and freedmen and honest expressions of contrition could accelerate a reconciliation process in America that could truly heal our country from Massachusetts to Mississippi to Arizona to California.

(I am grateful to Dr. Peggy Brooks-Bertram for her extensive advice and whose scholarship on the efforts of Drusilla Dunjee Houston, a fighter for African-American civil rights and dignity, has been inspiring.)

UNHEALED HISTORICAL MEMORY

We start with a proposition that suggests a direct link between political deadlock in Washington with the enduring impact of the losses in the South from the Civil War and the consequences of Reconstruction and what was called post-Reconstruction—that is, the end of the federal occupation of the Southern states. We examine the Southern white effort to put back into "their place" the freed slaves and the mechanisms of Jim Crow laws and the terror of lynching to achieve the structural and psychological re-enslavement of the African-American population.

On September 9, 2010, President Obama addressed a joint session of Congress on his proposed health-care legislation. He had just stated that the bill would not provide health care for illegal immigrants. Then suddenly, Rep. Joe Wilson, a Republican from South Carolina, shouted out to the president, "You lie!" shocking all present and presumably most everyone watching on television. Wilson later apologized for letting his "emotions get the better of me." But he also sent out a self-congratulatory fund-raising letter to his supporters shortly after the event.

My proposition is this. While Mr. Wilson said he disagreed with the president's health-care proposal, his unprecedented outburst in a joint session of Congress while the president was speaking was truly meant to say, "I cannot bear to sit here being lectured to by a black man." One can only speculate how much Mr. Wilson's outburst reflects an earlier expression of rage by another South Carolina member of Congress, Senator "Pitchfork" Ben Tillman, reacting to the news that President Theodore Roosevelt and his wife had entertained Booker T. Washington at dinner in the White House on October 16, 1901. Tillman said, "The action of President Roosevelt in entertaining that n...er will necessitate our killing a thousand n...ers in the South before they will learn their place again" (Kantrowitz 2000, p. 259). As we will see below, South Carolina has a long association with resentment generated by losses in the Civil War and subsequent history.

Let's take a walk through history to see what support there may be for the idea that African-Americans in high office remains highly offensive to a significant proportion to our country's white population particularly in the South and West Virginia.

(In the November 2012 presidential election, Mitt Romney received 59 million votes nationwide. Of this, total 38% came from the South and West Virginia. Of Romney's 206 electoral votes, 138 were from the South and West Virginia. In the Deep South, the white Democratic vote ranged from 26% in South Carolina and Texas to 14% in Louisiana, 11% in Mississippi, and 10% in Alabama. Former Democratic congressman from Alabama Artur Davis, an African-American now a Republican, said after the November election, "The Republican conservative base seems perilously close to shrinking to white southern evangelicals, senior white males, and upper income Protestants.")

Joel Williamson, professor of history emeritus at the University of North Carolina at Chapel Hill, is considered by his peers to be one of the preeminent scholars of the South. The *New York Times Book Review* called his 1984 book, *A Crucible of Race*, "a major reinterpretation of black-white relations since the Civil War [which] has deepened our understanding of [Southern history's] tragic dimensions and enduring legacies."

Williamson explains that the institution of slavery had been under relentless pressure. Congress had forbidden importation of new slaves from abroad in 1808 and the effect was to concentrate slave ownership southward below the Mason-Dixon Line, isolating it and in the end causing its extinction. This did not mean that American leaders embraced black Africans as respected and respectable human beings. They in fact considered the mixing of whites and blacks as threatening the superiority of European culture. They asked themselves if America's future might be made white through exclusion of blacks from society—recall in 1817 that the American Colonization Society, supported inter alia by John Jay, Thomas Jefferson, and James Monroe, created to send blacks back to Africa resulted in the establishment of the state of Liberia, with its capital named Monrovia. The problem was that the vast majority of blacks refused to leave America. This was home for them.

Then an earthquake struck in black-white relations in the slave states. In 1831, in Southside Virginia, Nat Turner, a slave and Methodist lay preacher absorbed in End Times themes from the *Book of Revelation*, said he heard a heavenly voice tell him to slay his enemies. Turner led a group of rebellious slaves who slaughtered 57 white men, women, and children with axes, knives, and guns before being caught and killed themselves. The white victims were slaveholders and nonslaveholders. Their common feature is that they were all white, and the message, Williamson writes, was that when blacks rebelled, all whites could be killed. It is very significant that Turner's evangelical fundamentalism seemed to be a mirror image of the white evangelical communities which later would be so prominent in the sacrificial lynching of African-Americans described below.

After the Nat Turner rebellion, white Southern males were mobilized into a home guard, responsible for armed, mounted patrols constantly moving among slaves and eying free blacks. They made sure that blacks did not look them in the eye, and that they were always polite. Williamson says patrols were like juries on horseback who could summarily try, judge, and punish blacks suspected of disrespect for whites or, worse, possibly threatening violence. If one wonders about the enduring emotional strength of the National Rifle Association in today's America, Williamson offers one explanation (all quotes are from his *A Rage for Order*):

> The militant South, the military South prone to shoot first and answer ques-
> tions later, did and still does exist. It sprang from the necessity of controlling
> a potentially explosive black population. In the nineteenth century South
> the key to control lay in possessing all the guns ....Negroes were well aware
> of the facts of life, and of death, and of the odds against them in an insurrec-
> tion (p. 11).

Protestant churchmen in the South played a different role in the effort to keep the black population under control in a more positive way than the patrols. Evangelicals especially worked to enroll slaves in their denominations or minister to them in their own black churches. But through theology and what then passed for science, the white ministers strengthened the argument for slavery, which was in fact racial. Simply put, black people were inferior to white people. God had made Negroes to be slaves and white Southerners fulfilled God's wishes. And in the last years of slavery, whites developed a stereotype of blacks as simple-minded, docile, children, often given the name of Sambo. (I remember as a child in the 1940s reading an illustrated book called *Little Black Sambo*.)
Williamson writes:

> It was ...in the last generation of slavery that all blacks came to look alike in
> the eyes of Southern whites, and the person they chose to see was Sambo.

The Sambo of imagination was a child adopted into the white family, an adult black body with a white child's mind and heart, simultaneously appealing and appalling, naturally affectionate and unwittingly cruel, a social asset and a liability. Sambo had within him two terrific and opposite capacities. Improperly cared for, he became bestial, an animal in human form and all the more dangerous because of his human capabilities. Properly managed, on the other hand, he was like a white child—and dear (p. 15).

Unsurprisingly, blacks played the Sambo role as a wary, survival defense against white potential panics over perceived Nat Turner-like threats. They kept their eyes looking down, shuffled their feet, spoke in soft, uncertain voices to convey the message that they were not a threat.

Another very important psychological fact of plantation slave society is the anxiety and indeed repressed but painful anger of Southern white women at the knowledge that their husbands, brothers, and sons were sexually exploiting slave women and girls simply because they could at no legal or, it seemed, moral cost. Mulatto children were constantly appearing. The image of the virtuous white wife and mother propagated by the masters of the house and plantation served the purpose of distracting the women from the reality of the rampant rape by their men of defenseless female slaves. As Williamson writes, "The Southern woman did sometimes internalize the image of the plantation lady, and sometimes grew blind to the fact that the darkling boys and girls with whom her children played were their own brothers and sisters and a living insult to her integrity" (p. 28). We will return to this theme.

After the War: Radical Reconstruction

For a good 20 years after the end of slavery, Southern whites worked to reestablish the black-white relationship before the Civil War. One dominant theme among white Southerners was that Reconstruction imposed by the victorious North was meant to turn social and race relationships upside down—to upset the idea of the "place" that naturally separated blacks and whites. "It was a horrendous effort...to make the social order in the South a monstrosity. In the reduction of the planter elite and in the liberation of the slave and his elevation in civil life, it was as if the conquerors had lopped off the head and sewn on a foot in its place" (p. 37).

Reconstruction was in Southern eyes a horror, negating their sense of the proper social order. They raged at the Radical state legislatures, with their black members eating peanuts during sessions and betraying their ignorance of parliamentary rules of order. "The democratic faith implicit in Radical Reconstruction was almost unthinkable to Southern minds; it sat crosswise over the molds of what ought to be racially and socially. In Southern eyes, Reconstruction was, in essence, an ordinance against nature and a denial of God" (p. 37).

South Carolina, Rep. Joe Wilson's state was particularly distressed. Fifty-eight percent of its population was black. Whites felt that they were losing—or had lost—control of their future and identity. They had a vision of perpetual domination by a black majority. The eager fighters who had started the Civil War by attacking Fort Sumter in Charleston harbor in 1861 were defeated. Many of the Southern whites who had been closest to large numbers of slaves and who affected to care for them as their protected children now began to displace the rage they might have been expected to direct to the Northern victors or Confederate leaders for the loss of the war on the freed slaves. This is important to understand because while former slaves had an understandably powerful sense of victimhood, the Southern whites also felt intensely victimized.

In Thomas Dixon's 1905 novel, *The Clansman* (more on Dixon below), a defeated white gentleman, gives his view of South Carolina under Reconstruction:

> Black hordes of former slaves, with the intelligence of children and the instincts of savages, armed with modern rifles, parade daily in front of their unarmed former masters. A white man has no right a negro* need respect. The children of the breed of men who speak the tongue of Burns and Shakespeare, Drake and Raleigh have been disarmed and made subject to the black spawn of an African jungle.....No people in the history of the world have ever before been so basely betrayed, so wantonly humiliated and degraded! (*Dixon refused to capitalize "Negro.")
>
> For a Russian to rule a Pole, a Turk to rule a Greek, or an Austrian to dominate an Italian, is hard enough, but for a thick-lipped, flat-nosed, spindle-shanked negro, exuding his nauseating animal odor, to shout in derision over the hearths and homes of white men and women is an atrocity too monstrous for belief (p. 290).

POST-RECONSTRUCTION AND THE RISE OF THE RADICALS

With the withdrawal of federal troops from the South effectively ending the era of Reconstruction, Radicalism became prominent in the South in 1889. Its rationale was that the Negroes, no longer restrained by the controls of slavery, were regressing to their original condition of bestiality. The new, young Negro was basically a savage, and he was a particular threat in his desire to rape white women. Radicals believed that in the end blacks and whites could not live together. They would have to go—back to Africa or someplace else.

The recession of the late 1880s and depression of the 1890s had a major impact on the minds of Southern whites. Men who had prided themselves on their ability to provide for their families suffered a significant loss of self-confidence and inevitably self-respect. The less advantaged among them came to believe it was impossible to have families. They felt inadequate and incompetent. It is psychologically plausible that in the face of white men's inability to meet the material needs of their families, they could at least compensate by militancy to physically protect their women from the perceived black animal rapist. Williamson writes:

> In the Radical mind, the single most significant and awful manifestation of black retrogression was an increasing frequency of sexual assaults on white women and girl children by black men. Above all else, it was this threat that thrust deeply into the psychic core of the South, searing the white soul, marking the character of the Southern mind radically and leaving it crippled and hobbled in the matters of race long after the mark itself was lost from sight (p. 84).

(It is remarkable how effectively the image of the black beast rapist was used in the 1988 presidential campaign consistent with the Republican Party's "Southern strategy." The late South Carolinian, Lee Atwater, used the story of Willie Horton, himself a black native of South Carolina, who was serving a life sentence without possibility of parole in a Massachusetts prison for the brutal murder—19 stab wounds—of a 17-year-old gas station attendant. In his capacity as governor of Massachusetts, Michael Dukakis, the Democratic candidate running against Republican George Herbert Walker Bush, had granted Horton a weekend furlough as part of a rehabilitation policy for prisoners. Horton did not return and ended up raping a white woman in Maryland after pistol whipping her. The Maryland judge who sentenced Horton to two life sentences plus 85 years refused to send him back to Massachusetts, the only state in the Union that granted furloughs to prisoners sentenced to life without possibility of parole. The ad was believed to have had a strong mobilizing effect in the South and no doubt parts of the rest of the country.)

THOMAS DIXON: THE BLACK RAPIST IN NOVELS, ON STAGE AND FILM

Joel Williamson says, "The one work nearest to codification of the [Southern white] Radical dogma came not at all in a scholarly form, but in a novel...*The Leopard's Spots*, written by Thomas A. Dixon, Jr. in 1902" (p. 96). Dixon had seen a stage adaptation of Harriet Beecher Stowe's *Uncle Tom's Cabin*, and he was outraged. Her novel is widely credited to have helped precipitate the Civil War. President Lincoln reportedly said when he met Stowe, "So this is the little lady who made this big war." One of the characters in *The Leopard's Spots* says of Simon Legree in *Uncle Tom's Cabin*, "The picture of that brute with a whip in his hand beating a negro caused the most terrible war in the history of the world. Three millions of men flew at each other's throats and for four years fought like demons. A million men and six billions of dollars worth of property were destroyed." Dixon determined to write a counternovel. In his last book, *The Flaming Sword* (1939), he wrote, "A novel is the most vivid and accurate form in which history can be written." Reality was to provide strong support for his view.

Thomas Dixon was born on January 11, 1864, in King's Mountain, North Carolina. He came from a Calvinist Presbyterian background but became a Baptist preacher, playwright, actor, and novelist. He had studied at Wake Forest University and Johns Hopkins in Baltimore where, significantly, he had met fellow student Woodrow Wilson. He had lived and worked in New York and Boston before settling back home in the South. Anthony Slide wrote a valuable biography, *American Racist: The Life and Films of Thomas Dixon* (2004), and Williamson has a fascinating chapter in *A Rage for Order*, that deals quite persuasively with Dixon's psychological complexity, especially with his anger, documented in his own hand, at the fact that his mother had been forced to marry his father at age 13. As we have seen and will continue to do so, rape of "pure" white girls and women was a dominant theme in justification of lynching blacks and white-led urban race riots.

It's important for the purposes of this chapter to extract portions from *The Leopard's Spots* that convey Dixon's sense of loss and injustice from the Civil War and Reconstruction and how he inspired millions of white Southerners to stand up and resist the depredations of the victorious federal government and to furiously and violently put the freed slaves back under white control. These texts can be seen in part as expressing some of the historical memory of the defeated and occupied white South but also a terrible record of abuse of blacks that has not been truly acknowledged and atoned for. They are also powerful expressions of victimhood psychology among white southerners.

On defeat:

> The ragged troops were straggling home from Greensboro and Appomattox …The men were telling the story of surrender…Surrender! A new word in the vocabulary of the South. Desolation everywhere marked the end of an era….Not a cow, a sheep, a horse, a fowl…save here and there a stray dog, to be seen. Grim chimneys marked the site of once fair homes….The tramping soldiers looked worn and dispirited….They looked worse than they felt, and they felt that the end of the world had come (p. 4).

On the threat of freed slaves:

> The town is swarming with vagrant negroes, bent on mischief. There are [white] camp followers…dealing out arms and ammunition to them, and… inflaming the worst passions against their former masters, teaching insolence and training them for crime….Gradually…the towering figure of the freed negro had been growing more and more ominous, until its menace overshadowed the poverty, the hunger, the sorrows and the devastation of the South, throwing the blight of its shadow over future generations, a veritable Black Death for the land and its people (p. 33).

On resentment of Northern liberals:

> Why is it that you good people of the North are sending your millions here now to help only the negroes, who feel least of all the sufferings of this war? The poor white people of the South are your own flesh and blood….They are, many of them, homeless, without clothes, sick and hungry and broken hearted. But one in ten of them ever owned a slave. They had to fight this

war because your armies invaded their soil. But for their sorrows, sufferings and burdens you have no ear to hear and no heart to pity (p. 48).

On the outrage of Radical Reconstruction:

The Confederacy went to pieces in a day, not because the South could no longer fight, but because they were fighting the flag of their fathers, and they were tired of it......They expected to lose their slaves and repudiate the dogma of Secession Forever. But, they never dreamed of negro dominion, or negro deification, of negro equality or amalgamation, now being rammed down their throats with bayonets (p. 136).

On the threat of race mixing:

My boy, the future American must be an Anglo-Saxon or a Mulatto! We are now deciding which it shall be. The future of the world depends on the future of this Republic. This Republic can have no future if racial lines are broken, and its proud citizenship sinks to the level of a mongrel breed of Mulattoes. The South must fight this battle to a finish. Two thousand years look down upon the struggle, and two thousand years of the future bend low to catch the message of life or death (p. 198).

More on Negro racial inferiority:

I am looking into the future. This racial instinct is the ordinance of our life.
     Lose it and we have no future. One drop of negro blood makes a negro. It kinks the hair, flattens the nose, thickens the lip, puts out the light on intellect, and lights the fires of brutal passions. The beginning of negro equality as a vital fact is the beginning of the end of this nation's life. There is enough negro blood here to make mulatto the whole Republic (p. 242).

On the superiority of the white South:

I love the South–the stolid, silent South, that for a generation has sneered at paper-made [federal] policies, and scorned public opinion. The South, old-fashioned, medieval, provincial, worshipping the dead, and raising men rather than money, family loving, home building, tradition ridden. The South, cruel and cunning when fighting a treacherous foe, with brief volcanic outbursts of wrath and vengeance. The South, eloquent, bombastic, romantic, chivalrous, lustful, proud, kind and hospitable. The South with her beautiful women and brave men. The South, generous and reckless, never knowing her own interest, but living her own life in her own way (p. 441).

The themes of *The Leopard's Spots* flowed into *The Clansman* published in 1905, which Dixon adapted as a stage play and performed sometimes himself in productions in Richmond, Raleigh, Columbia, Montgomery, Chattanooga, Knoxville, Nashville, and New Orleans. And he enjoyed great popular success in Columbus, Ohio; Indianapolis; and Topeka. D.W. Griffith, another Scots-Irish southerner, loved *The Clansman* and determined to turn it into an epic, though silent, film, which he did in 1915. Under its new name, *The Birth of a Nation*, which ran three hours with an intermission, had all of the major Dixon themes: a defeated, impoverished South; a brutal, unbelievably corrupt federal government occupation during Reconstruction; and gangs of unleashed, uncontrolled freed slaves, given the vote and armed, and most fearsomely beastly predators violating the flower of white Southern womanhood. But the Ku Klux Clan rides to the rescue of the degraded South and restores the natural order of the races.

Thomas Dixon excited by the box office success of *The Birth of a Nation*, contacted his old Johns Hopkins schoolmate, the new president of the United States, Woodrow Wilson, and under its first title, *The Clansman* became the first movie to be shown in the White House. Wilson was very impressed with the film and according to Anthony Slide he said, "It is like history with lightening. And my only regret is that it is all so terribly true."

The Leopard's Spots and *The Clansman* each sold a million copies. By 1930, according to one report, 90% of white southerners had seen *The Birth of a Nation*. Thomas Dixon must be judged a giant in the process of using art to illustrate a tragic and violent memory of the post–Civil War South. The film also strengthened the sense of southern white victimhood.

The Cross and the Lynching Tree

One of the most important and least discussed aspects of the black-white tragedy in the post–Reconstruction South is the role of Christianity. James H. Cone, the Arkansas-born, Distinguished Professor of Systematic Theology at New York's Union Theological Seminary, has written a powerful, devastating account of the terrorizing through lynching of blacks but also challenged the proclaimed Christianity of the white Southerners who justified lynching as a God-sanctioned, indeed religiously justified, method of preserving the peace and the virtue of white womanhood. In *The Cross and the Lynching Tree* (2011), and in only 164 pages of text, Cone, an African-American, has produced an indispensable account of white Christendom's disgrace—North and South—in perpetrating and standing by while God's black children were systematically humiliated, degraded, and murdered. He quotes a white Floridian telling a Northern critic, "The people of the South don't think any more of killing the black fellows that you would of killing a flea." A black from Mississippi is quoted saying, "Back in them days, to kill a Negro wasn't nothing. It was like killing a chicken or killing a snake" (p. 6). Whites lynched blacks in almost every state including California, New York, and Minnesota.

With the restoration of their authority, whites were able to "take back" the South—a familiar phrase in twenty-first-century political polemics and "to redeem it from what they called 'Negro domination,' through mob violence...excluding blacks from politics, arresting them for vagrancy, forcing them to work as sharecroppers, who never got out of debt, and creating a rigid, segregated society in which being black was a badge of shame with no meaningful future. A black person could be lynched for any perceived insult to whites." The lynching era is placed between 1880 and 1940. But there were many murders after that—most notably the killing of young Emmitt Till in 1955, which is seen as a major spur to the modern civil rights movement.

Cone writes that by the 1890s lynching fever seized the South like a plague. This was also the period of a deep, painful economic depression. White communities in the South made blacks their target for torture in an environment where they felt they had lost control—the classic scapegoat social mechanism.

> Burning the black victim slowly for hours was the chief method of torture. Lynching became a white media spectacle, in which prominent newspapers, like the *Atlanta Constitution,* announced to the public the place, date, and time of the expected hanging and burning of black victims. Often as many as ten to twenty thousand men, women, and children attended the event. It was a family affair, a ritual celebration of white supremacy, where women and children were often given the first opportunity to torture black victims—burning black flesh and cutting off genitals, fingers, toes, and ears as souvenirs. Postcards were made from the photographs taken of the black

victims with white lynchers and onlookers smiling as they struck a pose for the camera (p. 9).

Cone puts special emphasis on the failure of his teacher and colleague at Union Theological Seminary, Reinhold Niebuhr's dismaying reluctance to take a strong public stand in defense of the dignity and humanity of black Americans. Niebuhr was a gradualist, don't-rock-the-boat, white Christian, admittedly a giant among theologians. But he and most other white ministers seemed unable to be courageous on the race issue. Cone lays down a challenge to white Christians, North and South, to walk through the history of the lynching era and take retrospective account of their enormous sins of omission. It is a history that cries out for repentance. The author writes:

> They are crucifying again the Son of God. Both Jesus and blacks were 'strange fruit.' Theologically speaking, Jesus was the 'first lynchee,' who foreshadowed all the lynched bodies on American soil. He was crucified by the same principalities and powers that lynched black people in America.... God transformed lynched black bodies into the recrucified body of Christ. *Every time a white mob lynched a black person, they lynched Jesus.* The lynching tree is the cross in America. When American Christians realize that they can meet Jesus only in the crucified bodies in our midst, they will encounter the real scandal of the cross (p. 158).

And as Harvard sociologist Orlando Patterson reported in his monumental *Rituals of Blood* (1998), the mobs were often presided over by a Protestant minister of the gospel. While James Cone does not mention it, Patterson's research into eyewitness press accounts of lynchings, where black bodies were slowly burned—roasted really—suggested strongly the ancient ritual of burnt offerings to God or the gods. His research discovered lynching episodes in which small burned parts of the black victims' bodies were eaten by members of the lynch mob—like Holy Communion. There where powerful religious symbols in the lynching culture, suggesting that deep down the white mobs were making sacrificial offerings to the angry God who had permitted them to be humiliated by the Northern armies and then occupied by Northern forces.

As Orlando Patterson writes in *Rituals of Blood:*

> Jim Crow rose to power on, was suffused with, and had as the very center of its doctrine not just the permanent segregation and subjugation of

Afro-Americans but their demonization, terrorization, and humiliation. The central ritual of this version of the Southern civil religion...was the human sacrifice of the lynch mob....The brutally sacrificed Negro was the ultimate Christ figure of the narrative of aversion—Christ the scapegoat—spat upon, mocked, spiked, tortured, and accursed. In expelling 'the Negro,' all that was most evil and sinful and black and iniquitous and transgressing would be sent away: 'for the goat shall bear upon him all their iniquities unto a land not inhabited' (Leviticus 16:21).

These forgoing analyses need careful, respectful, deep study of the history of the era by black-and-white historians and especially Christian clergy if our country is to come to grips with this aspect of the American tragedy.

Both in broadly psychological and individual emotional terms, this walk through history will be extremely difficult and painful for Southern whites and African-Americans. It will require a fearlessly honest examination of the barbaric, sacrificial, savagery of systematic murder by lynching of freed slaves literally by consenting communities of white Southerners including women and their children. It will especially require critical analysis by white evangelical lay leaders and clergy of the place that conservative or fundamentalist evangelical Protestantism played in justifying the sacrifice of living, breathing human beings who were by any conception of Christianity precious in the eyes of God.

But there is a ray of hope.

A symbolically and psychologically very important event occurred in June 2012, with the election of the Rev. Fred Luter, Jr. as the first black president of the Southern Baptist Convention (SBC). The SBC was founded in 1845 because of a theological belief that the Bible supported the concept of slavery. Today, it represents some 16 million Southern Baptists. Hardheaded realists might say this happened because the SBC membership is declining and needs new faces even if they are not white. My personal view is that the election of President Obama in 2008 may very well have made Rev. Luter's election possible. And I also believe that a great majority of SBC members genuinely wanted to atone for the past.

One of the strongest inhibitors of this absolutely necessary task of facing history is the fact the white South has chafed and raged to this very day under the insults and disdain of the white North which has claimed from the earliest colonial times to be intellectually and morally superior to the people of the South. This is also a plausible basis for Southern victimhood psychology.

A detailed walk through their own harsh and hypocritical history by Northerners with acknowledgment of the unjustified hurts inflicted by their relentless contempt for almost all things Southern is essential to the North/South-Black/White healing process in a country that in the twenty-first century remains painfully torn. Such a process of Northern self-revelation—let's say confession—will also give Southerners a respite from the pressure of centuries of Northern disrespect to do their own difficult historical self-analysis. This chapter concludes noting the beginning of a Northern process of acknowledgment of moral debt to the South.[1]

Northern Arrogance and the Scandal of New England Slavery

Southerners had been very much aware of a Northern tradition of aggressive disrespect for their life style and culture. The Southern reaction was anger, frustration, and humiliation, as Pamela Creed, a George Mason PhD, documented in a 2007 research paper, "An American Conflict of Mind: Competing Narratives and Identity." She cites Lewis J. Simpson, a professor of American literature at Louisiana State University in his essential *Mind and the American Civil War: A Meditation on Lost Causes* (1989), on extensive evidence that well before the Civil War there were competing perspectives on the origins, birth, and future of the country among those who settled in New England, the South, and the frontier.

In his *Cavalier and Yankee: The Old South and American National Character* (1975), William R. Taylor wrote that in New England there was an evolving culture of great respect for literature and learning. The Southern planters were much less interested in Enlightenment innovations and more in preserving a way of life based on a slaveholding, feudal aristocracy.

Pamela Creed quotes Susan Mary Grant in her monograph *North over South* (2000), saying, "The South has always been regarded by non-Southerners as distinct and separate from the nation as a whole, and as differentiated in some mysterious and irrational way from the national experience—the national ideals." Grant quotes Samuel Nott, a Northern writer, saying, "The South is a lower civilization [solely by virtue of its] greater barbarism and poverty at the starting-point of emigration [from Great Britain]."

I would recommend the brilliant *Albion's Seed: Four British Folkways in America* (1985) by David Hackett Fisher as an indispensable source for understanding the strong ultimately tragic clash of identities between the middle-class Puritan settlers in New England from East Anglia and the impoverished Scots-Irish induced to go to the American colonies in large numbers—about 200,000 at the beginning of the 1700s. The latter formed the backbone of the Southern-indentured poor and later the cannon fodder for the Confederate armies. I also strongly suggest Senator Jim Webb's *Born Fighting: How the Scots-Irish Shaped America* (2004) as an up-to-date portrait of this core American community that in many parts of the country still smarts from perceived Northern (liberal) indifference and disdain some 300 years after arriving in America.

Pamela Creed's insightful analysis has a very useful quotation from Susan Mary Grant that is a good introduction to the final segment of this chapter. She wrote:

> Although it was a fictitious construction—and a destructive one—the idea that the North and South had separate origins helped Northerners distance themselves from a society they saw as an affront to American values; it absolved them, too, of any residual guilt on the maintenance of slavery and conveniently ignored the overt racism of Northern society.

THE LITTLE-KNOWN HISTORY OF NORTHERN SLAVE TRADING AND OWNERSHIP

At the beginning of this chapter, I noted that it is an exercise in healing wounded history using the tools of political psychology. One of the key beliefs in this approach is that all the parties who have hurt other people must be helped to acknowledge their misdeeds, crimes, and sins. We close with what can only be a brief glimpse of Northern—specifically New England—complicity in the kidnapping and enslavement of defenseless black Africans. This does not relieve the South of the burdens of historic brutalization of slaves and freedmen which must be acknowledged and documented in detail and atoned for. But this walk through America's tragic history must expose the moral crimes of Northern slave traders and slaveholders. And among those offenses are the intellectual arrogance and spiritual deformity of many New England leaders, clergy in particular, who neglected to mention their slave problem.

Here we draw from an eye-opening—for me astounding—expose by Francie Latour in the September 26, 2010 *Boston Globe*. The title is "New England's hidden history." Its subtitle is, "More than we like to think, the North was built on slavery." The article starts with an unforgettable story quoted here in full:

> In the year 1755, a black slave named Mark Codman plotted to kill his abusive master. A God-fearing man, Codman had resolved to use poison, reasoning that if he could kill without shedding blood, it would be no sin. Arsenic in hand, he and two female slaves poisoned the tea and porridge of John Codman repeatedly. The plan worked—but like so many stories of slave rebellion, this one ended in a brutal death for the slave as well. After a trial by jury, Mark Codman was hanged, tarred, and then suspended in a metal gibbet on the main road to town, where his body remained for more than 20 years.
>
> It sounds like a classic account of Southern slavery. But Codman's body didn't hang in Savannah, Ga.; it hung in present-day Somerville, Mass. And the reason we know how long Mark the slave was left on view is that Paul Revere passed it on his midnight ride. In a fleeting mention from Revere's account, the horseman described galloping past 'Charlestown Neck, and got nearly opposite where Mark was hung in chains.'

Latour continues, "When it comes to slavery, the story that New England has long told itself goes like this: Slavery happened in the South, and it ends thanks to the North. We had a little slavery in the North but the slaves were like family. We taught them to read, let them marry. And then freed them. New England is the home of abolitionists and underground railroads. In the story of slavery—and by extension, the story of race and racism in modern day America—we're the heroes. Aren't we?"

Yet Latour's research uncovered more and more stories of New England slavery and what she calls "its brutality, its staying power, and its silent presence in places whose names are symbols of American freedom." As we visit Lexington and Concord or walk in Cambridge or neighboring Somerville, where Harvard University spreads, we learn we are stepping on ground the slaves trod. (I was in Cambridge in May 2012, admiring the great homes clustered close together, wondering today how many of them were financed through the slave trade.)

Brookline, a close suburb of Boston, is one of the most politically and morally liberal communities in the United States. Once, nearly half of the town's land was the property of slave owners.

Joanne Melish, a historian at the University of Kentucky, who wrote *Disowning Slavery: Gradual Emancipation and 'Race' in New England, 1780–1860* (1998), said: "The absolute amnesia about slavery here on the one hand, and the gradualness of slavery ending on the other, work together to make race a very destructive thing in New England....If you have obliterated historical memory of actual slavery—because we're the free states, right?—that makes it possible to turn around and look at a [Southern] population that is disproportionately poor and say it must be their own inferiority. That is where New England's particular brand of racism comes from."

Connecticut abolished slavery only in 1848. There were thousand-acre plantations there. *Hartford Courant* journalist Anne Farrow wrote, "A mentor of mine has said that New England really democratized slavery. Where in the South few people owned so many slaves, here in the North, many people owned a few. There was widespread ownership of black people."

Perhaps the most notable of the New England slave owners was John Winthrop, of "City on a Hill" fame, who was the first governor of Massachusetts Bay Colony. Winthrop had slaves at his Ten Hills Farm, and in 1641 he helped pass a law making chattel slavery legal in the American colonies. Winthrop's house was bought by the Royall family, which made its fortune from slave plantations in Antigua. The Royalls helped endow the Harvard Law School, whose seal until May 2016 had a portion of the Royall family crest. The university officially retired the Law School shield in response to the revelations of the Royall family riches acquired in its slave plantations.

The family also endowed the prestigious Royall Professorship of Law, almost always held by the dean. When current Supreme Court associate justice Elena Kagan became dean of the Harvard Law School, she decided to pass on the Royall title. She reportedly didn't say why. But it may have been her contribution to the acknowledgment of the embarrassing and disgraceful heritage of slave trade-generated academic philanthropy.

In the last 15 years or so, there have been important new discoveries impacting the national consciousness of the buried history of the North's complicity in slavery.

Joanne Melish's 1998 book noted above was a key contribution. This was followed by:

- Uncovering of the African Burial Ground in lower Manhattan where 15,000–20,000 burials of Negroes—mostly slaves—occurred in the 1700s. Establishment of a U.S. national memorial at the site in 2007.
- Descendants of Rhode Island slave traders begin to publicly examine their family history in a journey that results in Katrina Browne's PBS documentary,
- *Traces of the Trade: A Story from the Deep North*, and Tom DeWolf's book, *Inheriting the Trade: A Northern Family Confronts Its Legacy as the Largest Slave-Trading Family in U.S. History.*
- Reparations activists file lawsuits based on the role of Northern banks, insurance companies, etc.
- "Slavery in New York" exhibit at New York Historical Society sets records for attendance.
- Major *Providence Journal* series on Rhode Island's complicity in slavery.
- Major *Hartford Courant* series on Connecticut's role in slavery, later made into a book, *Complicity: How the North Promoted, Prolonged, and Profited from Slavery.*
- Brown University president Ruth Simmons creates Slavery and Justice Committee to examine the role of slavery in the founding of the university and broader issues its raises for today.
- Aetna apologizes for its historic role in slavery as do Connecticut, New Jersey, and several southern states.
- Many local towns, churches, and families begin to uncover their complicity (often with the help of the Tracing Center on Histories and Legacies of Slavery.)

I am indebted to James DeWolf Perry, executive director of Tracing Center on Histories and Legacies of Slavery (www.tracingcenter.org) in Watertown, Massachusetts, for providing a broad contextual analysis of the economic incentives in the slave trade in the American colonies.

The colonial New England economy was critically dependent on what has often been described, innocently, as the "carrying" or "provisioning" trade, or simply trade to the West Indies. This was, in reality, a trade entirely to support slave plantations in the West Indies, and the North's share of the profits from that vast operation enabled the northern colonies to take hold, flourish, and eventually to play a critical role in the rebellion against Great Britain.

Similarly, the northern economy in the antebellum era profited handsomely from the cotton trade, with much of the income from southern cotton plantations flowing north to pay for financing, insuring, marketing, provisioning, and transportation for cotton production and the cotton trade. Clearly, there is much, much more to be uncovered, learned, and taught about America's shared heritage, North and South, in our original sin of wealth creation on the backs of kidnapped and enslaved black Africans.

Conclusion

I want to close with a reminder that in enduring racial, ethnic, and religious conflicts whose traumatic memories pass from generation to generation, we do not walk through history because it is merely intellectually interesting. We do it because there is cumulative experience in the broad field of psychologically sensitive conflict analysis and resolution practice that indicates that it is literally a categorical imperative.

The evidence is strong that the wounds of history can only begin to heal when they are uncovered and exposed to contemporary generations which have the moral commitment and wisdom to acknowledge the hurts inflicted on others by their forbears. And to express remorse for what their people did in the past. And finally to ask forgiveness of the victims and their descendants.

I began this chapter with a tribute to an African-American scholar, Peggy Brooks-Bertram, whose work has inspired me to dig deep. I close with a tribute to another scholar-filmmaker, Katrina Browne, who discovered that her forbears, the DeWolf family of Bristol, Rhode Island, were the biggest slave traders in America's biggest slave-trading state.

Katrina literally took a walk through history with family members and an African-American woman colleague in Bristol and to slave forts in Ghana and the ruins of a DeWolf family plantation in Cuba. As briefly noted above, she produced a historic feature-length documentary on the story called "Traces of the Trade: A Story from the Deep North." The film was shown at the Sundance Festival in 2008 and then on PBS's premier program *Point of View* (*POV*).

A final point: I am strongly committed to the "resolution" goals of the George Mason School for Conflict Analysis and Resolution. In the process

I search for signs of progress in healing our national wounds. On October 18, 2016, the *Washington Post* reported a very significant event, under the headline "Chiefs' group apologizes for 'darker periods' of policing." Terrence M. Cunningham, president of the 23,000 member International Association of Chiefs of Police, told a plenary session their annual meeting in San Diego, "While we obviously cannot change the past, it is clear that we must change the future....For our part, the first step is for law enforcement and the IACP to acknowledge and apologize for the actions of the past and the role that our profession has played in the historical mistreatment of communities of color."

When I read this report, I thought, this is a big deal. For a conscientious American white man or woman, it no doubt was.

But then I read my colleague Tony Gaskew's chapter, Chap. 6, "Transforming Systemic Humiliation of Crime and Justice: Reawakening Black Consciousness," and experienced the depth of the rage of a brilliant black scholar and professional in the American justice system and got a devastating sense of the enormity of black American wounds yet to heal.

I hang my head in a newly realized level of shame for my country.

Note

1. On February 14, 2013, during a Lenten Forum at the Washington National Cathedral, I emphasized the psychological importance of the election of Rev. Luter to the SBC presidency and cited press reports that most of the 7000 delegates at the New Orleans convention rose to their feet to cheer the election, many shouting Hallelujah. I also proposed that the Dean of the Cathedral consider inviting Rev. Luter to a discussion of America's unhealed wounds and a walk through the history of North-South and black–white relationships. (www.nationalcathedral.org/forums).

References

Cone, James H. 2011. *The Cross and the Lynching Tree*. Maryknoll: Orbis Books.
Dixon, Thomas. 1902. *The Leopard's Spots*. New York: Doubleday, Page & Company.
———. 1905. *The Clansman*. New York: Grossett and Dunlap.
———. 1939. *The Flaming Sword*. Lexington: University of Kentucky Press.
Fisher, David Hackett. 1985. *Albion's Seed: Four British Folkways in America*. New York: Oxford University Press.
Grant, Susan Mary. 2000. *North Over South*. Lawrence: University of Kansas Press.

Hampton, Jean, and Jeffrey Murphy. 1988. *Forgiveness and Mercy*. Cambridge: Cambridge University Press.

Kantrowitz, Stephen. 2000. *Ben Tillman & the Reconstruction of White Supremacy*. Chapel Hill: University of North Carolina Press.

Mann, Thomas, and Norman Ornstein. 2012. *It's Even Worse than It Looks: How the American Constitutional System Collided with the New Politics of Extremism*. New York: Basic Books.

Melish, Joanne. 1998. *Disowning Slavery: Gradual Emancipation and 'Race' in New England, 1780–1860*. Ithaca: Cornell University Press.

Patterson, Orlando. 1998. *Rituals of Blood*. New York: Basic Civitas.

Rochlin, Gregory. 1978. *Man's Aggression: The Defense of the 'Self'*. Boston: Gambit.

Simpson, Lewis J. 1989. *Mind and the American Civil War: A Meditation on Lost Causes*. Baton Rouge/London: Louisiana State University Press.

Slide, Anthony. 2004. *American Racist: The Life and Films of Thomas Dixon*. Lexington: University Press of Kentucky.

Taylor, William R. 1975. *Cavalier and Yankee: The Old South and American National Character*. Cambridge, MA: Harvard University Press.

Webb, James. 2004. *Born Fighting: How the Scots-Irish Shaped America*. New York: Broadway Books.

Worthington, Everett. 1998. *Forgiveness and Reconciliation*. New York: Routledge.

CHAPTER 6

Transforming the Systemic Humiliation of Crime and Justice: Reawakening Black Consciousness

Tony Gaskew

INTRODUCTION

On May 5, 2016, I participated with 12 other educators from around the nation in a roundtable discussion at the White House on criminal justice reform. During my 30-year journey in the smoke and mirrors of the criminal justice system, which includes working as a police detective at Melbourne Police Department (MPD), being assigned as a member to the Department of Justice's (DOJ's) Organized Crime Drug Enforcement Task Force, and as a tenured associate professor of criminal justice and founding director of a nationally recognized prison education program at the University of Pittsburgh (Bradford), there is very little that I have not seen, heard, or done in the business of crime and justice. I have relied upon the powerful metaphysics of my Blackness to navigate through the truths of thousands of arrests, convictions, and prison sentences, including death penalty cases, as a *mitigator of justice* (Gaskew 2014a). I brought W.E.B. Du Bois to every arrest, James Baldwin to every court proceeding, and Ralph Ellison to every sentencing. There was never a moment

T. Gaskew (✉)
University of Pittsburgh (Bradford), Bradford, PA, USA

131

throughout my career as a Black American criminal justice professional that Malcolm X was not with me. This roundtable discussion and all the subsequent meetings at the White House were no different. Regardless of the agenda, because there is always an agenda, the larger narrative always came back to an applied concept that I have researched, published on, and, more importantly, "collectively lived" as part of my Black American experience: the systemic humiliation of Black spaces within the constructs of crime and justice. The synergy of direct and structural violence directed at Black American diaspora by the criminal justice system is much more complex and destructive than it sounds. Over the past four centuries, the criminal justice system, specifically the policing culture, has been used to fictionally define and frame the Black American experience (Gaskew 2014a, b). As noted by the previous chapter, *The Civil War at 150 Years: Deep Wounds Yet to Heal*, the constructs of crime and justice have opened yet another unhealed wound in American history (Montville 2017).

Systemic humiliation is defined as a static set of institutionally owned and socially constructed set of rules, customs, and beliefs designed to create and sustain a culture that inherits the crippling effects of a politics of shame, self-segregation, and transgenerational learned helplessness (Gaskew 2017a, b). It intentionally strips away any level of dignity and respect and sets into motion a climate void of the universal tenets of connectivity, compassion, mercy, and social justice. Its recipients have always been America's indigenous populations, and none greater than its native sons, Black Americans. However, speaking the language of a social scientist, systemic humiliation is not the root cause of these killing fields but the insidious side effect of an invisible history of micro and macro-aggressions against Blackness. Born from the womb of our nation's *original sin* of chattel enslavement and the Black American Holocaust, the mental illness of White Supremacy is the fundamental "cause" in this social experiment of human suffering and continues to sit at the core of how Black spaces are "effected" through oppression, marginalization, and humiliation (Gaskew 2014a, b). The 400-year-old illusion of White superiority and Black inferiority has saturated the poisons of greed, anger, and ignorance (Williams 2000) into every single American social institution, infecting the hearts, minds, and souls of tens of millions of its willing host cells.

Arguably, there is no greater by-product of this psychosis than the racially constructed criminal justice system, specifically the policing culture, and the direct and structural violence it has inflicted on Black bodies. Today, despite making up less than 5 percent of the adult population, Black men occupy nearly 40 percent of our nation's prison cells (The

Sentencing Project 2015). Black American spaces are more likely to be stopped, more likely to be arrested, and more likely to be incarcerated. As a result, today a police officer can walk into any maternity ward in America, and with an almost statistical certainty, place handcuffs on one out of every three nameless newborn Black American infants. You see, crime is a corporately constructed poison. It is a tool of White Supremacy used to demonize Black American humanity.

The systemic humiliations inherited by the Black American experience through the policing culture are metaphysical in nature, scope, and understanding; thus, it's only logical that a Black ontological lens be used to examine *healing* solutions. In the brief space of this chapter, using an autoethnographic methodology, I will attempt to synergize the thousands of interviews and group discussions I've had as an active participant observer during my 30-year study of crime and justice. My collective input encourages the reawakening of a Black American consciousness drawn from applied concepts of *Black Cultural Privilege* (Gaskew 2014a, b; 2017a, b, c), a reawakening that will apply the essence of Black fearlessness and create the unwavering cultural demands of *truth, accountability, empowerment,* and *healing.*

THE REAWAKENING OF BLACK CONSCIOUSNESS: BLACK CULTURAL PRIVILEGE

James Baldwin (1965) believed that Black Americans are the conscience of America and to be Black and conscious in America is to be in a constant state of rage. You see, a strong and vibrant Black consciousness has always been the moral compass of saving America from itself. It has been at the forefront of fighting the war against the mental illness of White Supremacy for nearly four centuries in America. It has successfully won the physical, psychological, and spiritual battles of the holocaust of enslavement, the Black Codes, and Jim Crow. As a Black American man born in the early 1960s, I saw firsthand the incredible life force of Black consciousness with the awakening of the *Black Power Movement*, giving birth to a generation of revolutionaries who immersed themselves in the collective goals echoed by Karenga (2010): to solve pressing problems within the Black American community and to continue the revolutionary struggle being waged to end White Supremacy, racism, and oppression against Black spaces. Today, Black consciousness needs a reawakening. A reawakening I describe as

Black Cultural Privilege. Black Cultural Privilege is the physical, mental, and spiritual awareness that connects the rich diverse history of an African past with the ever-evolving journey into the legacy of the collective lived Black American experience. It's an unconscious bond that exists among a people whose roots share an indestructible cultural DNA that has only been strengthened by 400 years of direct and structural violence, enslavement, the Black Codes, and Jim Crow. BCP defines the essence of Blackness.

Without a doubt, we, as an entire universe of living beings, are one. Everything in it, around it, and shaped by it is alive, always in motion, and connected to everything else. We know this for a fact because our common senses are designed for the sole purpose of this synergy. When the sun shines, the wind blows, or the rain falls, it brings with it the same window of life to all beings. Nothing in the universe is spared. However, the human connection to this vast universe is only between 6000 and 150,000 years old, depending on which story you enjoy, science or faith. Regardless of the version, the human connection with the universe began in the rich cultural soil of Africa, the original Garden of Eden, and through the DNA of its Black African people, the original Adam and Eve. Black bodies were the first human students of the universe, and Black Americans are their living testament. Black bodies were the first human voices, and they created the first human languages and the first human civilizations. Black bodies were the first human beings to be taught the gifts of truth, humility, and forgiveness; that we all share the same duty of preserving life; that we are all connected under the universal principle that if one living being suffers, all living beings suffer. They were the first to absorb the life lessons of compassion, mercy, pride, empathy, righteousness, courage, unity, compromise, and love, and the first to apply the gift of the *fourth eye*. Black bodies were the first scholars of metaphysics, the ethnosphere, spirituality, enlightenment, faith, and karma (Karenga 2010; Williams 2000); the first to apply the philosophical concepts of awareness, morality, and wisdom (Williams 2000); the first to be taught about the poisons of greed, anger, and ignorance (p. 46); the first to use the family building blocks of teachers, teachings, and communities (pp. 33–35); the first to understand the universal rule of cause and effect, that pain and happiness, along with life and death, are all part of the interconnected cycle of life. Black bodies were the first to apply the principles of fearlessness (p. 166) as a life road map; the first to recognize the duty of not contributing to evil, doing good, and doing good for others (p. 91). The universe taught the world's first human beings, Black people, *the art of life* (p. 7).

Just to be clear, this reawakening is not just another layer of Afrocentricity (Asante 2003). Black Americans are no longer negotiating from a position of social, political, or economic weakness. Those days are over. We have the resources to frame and define the concepts of crime and justice. Kwame Ture (1967) once noted that "confusion is the greatest enemy of the revolution" (p. viii). There is no longer any confusion in our revolution. We know exactly what to do. We now simply have to do it. This reawakening is the natural evolution of the Black American conscience (Du Bois 1994). It's a visionary consciousness that filters, deconstructs, and eliminates the by-products of shame, self-segregation, and transgenerational learned helplessness (Gaskew 2014a) inherited by 400 years of White Supremacy. It empowers Black spaces in the ideological war against White superiority and Black inferiority. It produces a cultural fearlessness that challenges the legitimacy of any social construct in America that attempts to criminalize Blackness. It confronts the systemic actors of direct and structural violence, that use the mask of law and order to conspire against the Black American diaspora. It compels truth and demands accountability, holding institutional stakeholders responsible for maintaining justice to standards established and owned by Black American voices. As the founders of humanity, Black people must take responsibility for their own destiny. Black Americans must make peace with their own historical legacy. Black Americans must take ownership of either transforming or disposing of the current criminal justice system. Black Americans must wake up each morning and take full responsibility for the changes that we want to make in *our* lives and in *our* world (Williams 2000, p. 178). The reawakening of a twenty-first-century Black American conscience will end the life cycle of White Supremacy and place the moral compass back into the hands of the universe's first human beings (Gaskew 2017c). At the core of BCP sits a set of *cultural demands* that will foster transformative justice within the policing culture.

Cultural Truth

This first hurdle Black Americans must overcome after the reawakening is mastering truths about the criminal justice system and the policing culture. As a people, we need to stop lying to ourselves. We don't have either a good or bad relationship with the justice system. We simply don't have a relationship. The criminal justice system is not part of the connective bond of living beings within the universe. The criminal justice system does not recognize the cultural legacy of the first humans on the planet. The actors whose livelihood depends on criminal justice system do not recognize their duty to not spread evil, to do good, and to do good for others. Its inner core is based on the foundational poisons of greed, anger, and ignorance, all directed at the dehumanization of the Black American experience. Thus, as Black Americans we must first decide whether creating a relationship with the criminal justice system and its gatekeepers, the policing culture, is even worth the effort. Is the system even worth reforming or saving? The social construct which started off as slave patrols, conducting stop and frisks on Black bodies for over three centuries, has never morphed into anything other than a solidified tool of White superiority and Black inferiority. I ask again, is reforming the criminal justice system even worth the cosmic energy of the founders of humanity?

Additionally, there are two cultural truths about the criminal justice system that Black America should consider before moving forward. First, White Supremacy will always be embedded within the policing culture and the criminal justice system. Regardless of the sincerity of any reform efforts, the social institutions of policing, courts, and corrections were made by White Americans, are controlled by White Americans, only to serve and benefit White Americans and to dehumanize Black Americans. The criminal justice system in America is the *Great White Shark* (Gaskew 2014a), a corporately constructed 24-hours-a-day, 7-days-a-week eating machine and multitrillion-dollar-a-year business with the sole purpose of morally destroying Black bodies, Black culture, and Black potential (Karenga 2010). It will never willingly surrender its cultural influence to inflict systemic humiliations against Black spaces. Its power must be taken and its culture humbled.

Second, only a complete state of Black American hopelessness in the justice apparatus will usher in the opportunity for transformative justice. There is much more pain and suffering that needs to be absorbed. Please keep in mind that a nation that was founded on the universal evils of greed, anger, and ignorance (Williams 2000) has created a very high threshold for violence, which karmically does not bode well for the policing culture. Over the last four centuries, the mental illness of White Supremacy has very effectively enslaved a segment of the Black American population, convincing them that their Black lives, the lives of their Black families, and the lives of their Black communities are worthless and inferior, while at the same time convincing them that White lives, the lives of White families, and the lives of White communities are valuable and superior. Black inferiority and White superiority has resulted in the killings of Black bodies at the hands of other Black bodies as well as the attempted extermination of Black culture and Black potential through the holocaust of mass incarceration. For the most part, the policing actors who maintain its culture from the original sins of this nation, the colonization and criminalization of Black bodies, have escaped the cosmic wrath of their actions. However, those days are coming to an end. The metaphysics of violence has shifted. Black voices, whether they are framed by scholarship or clergy, that White fragility historically counted on to pacify young Black rage against state-sponsored violence, are now silent. You see, over the past several 100 years, the policing culture has demanded two basic needs from Black America: *respect* and *fear*. Black America never respected the policing culture and never will. It is impossible to respect anyone or anything that does not understand the oneness of humanity. However, some Black American communities provided the policing culture the *fear* they demanded. There are literally generations of Black American bodies who have been corporately conditioned not to make eye contact with the policing culture, to treat them as overseers on a plantation, to run and hide at the very mention of the police, for little or no justification. In fact, an argument can be made that the transgenerational trauma of *police fear* is regenerated every time Black parents have the legendary "talk" with Black sons or Black daughters on how to survive a police encounter.

The universal dilemma facing the policing culture today is that slowly but surely Black souls are being *woken*. The illusion of justice is being exposed and the primary tool of fear used to enslave Black people is quickly losing its effectiveness—too many unlawful stops, arrests, and shootings—too many excuses, lies, and cover-ups—too much greed, anger, and ignorance—too much death and indifference—too much evil. Black America has reawakened to the reality that there is nothing else the criminal justice system can inflict on their souls that has not already been tried to void their entire human condition: oppression, marginalization, alienation, subjugation, enslavement, incarceration, and even extermination. Economic, employment, medical, housing, and educational sanctions. Basic human rights denied. All modes of evil tried and failed. Now, fearlessness is beginning to take hold among Black spaces. The same Black spaces who once saw no value or worth in their own Black lives are beginning to see no value or worth in police lives. The same Black spaces who once saw themselves as active peacemakers are now sitting back and waiting for the universe to correct itself. Violence begets violence and the policing culture will no longer be bystanders to karma. The policing culture will never be safe as long as Black America is not safe.

Cultural Accountability

As Fanon (1967) suggested regarding the process of decolonization, "to tell the truth, the proof of success lies in a whole social structure being changed from the bottom up" (35). If Black America decides it is worth their human investment to decolonize the criminal justice system, then their full and unwavering cultural commitment is required. There will no longer be a moral middle ground on issues of Black humanity. It's either all or nothing, and Black America must be prepared to hold the criminal justice system fully accountable. Black America must be willing to *unfriend* the gatekeepers of the criminal justice system, starting with the police. The unfriending process involves cultural tough love. No different than managing the lifestyle changes of someone who is suffering from an addiction, Black America must stop enabling the policing culture—that is, eliminating all *Black funding*, *Black patronage*, and *Black empathy* for the policing culture.

First, Black America must withdraw all economic support for the policing culture; oppose any and all efforts that increase the monetary coffers of policing. Under no circumstances should any pay raises, new equipment, or new training receive Black support; oppose the hiring of any new officers or police staff; vote anyone out of office that supports any of these efforts. In any case of alleged police misconduct, Black America must report the incident by initiating an official complaint and levy federal civil litigation against the city, the agency, and the officers involved. Black America must file official complaints on every police contact. This includes any police encounter, whether a traffic stop, a pedestrian stop, and any level of verbal or physical force used by the police. Black America must make every single Black American contact with the police cost the justice system money. Second, Black America must entirely withdraw their community support for the policing culture; do not participate in police-community relations meetings, volunteer police academies, or the police athletic league; oppose any effort to establish community-oriented policing in Black neighborhoods; do not support the use of school resource officers in any educational setting that serves Black students. As well, Black

America must actively withdraw any future employment participation within the policing career field. Although Black Americans serving as police officers nationwide have always been sparse (Bureau of Justice Statistics 2015), the policing culture does not deserve the human potential and moral sacrifice of one more young, dignified, and talented Black American body among its rank and file. Black American police will no longer be caught in the crossfire between Black and Blue.

Third and finally, Black America must abandon all of its emotional support for the policing culture. The biggest advantage of being from a family of Black American police officers with over 70 years of combined participant observation experience is that you are completely immersed into the emotional makeup of the policing culture. Without a doubt, the absolute worst and most seductive vice the policing culture has ever inherited from Black communities across the nation is their emotional permission of *perceived entitlement*. Since the twilight years of the Black Power Movement, Black inferiority and White superiority in policing has successfully framed a narrative of *good* and *bad* Black America. The rules are simple. If you unquestionably believe the American system of justice is fair, equitable, and just, openly support the policing culture, and the most important, publicly criticize and degrade Black spaces that don't, you are a good Black American. If not, you are a bad Black American. As noted in *Rethinking Prison Reentry* (Gaskew 2014a), there is a segment of Black America that is very comfortable with this narrative because it allows them a psychosocial window to escape the weight of 400 years of dehumanization. Thus, good Black Americans have given the policing culture emotional carte blanche to police bad Black Americans—that is, the emotional permission to basically do whatever the policing culture wants, whenever the policing culture wants, and to whomever the policing culture wants, as long as they don't *incarcerate* good Black Americans; the emotional permission to do no wrong, and to never admit guilt, fault, or weakness about anything, anywhere, or anytime, as long as they don't *humiliate* good Black Americans; the emotional permission to embrace a pseudo-warrior mentality, where the policing culture is given hero-like status, have funeral processions reserved for mythical royalty, and openly rewarded for acts of direct and structural violence, as long as they don't *terrorize* good Black Americans; the emotional permission that has allowed police chiefs from Baltimore, Chicago, and New York to look right into the eyes of Black people and successfully frame the narrative that Black-on-Black crime is the fault of good Black Americans. Perhaps even more telling, the emotional permission that granted the policing culture unfiltered permission to unlawfully stop, search, arrest, and kill Black bodies and to know with a degree of absolute certainty that they will never be held accountable by good Black Americans. Thus, the emotional support for policing must be culturally rescinded by Black America.

Black America must allow the policing culture to fail; to take back the gift of Black forgiveness; to withdraw Black empathy, mercy, and compassion; to remove Black trust, dignity, and any sense of love. No more Black truth, righteousness, or wisdom. Black America must stop apologizing for and protecting the policing culture from Black America; to let White Supremacy, permeate and suffocate the policing culture; to admit that the policing culture has spread evil; to allow the universal poisons of greed, anger, and ignorance to completely consume the culture; to welcome the onset of fear and mortality within the policing culture; to concede that pain and suffering are universal truths that the policing culture must also face. Black America must get out of the way of karma. Police cultural fragility is the best-kept secret in the business of crime and justice.

Cultural Empowerment

The Black American experience must define and frame the policing culture. Black civilian-led policing, from bottom to top, must project its own sense of Black connective humanity into the policing role, purpose, and culture. Black voices must approve the hiring of every single new police officer across the nation. No pay raises, promotions, or union perks will go unchecked without Black oversight. The process of all citizen-initiated complaints regarding police misconduct toward Black bodies, and all subsequent internal investigations, will be managed by Black people. Every Black space will require every single police officer in the nation to retake their oaths and rededicate their allegiance to serve and protect under the tenets of dignity, mercy, and compassion. The purpose of policing will no longer be to serve the best interests of their fellow officers, their agency, or the corporate greed of the criminal justice system. Black spaces will shift the narrative of the policing culture. First, there are no *good* or *bad* cops. Over my 30 years as an insider of the policing culture, I've discovered there are simply *righteous, rotten, or riddled* people, all who happen to have badges. Those who are righteous, the mitigators of justice (Gaskew 2014a), simply try *to do the right thing*. Those who are rotten, the corruptors of justice, simply try *to do evil*. And those who are riddled, the cowards of justice, simply try *to do nothing*. Second, the overwhelming majority of police officers today and the true enemy of Black America live comfortably within the riddled spectrum of the policing culture. These are the police officers, primarily White, that witness the daily racial humiliations projected on Black bodies under the rule of the law and use the power of their silence to protect the police officers who engage in systemic dehumanization of Blackness from truth and accountability. Their cowardice must be exposed and punished. And third, more Black bodies must be willing to sacrifice and share their Black essence by serving as mitigators of justice. A reawakened Black consciousness will usher in an ultra-professional policing culture, which includes a synergized Black American police officer. More Black American police officers, serving in the role of mitigators, will actively *police* the officers who are seduced by the cultural offerings of greed (money, power, and sex), anger (punishing Blackness), or ignorance (assimilating to White Supremacy). The blue wall of silence will come to an end, and the policing culture as we know it will either shift toward the essence of Blackness or become extinct. However, a reawakening of Black consciousness without a sense of *healing* only sows the seeds of shame, self-subjugation, and transgenerational learned helplessness. That realm of psychological violence will no longer be accepted. This process also requires the policing culture to publicly confess and to publicly accept culpability for its *crimes against Black humanity*.

Cultural Healing

First, truth and accountability panels must be held across the nation, where police officers, police agencies, and the policing culture publicly admit the damage they have intentionally inflicted upon Black bodies. These actors of direct and structural violence must admit their crimes against Black humanity and accept full accountability for their actions. Without exception, every policing agency in America must submit to actively participating in this process of systemic healing. Second, every single Black body that has ever been shamed, self-segregated, or transgenerationally traumatized by the policing culture will be made whole again by investment in their human potential. Every single Black body that has been jailed or imprisoned will be compensated. Every single Black body that has come under the control of community corrections will be compensated. Every single Black child whose parent has been subjected to the corrupters or cowards of justice will be compensated. Every single police officer in America will understand that when they make a decision to enslave a Black body under the tenets of White superiority and Black inferiority, a price will be paid. Third and finally, the policing culture will be the source of the compensation. Every single dollar obtained through civil asset forfeiture, court fines, and associated fees nationwide will be used to make Black bodies whole again. According to the National Institute for Justice (2015) since 2001, nearly $30 billion has been seized through civil asset forfeiture and sits in the *drug war chest* of the policing culture. This number grows exponentially each year by $4 billion. Unfortunately, there is a dearth of research on the dollar amount collected by each of our 35,000 municipalities regarding the criminal court costs associated with the enslavement of Black bodies. But, if a town the size of Ferguson, Missouri, with a population of roughly 22,000, can issue nearly 33,000 warrants and collect $2.6 million in revenue during a single year (U.S. Department of Justice 2014), can you just imagine the hundreds of billions of dollars being generated annually by the policing culture from Black bodies? Can you imagine the trillions of dollars that the policing culture has pilfered by dehumanizing Black bodies, Black culture, and Black potential since the inception of slave patrols? The time has come for Black America to demand payment on a 400-year-old debt.

Final Thoughts

When Black America finally decides to choose the *red pill*, game over. The only plausible way that fewer than one million full- and part-time sworn members of the policing culture, given its level of fragility and its appetite for the universal poisons of greed, anger, and ignorance, can systemically humiliate 43 million Black bodies is because they choose the *blue pill*. The entire criminal justice system is just a magic trick, designed to hypnotize Black spaces into believing in the *illusion of justice*. All of its historic authority and entitlement rests on the assumption that Black America will continue to fear, pray, and forgive. Black Cultural Privilege calls on the essence of Blackness to reawaken its universal power of fearlessness; to defy the policing culture, exposing its weakness to enforce compliance; to confront the policing culture, demanding truth, accountability, empowerment, and healing; and to threaten the policing culture, forcing either its humility or humiliation. The only question remaining is when.

REFERENCES

Asante, M. 2003. *Afrocentricity: The Theory of Social Change*. Souk Village: African American Images.

Baldwin, J. 1965. Negro Leaders on Violence. *Time* 86: 17–21.

Bureau of Justice Statistics. 2015. *Employment and Expenditure*. Retrieved from http://www.bjs.gov/

Du Bois, W.E.B. 1994. *The Souls of Black Folk*. Mineola: Dover Publications.

Fanon, F. 1967. *The Wretched of the Earth*. London: Penguin.

Gaskew, T. 2014a. *Rethinking Prison Reentry: Transforming Humiliation into Humility*. Lanham: Lexington Books.

———. 2014b. The Policing of the Black American Male: Transforming Humiliation into Humility in Pursuit of Truth and Reconciliation. In *Crimes Against Humanity in the Land of the Free: Can a Truth and Reconciliation Process Heal Racial Conflict in America?* ed. I. Michelle Scott. Santa Barbara: ABC-CLIO Publishing.

———. 2017a. Do I Want Be a 30 Percenter or 70 Percenter?: Black Cultural Privilege. In *Race, Education, and Reintegrating Formerly Incarcerated Citizens: Counter Stories and Counter Spaces*, ed. Joni Schwartz and John Chaney. Lanham: Lexington Books.

———. 2017b. Unfriending the Policing Culture: The Reawakened Black Consciousness. In *Policing Black and Brown Bodies: Policing in the Age of Black Lives Matter*, ed. Sandra E. Weissinger and Dwayne Mack. Lanham: Lexington Books.

———. 2017c. Mindfulness, the Reawakening of Black Dharma, and Mastering the Art of Policing. In *Collective Dignity: Practices, Discourses, and Transformations,* eds. Chipamong Chowdhury, G. Saab, Z. Luckay, M. Britton, and J. Gerson. Germany: Dignity Press.

Karenga, M. 2010. *Introduction to Black Studies*. Los Angeles: University of Sankore Press.

Montville, J.V. 2017. The Civil War at 150 Years: Deep Wounds Yet to Heal. In *Power, Humiliation, and Suffering in America*, ed. Daniel Rothbart. New York: Palgrave Macmillan.

The National Institute for Justice. 2015. *Policing for Profit*. Retrieved from http://ij.org/report/policing-for-profit/executive-summary/

The Sentencing Project. 2015. *Black Lives Matter: Eliminating Racial Inequity in the Criminal Justice System*. Retrieved from http://sentencingproject.org/wp-content/uploads/2015/11/Black-Lives-Matter.pdf

The United States Department of Justice. 2014. *Investigation of the Ferguson Police Department*. Retrieved from https://www.justice.gov/sites/default/files/opa/press-eleases/attachments/2015/03/04/ferguson_police_department_report.pdf

Ture, K. 1967. *Black Power: The Politics of Liberation*. New York: Vintage Books.

Williams, A. 2000. *Being Black: Zen and the Art of Living with Fearlessness and Grace*. Berkley: Penguin Compass Press.

CHAPTER 7

Truth-Telling from the Margins: Exploring Black-Led Responses to Police Violence and Systemic Humiliation

Arthur Romano and David Ragland

INTRODUCTION

This chapter examines the layered, intersecting, and often overwhelming forms of injustice that shape experiences of systemic humiliation. We analyze systems the complex discursive, institutional, and material arrangements that significantly shape the lived experiences of Black people in the United States. In so doing, we seek to understand how the repetition of silencing, erasure, the (re)framing of Black people as a threat, as well as other forms of marginalization continue to contribute to this humiliation. We build on Tony Gaskew's theme developed in Chap. 6 that the systemic nature of the oppression of Black people in the United States involves a persistent existential threat, material inequality, and cultural and symbolic assault that intersect in ways that overwhelm and generate feelings of powerlessness. As Gaskew argues, the work of truth-telling supports the

A. Romano (✉)
School for Conflict Resolution and Analysis, George Mason University, Arlington, VA, USA

D. Ragland
Pacifica Graduate Institute, Carpinteria, CA, USA

© The Author(s) 2018
D. Rothbart (ed.), *Systemic Humiliation in America*,
https://doi.org/10.1007/978-3-319-70679-5_7

145

development of one's own voice as the resistance and autonomy necessary to overcome systemic humiliation.

It is this intersection of outrage and powerlessness that international researchers highlight as central to experiences of humiliation (Coleman et al. 2007; Leidner et al. 2012). As a result, it is of critical importance to not only draw attention to the systemic context in which persistent experiences of humiliation occur but to also highlight efforts aimed at constructing social spaces in which people that experience oppression explore ways to heal from and critically analyze and respond to those experiences. In particular, we highlight the Truth Telling Project (TTP), a grassroots effort founded by three St. Louis natives, activists, and educators in 2014—David Ragland, Anthony Neal, and Pastor Cori Bush—and supported by a core group of activists and academics that are committed to the idea that any attempt to engage with structural racism, systemic humiliation, and particularly issues of police violence, in Black communities must attend carefully to the opinions, perceptions, and experiences of those most directly affected. This approach seeks to move away from a more superficial model focused on "inclusion" and toward the centering of what Gaskew refers to in the previous chapter as a "Black ontological lens."In analyzing the TTP, we highlight the normative commitments, pedagogical orientation, and practices that have been employed over the past two years. The TTP has invited family members of those killed by police, as well as others who have experienced direct police violence, to a series of events in which they can share their experiences and join with people from a wide range of backgrounds who are interested in racial justice. This "testimony" is also often recorded and shared with other communities along with educational materials and dialogue frameworks which are then used to lead discussions focused on supporting those who experience or are at risk of police violence while working to influence social and institutional change in their own locales. In particular, we describe how TTP organizers and participants have attempted to: (1) create supportive and healing spaces for those who have experienced police violence to share their experiences; (2) engage in an analysis of systemic oppression and structural racism that takes those experiences seriously; and (3) explore ways of shifting or transforming systemic oppression and humiliation and seeking greater justice.

In examining the TTP, which grew out of the Ferguson protests, this chapter considers how communities that are deeply alienated from and targeted by the criminal justice system and other institutions are working to build alternative social institutions to address racialized oppression and humiliation while exploring the possibilities for realizing a more just society.

FRAMING HUMILIATION: DECOLONIZATION, CRITICAL RACE THEORY, AND CONTEXT

In order to understand the denial of dignity of Black people in the United States, it is necessary to consider the violent history of oppression and the complex set of overlapping systems (discursive, material, institutional, cultural) that impact the ongoing experiences of subjugation and humiliation today. While we do not offer an exhaustive account of those systems or how they function, we want to emphasize racial subjugation as a systemic power dynamic and social arrangement with a deep history that continues to shape Black experience in the United States (Alexander 2012; Bell 1987; Delgado and Stefancic 2012).

From a global perspective, decolonization and coloniality theorists examine the racialized power relations between the colonizers and the colonized, emphasizing that "coloniality refers to long-standing patterns of power that emerged as a result of colonialism, but that define culture, labor, intersubjective relations, and knowledge production well beyond the strict limits of colonial administrations" (Maldonado-Torres 2007, 244). Azarmandi (2016) argues that colonial occupations were grounded in structural violence which saw as primary new racialized classes of "other" and "subhuman" groups that were used to justify both direct and indirect forms of violence (161). This history of racial violence in the United States includes but is not limited to forced labor, rape, economic deprivation, material extraction, and the nonacknowledgment or trivialization of these forms of violence within the wider society.

Critical race theorists also attempt to account for the ways in which Blacks and people of color (in the United States) experienced the colonial project, slavery, and, most importantly, its ongoing legacy of structural racism and violence (Bell 1987; Delgado and Stefancic 2012). Understanding the palpable effect of these oppressive structures and understanding how they can produce experiences of powerlessness and indignity in the everyday lived experiences of Black people in the United States is of critical importance when considering ways of responding to systemic humiliation. In *Letter From the Regions of My Mind* (1962),

James Baldwin highlights a kind of existential anxiety that is all too common for Black people living in the United States today. He writes:

> For the girls… knew what the price would be, for them, of one misstep…
> One did not have to be very bright to realize how little one could do to change one's situation; one did not have to be abnormally sensitive to be worn down to a cutting edge by the incessant the incessant and gratuitous humiliation and danger one encountered every working day, all day long. The humiliation did not apply merely to working days, or workers; I was thirteen and was crossing Fifth Avenue on my way to the Forty-second Street library, and the cop in the middle of the street muttered as I passed him, 'Why don't you niggers stay uptown where you belong?' (2).

The humiliation of many Black people still includes for too many an anxiety born of the intersectional risks (in this case of race, class, and gender) that Baldwin describes in his cautionary tale of the insecurity felt and realized among the Black girls he knew in Harlem. The inability or limitation to affect one's life prospects in the face of persistent systemic marginalization, which Baldwin describes, along with the inescapable and elevated risks of being a Black person in the United States, we argue create the context for persistent experiences of powerlessness and humiliation.

In their recent research on the affective dimensions of intergroup humiliation, Leidner et al. (2012) examine the importance of anger and shame in understanding experiences of humiliation in their study of intergroup humiliation. While both anger and humiliation involve *a sense of outrage*, the authors suggest that anger differs from humiliation in several important ways. Unlike anger, the experience of humiliation involves a loss of feelings of power and agency according to the authors, which explains why "humiliation in intergroup contexts has been shown to lead to inertia rather than confrontation, despite humiliation leading to a desire/motivation for violence" (Leidner et al. 2012, 2).

Tony Gaskew (2014) articulates a framework for systemic humiliation that centers on the impact of intergenerational subjugation emerging from structural racism and the direct violence of policing and criminal justice processes to maintain injustice for Black people in the United States. As a result of this unequal treatment and dehumanization, he contends, "many share a deep-rooted anger, shame, resentment and mistrust for anyone involved in or around the criminal justice system" (Gaskew 2014, 222). This contextualization of humiliation takes issue with the frequent absence of recognition of historical and present-day trauma in the culture and practices of American institutions toward Blacks in the United States, creating "insurmountable psychosocial obstacles" (Gaskins cited in Scott 2014, 222) for far too many people in their engagement with these systems.

Building on Ginges and Atran's work (2008), Leidner et al. (2012) conclude, "Humiliation episodes are also characterized, however, by powerlessness as a result of the publicly observable power asymmetry between 'humiliator' and 'humiliatee' inherent to humiliating situations" (p. 4). We maintain that when focusing on interpersonal dynamics and the relationship between the humiliator and humiliatee, it is necessary to take into account the systemic context in which people feel stripped of their dignity, as power asymmetry is manifest across multiple axes simultaneously and is made possible in a systemic context. In the following section, we focus briefly on the criminal justice system and the school as sites where Black people are impacted by inequality, exclusion, and violence to provide context for how systemic racism shapes experiences of humiliation in the United States.

THE CRIMINAL JUSTICE SYSTEMS, INEQUALITY, AND EXCLUSION IN THE "NEW JIM CROW"

Michelle Alexander's book *The New Jim Crow: Mass Incarceration in the Age of Color Blindness* (2012) is a seminal work revealing the disenfranchisement of Blacks as a result of being targeted by a range of criminal justice policies that disproportionately target poor Blacks and people of color. Alexander builds on the vast body of research highlighting the impacts of the war on drugs and the targeting of nonviolent drug offenders on Black people in the United States. These and other policy changes resulted in what she terms the *New Jim Crow*, where more African-Americans are under the control of the criminal justice system today, either in prison or on probation or parole, than were enslaved in the 1850s. In this work, Alexander highlights the similarities between the legally sanctioned racial caste system of the Jim Crow period and the changes in laws and policies that led to the mass imprisonment of African-Americans in the United States over the past several decades. She writes, "As the rules of acceptable discourse changed, segregationists distanced themselves from an explicitly racist agenda. They developed instead the racially sanitized rhetoric of 'cracking down on crime'" (43). It was in the context of this racialized approach to "tough on crime" policies that the US prison population grew at an unprecedented rate disproportionately impacting Black people in the United States.

In 2015, African-Americans were incarcerated at 5.1 percent times the rate of Whites (Nellis 2016) and African-American youths comprised 35.1 percent of juvenile arrests (Bureau of Justice Statistics 2015). According to Pew Research Center, Blacks and Latinos constituted 29.2 percent of the U.S. population in 2012 (Lopez 2014) and, as of January 2017, they made up 71.3 percent of all prisoners (Federal Bureau of Prisons 2017). Felony convictions enable discrimination in housing (US Department of Housing and Urban Development 2016; Domonoske 2016; Berson 2013), education, employment, and voting rights (Berson 2013; Chung 2016). Such disproportionate numbers of men and women of color in the criminal justice system negatively impact Black communities, which are not only targets of state surveillance but also regularly traumatized by the loss of loved ones to incarceration (Alexander 2012). While Black boys and young men have been at the center of debates about racialized criminal justice practices, women of color and Black girls are heavily impacted by the criminalization of the Black body. Between 1980 and 2014, the number of incarcerated women increased by more than 700 percent, rising from a total of 26,378 in 1980 to 215,332 in 2014. Further, the number of Black women in prison in 2014 was nearly twice the rate of White women (The Sentencing Project 2014).

Acts of police brutality against Black people can hardly be considered an unfortunate coincidence. According to Rodriguez's (2012) research on police brutality and surveillance, these incidents are "systemic, legally supported, and absolutely normal" (Rodriguez 2012). Black youth are also most at risk of experiencing police brutality, persistent surveillance, and harassment by law enforcement. Recently, police shootings in the United States, especially of Black youth, have garnered increasing international attention following the shootings of Trayvon Martin and Michael Brown, resulting in one of the longest sustained periods of protest the United States has seen in nearly five decades. Some US record-keepers now estimate that an average of 928 people have been killed by police annually over the last eight years (McCarthy 2015). According to the Guardian Project, of the 1092 people killed by police shootings in the United States in 2016, 24.36 percent were African-Americans (The Guardian 2016).

Overall, in 2016 Black people were killed by police at almost three times the rate of Whites in the Unites States (The Guardian 2016). In addition, African-Americans constitute 37 percent of the unarmed population killed by the US police in 2015 (Mapping Police Violence 2016). According to the Centers for Disease Control and Prevention, African-Americans between the ages of 20 and 24 are more likely to be killed by law enforcement, with rates 4.5 times higher than any other group (Wales 2014). Additionally, recent research on racial profiling approaches such as "stop and frisk" demonstrates that these practices are ineffective and damaging toward youth of color (New York Civil Liberties Union 2016). While protests against police violence and structural violence have elevated the profile of these issues, police violence and structural violence remain persistent issues for far too many Black people in the United States (Ragland 2015).

Racial Inequality and Punitive Practices in Schools

The school-to-prison pipeline is a concept that is commonly used to describe the disturbing national trend in which youth are syphoned out of public schools and into the juvenile and criminal justice systems. Many Black youth and youth of color, as well as young people with learning disabilities or histories of poverty, trauma, or violence are disproportionately impacted by "zero-tolerance" policies in schools (Zweifler and Beers 2002; Stinchcomb et al. 2006; Brownstein 2009). Further, the increasing use of "school safety officers" (police) in schools commonly escalates minor school infractions into criminal offenses (Brown 2015), with the negative impacts felt most acutely by urban youth of color.

Students of color are most directly affected by the discriminatory application of discipline policies. In the 2011–12 school year, Black students were suspended three times more than White students and expelled three and a half times more often nationally (Wong 2016). Moreover, Black children are suspended, often for less serious disciplinary matters when compared with White students.

This double standard around school discipline has negative psychological and emotional impacts on Black children with lifelong repercussions. Skiba et al. demonstrate the connections between suspensions, lower academic achievement, and probability of incarceration later in life (Skiba et al. 2003). Apel and Sweeten (2010) note that the arrest of high school students increases the likelihood of them dropping out of school. If the student must appear in court, the probability of dropping out increases four times (Darden citing Apel and Sweeten 2010). Far too many Black children and youth are pushed out of the school system and enter the US criminal justice system and the consequences of incarceration are dire. The result of these harsher forms of exclusionary punishment and the criminalization of students of color is a reduction of life choices and educational and economic opportunities. Educational marginalization and criminalization limits one's life chances and well-being and often excludes these young people from broader inclusion in the democratic process later in life as a range of rights are permanently stripped from people that have been convicted of crimes or plea bargained on charges. This criminalization and the framing of Black youth as deviant sends a negative message to Black children and youth and other young people at risk at an early age. As Bernstein explains, "young people...generally get the message, they are at once disposable and dangerous—worth little to cultivate but anything to contain" (Bernstein 2014, 6).

In the next section, we examine the TTP, a grassroots response to systemic humiliation and the rash of police killings of Black people in the United States.

THE TRUTH-TELLING PROJECT

Indict. Convict. Send these killer cops to jail. The whole damn system...is guilty as hell

This chant was heard from protesters on the streets of Ferguson, Missouri immediately following the shooting death of Black teenager Michael Brown. The broader statement "Black Lives Matter" came to represent a moral claim of human dignity and full personhood in opposition to systemic practices of indignity and humiliation. "Black Lives Matter" is a declaration drawing attention to the continued chasm between "guaranteed" rights and the lived experiences of Black people in the United States today. Further, this statement expresses an awakened consciousness and a sense of agency in seeking to redress centuries of systemic violence. Fuad Al-Daraweesh and Dale Snauwaert (2015) explain, "If we are moral equals, and if our identity is inseparable from our culture, then what follows in principle is a right to cultural recognition. In turn, if we have a right, justified claim, to cultural recognition, then the others are obligated to respect our cultural heritage" (22).

As we highlighted earlier, the systemic nature of oppression involves power asymmetry that is present in humiliating experiences and manifested through complex social mechanisms that negatively and disproportionately impact Black people in the United States. Such accumulated trauma is widely recognized among those in the Black community, but rarely acknowledged by the broader society. Nearly 50 years ago, Dr. Martin Luther King Jr. (MLK) highlighted the depths of this problem:

> When the Constitution was written, a strange formula to determine taxes and representation declared that the Negro was sixty percent of a person. Today another curious formula seems to declare he is fifty percent of a person. Of the good things in life, the Negro has approximately one half those of whites. Of the bad things of life, he has twice those of whites. Thus, half of all Negroes live in substandard housing. And Negroes have half the income of whites. When we turn to the negative experiences of life, the Negro has a double share: There are twice as many unemployed; the rate of infant mortality among Negroes is double that of whites; and there are twice as many Negroes dying in Vietnam as whites in proportion to their size in the population (Quote appears in Zinn and Anthony 2004, 418).

The shooting of Michael Brown Jr. and the indignity experienced by residents in his community in Ferguson and by Black people around the country as they witnessed his body lay in the street for four hours in the hot sun became a contemporary tipping point in relation to these forms of structural violence. Many Black people decided that day that they could not take this assault to their lives any longer. This moment also built on the recent experiences of anger, humiliation, and outrage following the shooting of Trayvon Martin just a few months earlier and is contextualized within centuries of abuse of Black people at the hands of state and private interests. Yet, the disregard and demonization of Black bodies, even in death, as was the case with Michael Brown and Travon Martin as they were inaccurately portrayed as criminals, symbolizes for many a larger message and experience of disregard for Blacks in this society. There is additional resentment that continues to build as many White actively support or remain silent in the face of racist behaviors, institutional practices, and policies.

It was in this context that the Truth Telling Project began, inspired by the ongoing uprisings in Ferguson and growing outrage across the country. TTP explored the possibilities to continue building on the work of these social movements in terms of supporting Black people impacted by police violence, analyzing the causes and impacts of systemic oppression on Black lives, and discussing ways of influencing and demanding change. Fundamental to this approach was an attempt to explore healing and justice that centered and affirmed the dignity of Black lives and the power of movements for racial justice. During these events, some of the stories of people who had experienced police violence and their reflections on the impacts of violence more broadly were recorded in order to educate others about the impacts of systemic racism.

The TTP, which began in the St. Louis/Ferguson community following the shooting of Michael Brown in 2014 grew quickly as founders were joined by St. Louis residents, activists, advocates, and members of the Ferguson protest community along with a core group of social justice educators and restorative justice researchers from around the country. The experience of the conveners of the TTP included working in areas ranging from peace and justice studies, conflict resolution, and transitional justice, to peace education and philosophy. The group was committed to the idea that any attempt to engage with structural racism, particularly issues of police violence in Black communities, must develop processes for dialogue and learning that engage seriously with the knowledge, experiences, and voices of those most directly affected. It was in the context of working on the TTP during its inception that the authors of this article first met each other in 2014.

The first TTP event "Truth Telling Weekend: Ferguson, TRC Summit" was held March 13–15, 2015. TTP organizers extended invitations to educators, activists, and community members impacted by police violence from across the country to discuss the possibilities for a truth and reconciliation (TRC) process emerging from Ferguson. The interest in truth and reconciliation, as well as transitional, transformative, and restorative justice was high following the uprisings in Ferguson which became a flashpoint for conversations addressing racial injustice in the United States. This interest in justice in the United States extended globally as members of TTP received messages from people around the world. Bishop Tutu sent a message prior to the Truth-Telling Weekend to the team, writing:

> From friends I have learned that already due to your courageous presence and unbowed spirit – in the streets and halls of power – over the last 8 months that you have begun to be heard. And that you have changed the nature of the national conversation about racist police violence, bringing to

light the unfortunate pattern that until you stood up had largely been understood as isolated events. But now the nation is debating the deep problems of structural racism and militarized policing tactics. This reframing of the problem is the first step toward true and lasting transformation (Personal Communication, March 2015).

Through a wide constituency of community members across the St. Louis region who convene to listen and offer support to those offering testimony, the TTP facilitates hearings where individuals testify about the violence they have experienced. The TTP also includes workshops and other participatory processes that support analysis of systemic racism and police violence as an entry point for connecting these stories to larger social dynamics and working toward change in their communities. Each day of the Truth-Telling Weekend focused on a specific theme. Day one included two main panels that explored the questions "What does truth and reconciliation look like for Ferguson and beyond" and "what is truth telling and where can it take us?" There were breakout sessions afterwards and three concurrent workshops: Listening and Learning: Tools for Creating Antiracist Counter-Storytelling Communities; Skills for Truth and Reconciliation, Dialogue and Mediation; and Civil Disobedience and Nonviolent Resistance. Day two began with a keynote plenary entitled "Truth Telling and its Impacts on the Civil Rights Movement, The Prison Industrial Complex and International Human Rights," which included SCLC board chairman and close MLK associate, Dr. Bernard Lafayette.

Throughout the first day, individuals who experienced police violence shared their experiences in private rooms and had an option to record their testimony if they wished to share it more widely. The day concluded with a silent march focused on the lack of justice experienced by marginalized communities in the Ferguson area and across the country. Day two included an interfaith service and a question-and-answer session with protest leader Reverend Sekou on the theme of "the Movement & Transforming Communities." The concurrent workshops on Day two included "Schooling, Restorative Justice, and Transforming Policing and our Communities" and "Solidarity, Self Determination and Community Organizing for Liberation" and closed with a panel discussion/workshop named "From Truth Telling to Transformation: Envisioning the Future." The weekend was designed to move from analysis of truth-telling as a process and activity that had been used in communities around the world to one that could engage participants in the Ferguson/St. Louis areas in exploring the goals they had voiced in prior meetings for transformative justice and greater self-reliance. The concurrent workshops helped to deepen the conversations began during plenary panels, while also providing skills and resources for participants interested in racial justice work and continuing the work of truth-telling.

Over 300 people were in attendance throughout the first weekend, and following this event, participants from across the country reached out to team members to share how they were influenced by participating in the process and offering support and encouragement for the project to move forward. One of the participants, for example, reached out to share that her daughter's attendance in the nonviolence training workshop during that first Truth-Telling Weekend inspired her activism during the University of Missouri student protests, which saw the institution's president resign in response to organizing that took place regarding racial justice issues on campus. With the boost in attention from a follow-up event that June with Dr. Angela Davis and growing support for the project, TTP launched its Truth Initiative, which hosted public hearings, recording testimony and providing opportunities for testimony on experiences of police violence and its root causes on November 13 and 14, 2015, in Ferguson. To date, the TTP and communities around the country have held over 30 workshops, panel discussions, living room conversations, and other events focused on truth-telling connected through an intention to value and learn from the experiences of victimized community members. These events have included living room conversations with White allies discussing issues of race and police violence in Saint Louis suburbs, the truth-telling hearings in Ferguson, and the Night of a Thousand Conversations (where communities listened to live streaming testimony from the Ferguson hearings) and explored themes related to systemic racism and the Voices of Freedom Concert (which explored truth-telling through the arts).

WHY TRUTH-TELLING?

Imani Scott's groundbreaking work in *Crimes Against Humanity: Can a Truth and Reconciliation Process Heal America's Racial Divide* (2014) argues that "Truth Telling" provides a necessary social moral inventory that seeks to generate opportunities to reflect and respond to historical and contemporary racial injustice. This acknowledgment of systemic violence against Black people and other marginalized groups is first step for any society interested in a TRC work. This need for acknowledgment of the impacts of oppression and awareness of erasure of violence against Black people in the wider US society was consistent with the sense that many in St. Louis/Ferguson protest community had made when they emphasized the need to make oppression more visible and to hold contemporary institutions accountable. It was this context in which we began to have conversations with community members impacted by violence, activists, academics, and others during the Ferguson uprising exploring the possibility for TRC processes in the United States starting in the St. Louis area.

It was clear from the start that many workshop participants were uncomfortable with the notion of a state-led TRC process. These misgivings were grounded in Black people's contemporary experiences with the state, which is still complicit in the disproportionate murder and incarceration of Black people. Further, many of the protestors had recently experienced being shot with rubber bullets, assaulted with tear gas, arrested for arbitrary injunctions, and met with militarized police during peaceful protests in Ferguson and St. Louis. In a series of passionate discussions about whether there should be a US government-sponsored process, residents and organizers also raised concerns about other models, such as the one used in South Africa, questioning whether it had or could have led to a deeper structural transformation of inequality.

Activists, students, and community members often talked about the ongoing traumatization that occurred after each killing of a Black person in the United States and a sense of overwhelm, expressed in terms of not being "able to even keep up with the hashtags"[1] (re: anxiety from continuous Black people killed by police). In these discussions, it was clear the United States was not a postconflict context in which the direct violence had subsided. Instead, each day brought more trauma and disappointment to the St. Louis/Ferguson community and others across the country because of the nonindictment of Darren Wilson, police response to protesters, ongoing police shootings, and the invalidating responses of "all lives matter" and "blue lives matter" across the country. On one conference call for the TTP, restorative justice scholar and practitioner Erin Dunlevey reported that her former student, Kimani Gray, was murdered by the NYPD. Erin was facilitating restorative circles with students at the time and offered to have a proxy for the officer who murdered Kimani join the circle to offer students a chance at cathartic forgiveness and possible long-term healing. The students protested because they viewed the police violence as an ongoing threat, viewing the interpersonal resolution (or reconciliation) attempts within restorative justice as too contentious, while the truth-telling and self-expression of these restorative circles were embraced by students.

In their research on Palestinians in the West Bank, Ginges and Atran (2008) note that persistent experiences of violence and humiliation "[do] not seem to contribute to political violence" as many commentators assume; however "it does seem to suppress support for conflict resolution," given the mistrust, inertia, and resentment that follows from the repetition of humiliating experiences (1). In the truth-telling process in St Louis, the introduction of narratives about conflict resolution were met with similar resistance and distrust initially, given that these processes were sometimes seen as an attempt to gloss over differences or as a naive attempts to change dynamics that were not yet ripe for resolution, given their deep historical and structural roots. Similarly, this resistance to attempts at conflict resolution was clearly present in our meetings and is not surprising, given the stress associated with living with the *ongoing* existential threats that many participants faced. In response to these discussions, the name "Truth Telling" was adopted to privilege the need to acknowledge oppression and to push back on what was seen as a rush on the part of some Whites to push forgiveness in the context of ongoing systemic racial conflict without first accounting for the impacts of racialized violence. The TTP was understood by organizers as the beginning of (and a part of) a much larger, long-term approach of creating an environment in which to consider ways of responding to these injustices that centered the voices of the people deeply impacted. St. Louis/Ferguson community members were invited as a central part of the TTP to share their stories of police brutality and to join with others interested in social justice in examining the causes of that violence and how people were working to impact social change.

The TTP started with this political and normative commitment of valuing experiences rendered silent because of dominant discourses of race in the United States which often questioned a priori the legitimacy of Black people's claims of injustice. The TTP project team chose not to pursue an official Truth Commission focused on gaining legitimacy in the eyes of the state but rather an initiative drawing its validity from a growing community working to sustain a movement for Black lives.

As a result, the TTP differs from TRC processes in several key ways. First, the TTP is not a state-led process and grows out of a "movement moment" in which people are deeply skeptical of the criminal justice system—and the state more broadly—and as a result are searching for alternative ways of building greater social justice at the community level. Further, rather than having a primary focus on bringing together victims and perpetrators, the TTP seeks to bring people whose experiences are often marginalized or silenced together with people that are supportive so that those experiences can be heard and reflected upon in a collective process of recognition and critical reflection about building power for future change. The TTP also seeks to explore collective political efficacy in regard to disrupting the status quo of structural racism and violence by exploring and developing models for connecting analysis with grassroots political action.

In discussions leading up to the Truth-Telling Weekend, local organizers worked closely with potential truth-tellers (community members that were interested in testifying about their experiences of police violence) regarding who they might like to have in a group of witnesses listening to their testimony and asking questions about their experiences. A variety of ideas were discussed, including the need to have witnesses who personally knew what it was like to experience systemic racism. Others were interested in having people be witnesses to testimony that had been supportive of the protest movement; those that had come out on the streets with protesters or provided support for protesters were favored as witnesses. There was also an interest in inviting "elders" who had experienced police brutality or had worked for years to change these systems. Given the intergenerational tension between civil rights generation activists and Ferguson protesters, the TTP leadership offered support in connecting elders such as Dr. Angela Davis, her sister Dr. Fania Davis, and Dr. Bernard Lafayette to activists.

In terms of making space for people to feel comfortable to share, given the ongoing incidents of police violence and brutality and the freshness of these experiences for many of the participants, organizers also decided not to include police as witnesses nor to request any police presence at the events. The organizers understood that numerous people expressed that they were harassed and targeted by police for their participation in the protests, and so no requests were made to have police present or participating in the events at that stage.

At the same time, truth-tellers (those who offered formal testimony at TTP events) such as Michael Brown Sr. and Toni Taylor, mother of Carry Ball Jr., expressed the need for their stories to have a wider reach outside of the St. Louis area in hopes that it might expand people's understanding of the impacts of police violence on Black families in the United States. To extend the reach of the testimony further than traditional TRC reports, TTP members also decided that testimonies gathered would be a part of an online learning platform available through the Truth Telling Project webpage that would utilize video testimonial and interviews and connects viewers to resources on related to racial and social justice. That learning portal with direct testimony of police violence in the United States and educational materials became available in 2017 as part of the "Truth Telling Commons" (http://ttpcommons.businesscatalyst.com).

COMMUNITY GROUNDED EDUCATIONAL APPROACHES: CRITICAL RACE PEDAGOGY

In truth-telling, both didactic and participatory pedagogical methods are employed to critically examine the mechanisms and processes that generate, sustain, and escalate poverty, militarism, racial injustice, White supremacy, patriarchy, homophobia, and other forms of oppression. While critical pedagogy offers a robust body of analysis and engaged approaches to learning, scholars point out that it often does not go far enough—frequently minimizing race and focusing primarily on class analysis, which gives primacy to Eurocentric Marxist approaches (Allen 2005; Gaskew 2014; hooks 1994; Lynn et al. 2013; Shimomura 2015).

This approach to critical pedagogy is aptly described by Pollock (2004) not as a colorblind approach but rather as color muteness, does not erase but instead glosses over the centrality of race for understanding subjugation in the United States. Minimization of race in analysis maintains the status quo by leaving uncomfortable or inconvenient issues uninterrogated by those with progressive educational commitments (Choi 2008; Ragland 2015). We maintain that it is critically important to explore the silence about race within pedagogical approaches employed by critical social justice traditions (Delpit 1988; Ladson-Billings 1996). The minimization of race among those who considered them at the vanguard of movement of for equality and justice has a long history in the United States. The U.S. founders, per historian Joseph Ellis (2000), purposely maintained silence about the debate over the morality of slavery in the continental congress to obscure the fact that the final decision to maintain the status quo was based on economic expediency and a refusal to relinquish free Black labor. Critical race pedagogy, especially in this context, acknowledges the unsaid about race as a core part of transformational learning and highlights the need to connect race analysis to other axis of oppression. Gaskew argues further that despite a general concern with oppression, critical pedagogy in practice most often privileges the voices of White academics. He notes that even critical pedagogical approaches to teaching in prisons rarely include teachers of color even while trying to interrogate racial inequality (Scott 2014). Critical race pedagogy, applied to truth-telling, seeks to challenge silence about racial oppression, to engage with structural racism and to recognize the intersectional nature of systemic oppression by attending to the ways of knowing expressed by Black people that have experienced injustice.

Bell hooks (1994) describes an approach to learning that centers the understanding of race as part of an emancipatory practice and draws on the use of storytelling and engaged learning as key processes for the self-empowerment of Black people in exploring themes of oppression. Lynn et al. (2013) make a case for those engaged in critical educational activities to understand more deeply the central role of race in invalidating the knowledge and experiences of people of color in education. This approach then also takes seriously the Black wariness of both White conservative and progressive educational traditions in the United States (Choi 2008; hooks 1994; Young 2010), which have often failed to deliver on promises of empowerment. The truth-telling approach to community education can best be described broadly as striving for a critical race pedagogy that sees community members simultaneously as both educators and learners and which centers analysis of systemic racism in connection with other axis of oppression.

Critical race pedagogy is not a singular approach but rather a broad orientation where people critically explore issues of oppression and inequality and examines forms of resistance and the possibilities for the transformation of oppressive systems. Critical forms of education and analysis that center race have been developed by a wide range of educators, including Black educators, writers, and scholars, such as bell hooks, Kimberlé Crenshaw, Alice Walker, and Audre Lorde. "The 'critical' in critical pedagogy refers to the ability to analyze, expose, and challenge the hidden social, cultural, and political processes that are a part of knowledge production, including how one's own views and assumptions come from a particular cultural and historical formation" (New York University Steinhardt 2016). Critical pedagogy encourages educators to not only be aware of injustices but to take action to transform the practices and structures that perpetuate them.

In terms of pedagogical approaches that have been employed as part of the truth-telling process, a wide range of methods have been utilized thus far, including storytelling for social justice, educational theater, arts-based approaches including community murals and other participatory pedagogical approaches. These approaches allow for multiple pathways to engage with the life experiences and knowledge of people impacted by injustice. This approach involves forming critical questions with those impacted by injustice in ways that are meaningful to the challenges people experiencing violence face in their lives and exploring opportunities that they see as viable moving forward. Paulo Freire highlights the importance of this approach which supports communities in identifying issues they see as important, as opposed to banking or top-down approaches to education that "download" key problematics. At the same time, hooks (1994) deepens this liberatory approach, as she argues that learning must engage the mind, body, and spirit in exploring possible futures.

Truth-telling events, which are part of the larger process of truth-telling, have included a wide range of pedagogical approaches including workshops on storytelling, qualitative social justice research, nonviolent action, and restorative justice. Facilitators draw on a range of approaches including role play and educational theater as well as other experiential activities and discussions to create a forum for introspection, analysis of social conditions, personal story sharing, and community building. Educators in this context include community members, activists, and other informal as well as professional educators. Over the course of the last three years since August 9, 2014, the TTP has continued to develop an approach that utilizes workshops, brainstorming sessions, and discussions about racial justice issues in ways that attempt to shift the power dynamics of formal education in ways that support people in playing an active role in analyzing systemic racism and oppression and other possible futures.

The arts have also played a critical role in this emergent grassroots pedagogical approach to truth-telling. In March 2016, the TTP organized an event in New York in collaboration with the Maxine Green Center for Aesthetics and Social Imagination entitled *Voices of Freedom*. Local and national artists offered presentations centered on the Movement for Black Lives, with the goal of supporting an inquiry into hidden stories, who holds power, and who is excluded from conversations about justice in the United States. The event featured the music of Holy Ghost, a band formed out of the protests in response to police killings, and included songs focused on the lived experiences of generations of Black people that have experienced police violence and the ways they have resisted and survived. There were also dance and theatrical performances that celebrated imaginative ways of organizing for social justice and explored the role of the arts in developing strategies for connecting people across various communities living within the *New Jim Crow.*

Dr. Tony Jenkins, an advisory board member of the TTP notes in his recent article "Facing Realities of Race" that truth-telling is "a form of critically reflective storytelling, and as personal narrative it humanizes the social dilemma by rooting it in human experience." This participatory approach to pedagogy then can help to build connections between personal stories and the larger systemic context in ways that bring into focus the direct impact of structural violence and systemic humiliation and allow people from varied communities to see the scope of these problems and ways people are responding. While people who participated in truth-telling processes often reported feeling supported, attempts to share their experiences of police violence more broadly were often met with resistance as they largely left unquestioned historical narratives that dominate our institutions and larger social discourse about race and justice. Further, discussions of victimization, oppression, and a privileging of speech acts (testifying) as transformative political action can serve to reinforce or leave largely unchanged the structural arrangement and power dynamics that make possible persistent experiences of systemic humiliation and experiences of powerlessness.

CRITICISMS AND OBSTACLES

Over the past two years, there has been a range of critical questions raised about the use of truth-telling processes to address issues of police violence and systemic humiliation and racism in the United States. For example, the first TTP event was critiqued on the grounds that there were too many academics and "experts" and not enough local residents and activists involved. The composition of the event influenced the ways in which the issues were discussed as local participants participated primarily by offering testimony but were underrepresented in the panels, affecting the ways that people made meaning of those experiences. Participants and core organizers both expressed concern about the power dynamics of privileging academic and professional voices when it came to framing systemic dynamics through analysis presented on the panel within substantive engagement with those working in the movement locally. Given that the TTP's core organizers were people of color from the St. Louis/Ferguson area and participated in the protests, they shared the concern raised by the participants that those with less formal education were, at various points, on the outside looking in on this process. Giving local participants the momentary recognition of expertise in the process by testifying was not sufficient in terms of generating pathways for those most impacted to be involved in analyzing and thinking through next steps for responding to injustice.

Given that TTP strives to establish an ethos of care and solidarity that takes seriously the epistemic insights of those who have experienced police violence and systemic racism, these critiques accelerated ongoing conversations about the need to deepen ongoing organizing in the community. Further it contributed to the evaluation of the pedagogical environments in which testimony would be shared (both at our events and virtual events hosted by other organizations) and in which analysis and future action would be explored so as to deepen opportunities for participation and create communities of support and care. Shawn Ginwright (2009), reflecting on his work with Black youth for over a decade in Oakland in the context of challenging systemic oppression, aptly notes that relationship building can be transformative as, "caring relationships can confront hopelessness and foster beliefs about justice among young people. These caring relationships are not simply about trust, dependence, and mutual expectations. Rather, they are political acts that encourage youths to heal from trauma by confronting injustice and oppression in their lives" (56).

In the TTP, care takes the form of coconstructing our approaches to truth-telling with community members while also focusing on building relationships among people that experience police violence and their allies in seeking social change. In addition to the composition of panels, TTP core organizers added more local leadership to the advisory group and focused on diversifying the pedagogical spaces that were used. As a result, the hearings in November 2014 and August 2016 included participatory and experiential educational processes, informal discussion, the use of arts and ritual, and other methods that broadened the ways in which people engaged with each other around these themes and the types of knowledge and expertise that were valued.[2]

Davis et al. point out the risks of circumventing difficult conversations and avoiding consideration of multiple viewpoints when they write:

truth-telling easily devolves into retributive constructions of justice defeating the goal of reconciliation. Geared to looking backwards to focus on blame and punishment, this kind of "truth" tends to leave the broader systems of injustice unchallenged (Davis and Scharrer 2017).

At the heart of the pedagogical challenge of grassroots truth-telling is this tension between creating supportive environments that take seriously those who are deeply impacted by racialized violence and oppression (especially given they are often marginalized within the wider society), and this need to deeply interrogate and explore differing notions of justice, liberation, and reconciliation. We see this as a generative tension requiring ongoing critical reflection that is conscious of how power manifests in these processes and impacts the production of knowledge.

Further, truth-telling and TRC processes are also often critiqued in the literature on the grounds that the subjective testimony of participants is used by the state to bolster preconceived models of a more tolerant and liberal state. In this way, TRCs are also often prefigurative of political arrangements that newly empowered elites and international actors favor in the postwar context. While the TTP does not take place in a postconflict setting, we face similar challenges in terms of needing to critically evaluate assumed ends of truth-telling processes.

Given the fact that the TTP emerged from the protest movement and that many people have experienced state-sanctioned violence, there was a degree of skepticism and opposition to the state-led processes of truth-telling that inform the TTP's approach. This does not mean, however, that engagement with state judicial processes and institutions is dismissed altogether or that the grassroots processes are without their own power dynamics. The work of connecting personal stories to larger narratives of liberation and structural violence can be fraught with challenges whether that be in a state-sanctioned process or at the grassroots level. For example, those who have the most credibility to talk about larger systems can favor those with educational privilege or those with clear and consolidated political organizing agendas or who make claims to have suffered the most. Thus, the personal story sharing can be leveraged in various ways by activists, academics, not for profits, and others for the purposes of a specific political project that participants may or may not agree with or which strips people of agency in terms of understanding how best to respond to larger oppressive systems. While truth-telling provides opportunities for engagement with a range of grassroots racial justice agendas and organizations within an "ecosystem" of Black-led organizing approaches, power is still negotiated in often subtle and complex ways as a result of more horizontal power relations.

Truth-telling as a process of truth and reconciliation work also runs the risk of making vulnerable those who have already experienced violence. King (2011) argues that those who participated in previous TRC commissions were likely to experience ongoing depression and further traumatization (139). Moreover, TRC processes have not been systematically evaluated in terms of their impacts on those who have experienced violence (Brouneus 2011). Similarly, Ferguson activists such as Taylor Payne and Kristine Hendrix have been drawing needed attention to the pressures that activists who have experienced trauma in relation to police violence face when retelling their stories and engaging with new cases where Black people have been shot. Eric Brahms (2004) similarly points out the problematic nature of truth-telling in reigniting trauma, but suggests that long-term support, which truth commissions do not often offer, could support better healing.

These critiques continue to be a source of critical reflection in the context of the TTP. It is worth noting that the context of Ferguson is different from approaches to truth and reconciliation that have been conducted outside of the United States in important ways. TTP offers a limited approach, focusing on highlighting marginalized voices for the purposes of supporting those impacted by violence, working toward grassroots community empowerment and education. Further, some of those leading the implementation of these processes abroad are removed from the communities that experienced violence and the contexts in which the violence took place. As a result, the cultural approaches used for dealing with trauma and the ways that local relationships were utilized for support were in some cases problematic.

The TTP in Ferguson and St. Louis grew as a community-initiated process, which unlike most state-initiated processes had local buy-in and leadership in the early phases of developing its approach. When questions about how to support truth-tellers arose, conversations were held with community members about ways this could be accomplished. In addition to the considerations discussed earlier about the composition of the witnesses, participants and organizers informally mapped resources in the community. As a result, local artists and those who led ceremonies and rituals during protests were also invited to contribute to the processes focusing on healing, while other community members provided meals and helped create spaces for informal conversation. This approach draws on networks of support that were already in place within the community and were further activated during the protests and TTP. The TTP also works with families who testify on an ongoing basis, as the organizers are deeply embedded in the Ferguson community. Arguably, trauma is also more likely when individuals recounting experiences have expectations beyond what TRC commissions could offer. To this point, participants in TTP shape the expectations and outcomes as the TTP events provide new opportunities to revisit what is being done with testimony and chart the direction of future activities drawing on participatory pedagogy.

Conclusion

This is a dynamic moment for racial justice movements in the United States. The uprising that took place in Ferguson in 2014 brought into sharp focus the systemic humiliation and violence that Black people experience regularly across the country and demonstrated that there were many people willing to take action to challenge systemic racism through creative forms of resistance. The TTP grows out of that "movement moment" in which many activists and community members are deeply skeptical of the criminal justice system—and the state more broadly—and as a result are searching for alternative ways of building greater social justice at the community level. Scholars Alexis Pauline Gumbs et al. (2016), in *Revolutionary Mothering*, draw attention to some of the commitments needed to sustain these kinds of grassroots efforts and building alternative spaces to heal and work for change in communities facing systemic injustice. Drawing on the insights and lived experiences of Black queer feminists Audre Lourde, June Jordan, and others, she writes, "in order to participate in and demand a society where people help to create each other, instead of too often destroying each other, we need to look at the practice of creating, nurturing and affirming, and supporting life" (9).

The TTP attempts to cultivate communities of care by affirming the dignity of those impacted by police violence and confronting hopelessness, humiliation, and despair by examining that violence in a larger social political context that challenges both the legitimacy and inevitability of these systems of racial oppression. Rather than having an initial focus on bringing together victims and perpetrators, the TTP sought to bring people whose experiences are often marginalized or silenced together with people that are supportive so that those experiences can be heard and reflected upon in a collective process of recognition and critical reflection about building power for future change.

As we highlight in this chapter, grassroots approaches to truth-telling are not outside the problematic dynamics that critics of TRCs raise about approaches to local engagement around issues of justice. However, our experience working with the TTP has been that many individuals who participated in the TTP hearings by witnessing and truth-telling, as well as those involved in organizing events, facilitating workshops, and offering artistic interventions, reported feeling an expanded sense of possibility for the future social justice action, and broader solidarity with other people involved in the truth-telling process. In this sense, truth-tellers can come away with an enlarged community of support that teaches and cares in ways that are recognizable as connected to everyday community life and to larger protest movements committed to affirming of the dignity of Black lives.

NOTES

1. Ferguson activist discussion in We Stay Woke Podcast, Episode 1.5 http://westaywoke.blogspot.com/2016/11/episode-15.html
2. For example, the August 2016 Youth Speak Truth, which opened the Michael Brown Jr. Memorial weekend, included verbal testimony from youth, as well as an art exhibition the community assisted in developing and hosting. The youth and other truth-tellers also participated in storytelling for social justice workshops which explored the power of narrative in healing from trauma and working for larger social change.

REFERENCES

Al-Daraweesh, Fuad, and Dale Snauwaert. 2015. *Human Rights Education Beyond Universalism and Relativism: A Relational Hermeneutic for Global Justice.* New York: Palgrave Macmillan.

Alexander, Michelle. 2012. *New Jim Crow: Mass Incarceration in the Age of Colorblindness.* New York: The New Press. http://site.ebrary.com/lib/alltitles/docDetail.action?docID=10556533

Allen, Ricky Lee. 2005. Whiteness and Critical Pedagogy. In *Critical Pedagogy and Race 2005*, ed. Zeus Leonardo, 53–68. Malden: Blackwell.

Apel, Robert, and Gary Sweeten. 2010. The Impact of Incarceration on Employment During the Transition to Adulthood. *Social Problems* 57 (3): 448–479. https://doi.org/10.1525/sp.2010.57.3.448.

Azarmandi, Mahdis. 2016. Colonial Continuities. *Peace Review* 28 (2): 158–164.

Baldwin, James. 1962. Letter from a Region in My Mind. *The New Yorker Magazine*, November 17. http://www.newyorker.com/magazine/1962/11/17/letter-from-a-region-in-my-mind

Bell, Derek. 1987. *And We Are Not Saved: The Elusive Quest for Racial Justice.* New York: Basic Books.

Bernstein, Nell. 2014. *Burning Down the House: The End of Juvenile Prison.* New York: The New Press.

Berson, Sarah B. 2013. Beyond the Sentence – Understanding Collateral Consequences. *National Justice of Justice Office of Justice Programs*, May. https://www.nij.gov/journals/272/Pages/collateral-consequences.aspx

Brahm, Eric. 2004. Truth Commissions. In *Beyond Intractability*, eds. Guy Burgess and Heidi Burgess. Conflict Information Consortium, University of Colorado, Boulder. Posted: June 2004 http://www.beyondintractability.org/essay/truth-commissions

Brouneus, Karen. 2011. The Trauma of Truth Telling: Effects of Witnessing in the Rwandan Gacaca Courts on Psychological Health. *Journal of Conflict Resolution* 54 (3): 408–437.

Brown, Emma. 2015. Police in Schools: Keeping Kids Safe, or Arresting Them for No Good Reason? *The Washington Post*, November 8. https://www.washingtonpost.com/local/education/police-in-schools-keeping-kids-safe-or-arresting-them-for-no-good-reason/2015/11/08/937ddfd0-816c-11e5-9afb-0c971f713d0c_story.html

Brownstein, Rhonda. 2009. *Teaching Tolerance* 36: 58–61. https://eric.ed.gov/?id=EJ866738

Choi, Jung-ah. 2008. Unlearning Colorblind Ideologies in Education Class. *Educational Foundations* 22 (3–4): 53–71.

Chung, Jean. 2016. Felony Disenfranchisement: A Primer. *The Sentencing Project*, May 10. http://www.sentencingproject.org/publications/felony-disenfranchisement-a-primer/

Coleman, Peter T., Katharina G. Kugler, and Jennifer S. Goldman. 2007. The Privilege of Humiliation: The Effects of Social Roles and Norms on Immediate and Prolonged Aggression in Conflict. Paper presented at IACM 2007 Meeting, February 2. http://ssrn.com/abstract=1111629 or https://doi.org/10.2139/ssrn.1111629.

Davis, Fania, and Jennifer Scharrer. 2017. Reimagining and Restoring Justice: Toward a Truth and Reconciliation Process to Transform Violence Against African-Americans in the United States. In *Transforming Justice, Lawyers and the Practice of Law*, ed. Marjorie A. Silver, 89–132. Durham: Carolina Academic Press.

Delgado, Richard, and Jean Stefancic. 2012. *Critical Race Theory: An Introduction.* 2nd ed. New York: New York University Press.

Delpit, Lisa D. 1988. Silenced Dialogues: Power and Pedagogy in Educating Other People's Children. *Harvard Educational Review* 58 (3): 280–298.

Domonoske, Camila. 2016. Denying Housing Over Criminal Record May Be Discrimination, Feds Say. *The Two-Way NPR*, April 4. http://www.npr.org/sections/thetwo-way/2016/04/04/472878724/denying-housing-over-criminal-record-may-be-discrimination-feds-say

Ellis, Joseph J. 2000. *Founding Brothers: The Revolutionary Generation*. New York: Alfred A. Knopf.

Gaskew, Tony. 2014. The Policing of the Black American Male Transforming Humiliation in Pursuit of Truth and Reconciliation. In *Crimes Against Humanity in the Land of the Free 2014*, ed. I. Scott, 219–240. Santa Barbara: Praeger. https://consortiumnews.com/2014/12/10/facing-realities-of-race/

Ginges, Jeremy, and Scott Atran. 2008. Humiliation and the Inertia Effect: Implications for Understanding Violence and Compromise in Intractable Intergroup Conflicts. *Journal of Cognition and Culture* 8 (3–4): 281–294. https://doi.org/10.1163/156853708x358182.

Ginwright, Shawn A. 2009. *Black Youth Rising: Activism and Radical Healing in Urban America*. New York: Teachers College Press.

Gumbs, Alexis Pauline, China Martens, Mai'a Williams, and Loretta J. Ross. 2016. *Revolutionary Mothering: Love on the Front Lines*. Oakland: PM Press.

hooks, bell. 1994. *Teaching to Transgress: Education as the Practice of Freedom*. New York: Routledge.

Incarcerated Women and Girls Report. 2014. *The Sentencing Project*.

Inmate Statistics. 2017. *Federal Bureau of Prisons*. Last Modified January 28. https://www.bop.gov/about/statistics/statistics_inmate_age.jsp

King, Regine U. 2011. Healing Psychosocial Trauma in the Midst of Truth Commissions: The Case of Gacaca in Post Genocide Rwanda. *Genocide Studies and Prevention: An International Journal* 6 (2): 134–151.

Ladson-Billings, Gloria. 1996. Silences as Weapons: Challenges of a Black Professor Teaching White Students. *Theory into Practice* 35 (2): 79–85.

Leidner, Bernhard, Hammad Sheikh, and Jeremy Ginges. 2012. Affective Dimensions of Intergroup Humiliation. *Plos One*. http://journals.plos.org/plosone/article?id=10.1371/journal.pone.0046375

Lopez, Mark Hugo. 2014. In 2014, Latinos Will Surpass Whites as Largest Racial/Ethnic Group in California. PewResearchCenter, January 24. http://www.pewresearch.org/fact-tank/2014/01/24/in-2014-latinos-will-surpass-whites-as-largest-racialethnic-group-in-california/

Lynn, Marvin, Micheal E. Jennings, and Sherick Hughes. 2013. Critical Race Pedagogy 2.0: Lessons from Derrick Bell. *Race, Ethnicity and Education* 16 (4): 603–628.

Maldonado-Torres, Nelson. 2007. On the Coloniality of Being. *Cultural Studies* 21 (2): 240–270.

Mapping Police Violence. 2016. Police Killed More Than 100 Unarmed Black People in 2015. *Mapping Police Violence.* https://mappingpoliceviolence.org/unarmed/

McCarthy, Tom. 2015. Police Killed More Than Twice as Many People as Reported by US Government. *The Guardian,* March 4. http://www.theguardian.com/us-news/2015/mar/04/police-killed-people-fbi-data-justifiable-homicides

Nellis, Ashley. 2016. The Color of Justice: Racial and Ethnic Disparity in State Prisons. *The Sentencing Project,* June 14. http://www.sentencingproject.org/publications/color-of-justice-racial-and-ethnic-disparity-in-state-prisons/

New York Civil Liberties Union. 2016. Stop-and-Frisk Campaign: About the Issue. *NYCLU Racial Justice.* New York Civil Liberties Union. http://www.nyclu.org/issues/racial-justice/stop-and-frisk-practices. Accessed 4 Feb 2016.

New York University Steinhardt. 2016. Definitions. NYU Steinhardt. http://steinhardt.nyu.edu/art/education/definitions

Office of General Counsel Guidance on Application of Fair Housing Act Standards to the Use of Criminal Records by Providers of Housing and Real Estate-Related Transactions. 2016. U.S. Department of Housing and Urban Development, April 4. https://portal.hud.gov/hudportal/documents/huddoc?id=hud_ogcguidappfhastandcr.pdf

Pollock, Mica. 2004. *Colormute Race Talk Dilemmas in an American High School.* Princeton: Princeton University Press.

Ragland, David. 2015. Challenging the Silence Racism Creates. *Counterpunch,* April 2. http://www.counterpunch.org/2015/04/02/challenging-the-silence-racism creates/

Rodriguez, Dylan. 2012. Beyond 'Police Brutality': Racist State Violence and the University of California. *American Quarterly* 64 (2): 301–313.

Scott, Imani M. 2014. *Crimes Against Humanity in the Land of the Free: Can a Truth and Reconciliation Process Heal Racial Conflict in America?* Santa Barbara: Praeger.

Shimomura, Fuyu. 2015. Can Critical Race Pedagogy Break Through the Perpetuation of Racial Inequity? Exploring What Is Behind the Structural Racism and Potential Intervention. *International Journal of Sociology and Anthropology* 7 (12): 254–260.

Silver, Marjorie A. 2017. *Transforming Justice, Lawyers and the Practice of Law.* Durham: Carolina Academic Press. Print.

Skiba, Russell, Ada Simmons, Lori Staudinger, Marcus Rausch, Gayle Dow, and Renae Feggins. 2003. Consistent Removal: Contributions of School Discipline to the School-Prison Pipeline. School to Prison Pipeline Conference, Harvard Civil Rights Project, Indiana University Policy Center, Indiana, May 16–17.

Stinchcomb, Jeanne B., Gordon Bazemore, and Nancy Riestenberg. 2006. Beyond Tolerance: Restoring Justice in Secondary Schools. *Youth Violence and Juvenile Justice* 4 (2): 123–147.

The Guardian. 2016. The Counted: People Killed by the Police in the US. *The Guardian*, September 20. https://www.theguardian.com/us-news/ng-inter-active/2015/jun/01/the-counted-police-killings-us-database

Wales, Mike. 2014. Who Are Police Killing? *Center on Juvenile and Criminal Justice*, August 26. http://www.cjcj.org/news/8113

Wong, Alia. 2016. How School Suspensions Push Black Students Behind. *The Atlantic*, February 8. https://www.theatlantic.com/education/archive/2016/02/how-school-suspensions-push-black-students-behind/460305/

Young, Evelyn Pullin. 2010. Grounding Critical Race Theory in Participatory Inquiry: Raising Educators' Race Consciousness and Co-constructing Antiracist Pedagogy. Dissertation, Boston College.

Zinn, H., and A. Arnove. 2009. *Voices of a People's History of the United States.* 2nd ed. New York: Seven Stories Press.

Zweifler, Ruth, and Julia De Beers. 2002. The Children Left Behind: How Zero Tolerance Impacts Our Most Vulnerable Youth. *The Michigan Journal of Race & Law* 8: 191–529.

PART III

Mental Health, Stigma and Dignity

CHAPTER 8

"To Wander Off in Shame": Deconstructing the Shaming and Shameful Arrest Policies of Urban Police Departments in Their Treatment of Persons with Mental Disabilities

Michael L. Perlin and Alison J. Lynch

Introduction

We must take seriously the complexity of interactions between persons with mental disabilities and the police. Although for some years we have been repeating the bromide that the nation's largest mental health facility is—depending on where you live—Rikers Island (New York), Cook County Jail (Illinois), or the Los Angeles County Jail (California) (Perlin 2013c; Acquaviva 2006), comprehending that reality has not, until recently, led us to comprehend (1) how these interactions lead to the deaths and serious injuries of persons with mental disabilities far more than other citizens, (2) how there is valid and reliable research telling us

Our thanks to Daniel Rothbart for his insightful and helpful comments.

M. L. Perlin (✉)
New York Law School; Mental Disability Law and Policy Associates,
New York, NY, USA

A. J. Lynch
Disability Rights New York, Brooklyn, NY, USA

175

about alternative ways of dealing with the underlying issues, and (3) the extent to which these interactions typically involve humiliation and shame, usually entirely obscured from the public discourse.

In two recent articles, the authors of this chapter have begun to consider these issues, from the perspective of therapeutic jurisprudence (TJ) and from the perspective of the need for trained and dedicated counsel to be assigned to the persons at risk (Perlin and Lynch 2016a; Lynch and Perlin 2017). In these articles, we argue for the need for "providing options and opportunities for individuals in crisis that will empower them, rather than relegate them to the nation's largest mental health facilities" (Perlin and Lynch 2016a, p. 690) so as to break the ongoing and deadeningly familiar "never-ending cycle of arrest-institutionalization-release-repeat" (Lynch and Perlin 2017, p. 354; Fradella and Smith-Casey 2014; Schug and Fradella 2015) and to provide authentic advocacy-based representation (Perlin and Weinstein 2016–2017). In this chapter, we have chosen to consider the same underlying problem from a different perspective: how the decision-making process engaged in by many police officers leads to the effectuation of arrests by consistently and strategically deploying humiliation as a means of controlling this stigmatized cohort of the population. (Regarding "the largely invisible operations of institutional abuses of power, social neglect, and infrastructure failures" that are reflected in police interactions with marginalized persons, see Hartling and Lindner, Chap. 2, this work, manuscript, p. 11). The shaming nature of these encounters and arrests often leave already-vulnerable individuals feeling unheard and potentially traumatized.

Here, we thus focus on how the decision-making processes made "on the street" by police officers who choose to apprehend and arrest certain cohorts of persons with mental disabilities, rather than seeking other, treatment-oriented alternatives in dealing with them, reflect the persistent use of humiliation and shame, in ways that robs their targets of the dignity to which they are entitled as an aspect of legal and human rights. And this happens in spite of the robust valid and reliable literature that demonstrates that certain methods of training programs designed for police officers—the "Memphis Model" of crisis intervention training (CIT) is the most well known (e.g., Steadman et al. 2000; Teller et al. 2006)—have resulted in dramatic reductions of arrests for "nuisance crimes" and help avoid contributing to the overincarceration of this population. Yet, these approaches are far from widespread, so far appearing in only a handful of cities with any consistency, and, as a result, populations of persons with mental disabilities in urban jails like Riker's Island continue to skyrocket (Perlin and Lynch 2016a, p. 690). We believe that this state of affairs—the rejection of interventions like the Memphis Model (or "crisis intervention teams" (CITs)—flows directly from the ways that shame and humiliation are regularly, overtly, and consciously used against the population in question.

As we have done in our other pieces on this topic, we will examine these issues through the filter of therapeutic jurisprudence (TJ), a new modality of solving a full range of seemingly intractable social problems. TJ teaches us that voice, validation, and voluntariness, embracing an "ethic of care," and privileging—rather than subordinating—dignity are central to any efforts to remediate the sort of issues we discuss here (e.g., Perlin and Lynch 2016b; see generally, Wexler 2000; Winick 2009). We believe that, if we adopt TJ as a tool in our efforts to come to grips with the underlying social problems, we will have the best chance of making significant and measurable changes in the lives of the persons under attack.

We will proceed in this manner. First, we will discuss the policies that have led to mass arrests of persons with mental disabilities for minor offenses (often the sort of behavior that would be ignored if engaged in by other individuals), including a consideration of the often-bigoted attitudes by police toward this population. Then, we will consider the valid and reliable evidence that offers alternative solutions (the Memphis Model; CITs) to the current state of affairs. We next look at the role of shame and humiliation in this process: first, by considering the structural of shameful and humiliating behavior and, next, by contextualizing it in terms of the behavior that we are examining. After this, we explain the meaning of therapeutic jurisprudence and how we see it as a redemptive tool to be used in efforts to solve the problems we face. We conclude with some modest suggestions.

Our title comes, in part, from Bob Dylan's song *I Am a Lonesome Hobo*. It begins mournfully:

I am a lonesome hobo
Without family or friends
Where another man's life might begin
That's exactly where mine ends

And its second verse ends with the words of our title:

> But I did not trust my brother
> I carried him to blame
> Which led me to my fatal doom
> *To wander off in shame* (Dylan 1967).

There is "no redemption" for the hobo in this song, according to Oliver Trager, one of the preeminent Dylanologists (2004, p. 270). He "wander[s] off in shame" as a reflection of his "fatal doom." Our hopes, in writing this chapter, is that the population on whom we focus—persons with mental disabilities entrapped in the criminal justice system—will, finally, be able to escape both their "shame" and their "doom."

Persons with Mental Disabilities in the Justice System

We know that individuals with mental illness are often at higher risk of becoming involved in the justice system. We also know that urban jails serve as some of the nation's largest mental health providers (Acquaviva 2006, p. 978) and that deinstitutionalization is still viewed in much of the community as a dangerous and "failed" experiment (Torrey 1995, p. 9; on the flaws in Torrey's arguments, see e.g., Perlin 2013b; Bagenstos 2012). As a result, individuals with mental illness regularly face subpar mental health care in prisons and jails (Perlin 2017), face further loss of liberty via civil commitment, and subsequently lose myriad due process and other civil rights via that process (see e.g., Perlin and Douard 2008–09, discussing the institutional civil rights litigation of *Falter v. Veterans Administration*, 1980, 1986). The shame of this loss of rights and liberty is rarely, if ever, discussed in the context of sweeping, systemic mental health care reform, even though the shame faced by many within the system is so readily acknowledged after the fact by individuals who have faced these circumstances.

One area in particular where we believe a more directed and targeted look at the ways in which shame impacts mental health treatment is in the role of crisis intervention by police officers for individuals in mental health crisis. Crisis intervention training has become a formal method of educating law enforcement officers about how to appropriately work with someone in a mental health crisis, and frequently these programs are paired with services that emphasize maintaining individuals with mental illness in the community, rather than arresting them for nuisance crimes that may happen as a result of their psychiatric symptoms (Perlin and Lynch 2016a). This training is especially critical, given the appalling reality that "a significant number of police officers hold on to the idea that [mentally disabled] persons are completely irrational and cannot be reasoned with" (Panzarella and Alicea 1997, pp. 335–36). In particular, programs may implement a "drop off center" where an individual with mental illness would be brought by police officers; rather than face a ticket for a minor violation, the individual would be brought to a center with community supports for housing, mental health services, treatment programs, and more (see generally, Compton et al. 2014; Watson and Fulambarker 2012).

On Crisis Intervention Training

Crisis intervention training (CIT) remains in an uncertain position within police departments around the country. Although cities that have implemented this program generally report positive results (e.g., Steadman et al. 2000; Teller et al. 2006), however issues of implementation—e.g., financial requirements (Murphy et al. 2012) and the difficulty of training a rural police force (Deane et al. 1999)—have kept CIT from becoming a more prevalent part of national police training schemes.

The most well-known and frequently employed by police departments is the Memphis Model of training. This particular method of training was developed in 1988 by the Memphis Police Department, in partnership with the National Alliance for the Mentally Ill (NAMI), the University of Memphis, and the University of Tennessee (Steadman et al. 2000). The Memphis Model utilizes a combination of lecture, role-playing exercises, and interactions with individuals with mental illness over a 40-hour training course to prepare an officer to handle what many police officers refer to as an EDP call, or a call for assistance with an emotionally disturbed person (Ibid.). The CIT training program also supports partnerships between psychiatric emergency departments and police departments, which increases the likelihood that people in psychiatric crisis will be directed to an emergency room rather than a jail, if an officer with crisis intervention training responds to the call (Compton et al. 2006).

Today, there are more than 2800 CIT programs in operation in 47 states and in Washington, DC (http://www.thearc.org/document.doc?id=4925). While some states have implemented CIT along with improved community mental health services as part of a general plan to address the issues of mental illness in the criminal justice system, others have implemented crisis intervention training only after particularly troubling interactions between individuals with mental illness and police officers (http://www.wweek. com/portland/article-6212-why_did_james_chasse_jr_die.html). By way of example, in Oregon, the death of James Chasse prompted Portland mayor Tom Potter to pledge $500,000 to initiate a CIT program. Chasse, who had schizophrenia, suffered broken ribs, a broken shoulder and sternum, and internal injuries. Officers reported that when they responded to a call about his behavior, he was "doing something suspicious or acting just, um, odd" (Ibid.). Chasse was killed after he ran from officers who were approaching him. His death prompted an outcry from local media and advocates about the treatment of individuals with mental illness, eventually leading to the Portland CIT program (Schwartz 2012).

Most departments initially choose to train around 20 percent of their staff (Perlin and Lynch 2016a); however, the area of training is one in which the disparities between urban and rural departments becomes clear. An urban department such as the New York Police Department has the resources to take some members of the police force off the streets to train them, while still having the necessary manpower for street patrols. However, a rural department with a limited number of officers will have much greater difficulty taking 20 percent of its force offline at one time to put them through training.

The logistics of the current CIT programs all have some variations, but generally follow a set pattern. Most CIT initiatives also come with an increased awareness of and resources for community mental health services. For example, in New York City, officers trained in CIT will be taught that individuals with mental illness can be brought to a "diversion center" where that individual will not face charges for whatever nuisance crime he was picked up on, but instead will be able to meet with staff including social workers, counselors and nurses to assist in connecting that individual to mental health services (http://www1.nyc.gov/assets/criminaljustice/downloads/pdf/annual-report-complete.pdf).

In considering this issue from the perspectives of shame and humiliation, it is essential to simultaneously consider the level of disdain many police officers have for mental health facilities and their "contempt" for the mental health system, which they perceive as "doing nothing" (Cooper et al. 2004, p. 306), a contempt that is even more important because of the extra time it regularly takes (estimates are 2½ times) to process an individual in a hospital rather than a jail (Green 1997). By way of example, in response to a survey, multiple police officers commented, spontaneously,

"It is too much of a hassle to get someone involuntarily committed" (Cooper et al. 2004, p. 303). Perhaps even more tellingly, a significant percentage of police officers who were questioned by researchers had no idea if there was a mental health liaison in their department (Ibid. at 304).

Also, significantly, there is evidence that, in some jurisdictions, at least, "[police] officers' stereotypes included the idea that it is not possible to have a meaningful conversation with [persons with mental disabilities]," and "officers hold on to the idea that [mentally disabled] persons are completely irrational and cannot be reasoned with" (Panzarella and Alicea 1997, pp. 335–36). Such attitudes are demonstrably wrong. Studies done by the MacArthur Foundation's Network on Mental Health and the Law dramatically conclude, on "any given measure of decisional abilities, the majority of patients with schizophrenia did not perform more poorly than other patients and non-patients" (Grisso and Appelbaum 1995, p. 169; see generally, Perlin and Lynch 2016c).

ON SHAME AND HUMILIATION

"Humiliation and shaming contravene basic fundamental human rights and raise important constitutional questions" (Perlin and Weinstein 2014, p. 5). These practices lead to recidivism, inhibit rehabilitation, discourage treatment, and injure victims (Ibid., p. 2; see e.g., Wagner 2009; Scheff 1998; Brett 2012; Leasure 2012). As we discuss below, they also directly contravene the guiding principles of TJ, especially in the context of its relationship to the importance of dignity in the law (Perlin 2013b; see also, Cucolo and Perlin 2017). We believe this is especially significant in the context of the problem we discuss here: the inappropriate arrests of persons with mental disabilities for "nuisance crimes" (Kondo 2004, p. 258).

Shame forces a downward redefinition of oneself (Massaro 1991); "the thrust of [shame's] aggression is to *dehumanize*" (Wurmser 1981, p. 81, emphasis added). It is bordered by "embarrassment, humiliation, and mortification, in porous ways that are difficult to predict or contain" (Massaro 1997, p. 665), and is "one of the most important, painful and intensive of all emotions" (Svensson et al. 2013, p. 3). Shaming is *public*; its dehumanization and social demotion occurs when a shameful trait or act becomes "visible, and is exposed to others" (Massaro 1991, p. 1902, citing Schneider 1977, pp. 34–35).

According to Professor Martha Nussbaum, when "shame is a large part of their problem…expos[ing] that person to humiliation may often shatter the all-too-fragile defenses of the person's ego. The result might be utter collapse" (2004, p. 236). By marginalizing the rights of those who are shamed and humiliated, such individuals are treated as less than human (Bernstein 1997, pp. 489–90).

Shaming sanctions may be psychologically debilitating.[1] The director of a mental health program for juveniles has directly criticized the shaming approach stating that "[a]ll of our mental health programs end up having more and more people come in with trauma at the hands of humiliation… the behavior [will] show up in different ways…[and] unfortunately, the morgue may see that person" (Coyne 2012, p. 557). Importantly, in the context of both this chapter and the practices under discussion, shaming "exploits one's fear of shunning by others, or [of] banishment from the community" (Massaro 1991, p. 1903).

In addition, proponents of shaming sanctions fail to recognize that shaming sanctions convey the message that offenders are less than human and deserve our individual and collective contempt (Massaro 1997, p. 659). "Sending this kind of message, even about criminal offenders, is, and should be, jarring in a political order that makes equality a cultural baseline" (Ibid., p. 700). It is hard to imagine how crude and degrading shaming policies can possibly foster respect for the law (Ziel 2005). It is far more likely that they will be counterproductive.

We need to consider this in the specific context of the population in question—persons with mental disabilities. Three common maladaptive responses to shame are depression, hiding/avoidance, and anger (Lazare and Sogg 2001). Depression will exacerbate already-existing conditions. Hiding avoidance can often lead to a denial of the problem (Ibid.). And anger may lead to acts of revenge (Ibid.). These behavioral responses to shame inevitably undermine the goals of shaming (Massaro 1999). This is no wonder, since the natural response to shame is to cover the source of the shame (Fletcher 2003). And, the all-too-frequent "response to shame seems to be: more shame" (Warner 1999, p. 3).

While humiliation and shame share many characteristics, humiliation involves more emphasis on an interaction in which one is debased or forced into a degraded position by someone who is, at that moment, more powerful (Hartling and Luchetta 1999). Humiliation is also, *interpersonal*, rather than wholly internal to a person (as shame may be), and often triadic, "requiring one who humiliates, one who is humiliated, and one witness (or more) whose good opinion is important to the one humiliated" (Fisk 2001, p. 77). Also, a humiliated person refuses to accept the legitimacy of the attempted debasement by others; a person experiencing shame takes their own debasement as well deserved, acknowledging their indiscretion or offense and so conceding the validity to their degradation in the eyes of others (Miller 1993, p. 43). Studies show the devastating consequences of systematic humiliation (Ibid.) and demonstrate that humiliation can cause depression, paranoia, violence, generalized and social anxiety, and suicide (Klein 1991). What behavior could be more counterproductive in dealing with persons with mental disabilities? (On the strong causal relationship between incarceration and major depressive disorder and bipolar disorder, see Schnittker et al. 2012.)

In recent years, scholars and activists from multiple disciplines have begun to devote themselves to the study of humiliation and how it robs the legal system and society of dignity (Perlin and Weinstein 2014, p. 5; Hartling and Lindner, Chap. 2, this work). The Human Dignity and Humiliation Studies Network explicitly underscores this in its mandate: "We wish to stimulate systemic change, globally and locally, to open space for dignity and mutual respect and esteem to take root and grow, thus ending humiliating practices and breaking cycles of humiliation throughout the world" (Ibid., pp. 5–6; see also, http://www.humiliationstudies.org; Hartling and Lindner, Chap. 2, this work).

It is important to note that there is almost no empirical evidence that shows that shaming sanctions improve society and no empirical evidence supporting the position that shaming sanctions are beneficial to the victims of the offense (Coyne 2012, pp. 25–26). There have been no comprehensive studies as to whether they are even effective, nor is there any empirical work through which the practical impact of such sanctions can be tested (Perlin and Weinstein 2014, p. 24; Netter 2005).

However, if we as a society reflect on the myriad ways in which shame and humiliation infiltrate everyday encounters, it seems eminently reasonable to actively work to reduce behaviors that lead to these negative factors. Shame and humiliation are not just products of arrest and conviction; in fact, "for violators of the criminal law, the process of stigmatization begins with their arrest and conviction, public events that are intended to produce shame" (Katz 2014, p. 231). Police are daily put into a position to engage with individuals with mental illness at their most vulnerable; this can and does lead to public confrontations that, even if not directly intended to shame and humiliate, can have that consequence if efforts by law enforcement are not affirmatively made to mitigate or avoid such outcomes.

Judges and legislators have started to recognize generally that police stops and escalated encounters with law enforcement can be shaming and humiliating for individuals, though those with mental illness have not been cited in judicial opinions as an individual population particularly at risk. In her recent magisterial opinion, holding the New York City Police Department's stop-and-frisk policies unconstitutional, Judge Shira Scheindlin focused on the issue of humiliation:

> While it is true that any one stop is a limited intrusion in duration and depri-vation of liberty, each stop is also a demeaning and humiliating experience. No one should live in fear of being stopped whenever he leaves his home to go about the activities of daily life. Those who are routinely subjected to stops are overwhelmingly people of color, and they are justifiably troubled to be singled out when many of them have done nothing to attract the unwanted attention. Some plaintiffs testified that stops make them feel unwelcome in some parts of the City, and distrustful of the police. This alienation cannot be good for the police, the community, or its leaders. Fostering trust and confidence between the police and the community would be an improvement for everyone (*Floyd v. City of New York* 2013, pp. 556–57).

Importantly, Judge Scheindlin approvingly cited a Ninth Circuit deci-sion focusing on how such stops "are humiliating, damaging to the detain-ees' self-esteem, and reinforce the reality that racism and intolerance are for many African-Americans a regular part of their daily lives" (Ibid., pp. 602–03, citing *Washington v. Lambert*, 98 F.3d 1181, 1198 (9th Cir. 1996)). While the long-standing issues related to race-based police stops is fraught with its own difficult and often-painful history and its concomi-tant impact on communities that are predominantly composed of racial minorities (on disparities in the ways that racial minorities are treated in the involuntary civil commitment system, see Perlin and Cucolo 2017), similarities to stops of individuals with mental illness can be gleaned from Judge Scheindlin's opinion. For example, for many with mental illness and visible symptoms, police stops may also be "a regular part of their daily lives," based solely on those visible characteristics of their illness. For many, this type of stop could result in feelings of shame or humiliation, especially when done so publicly. The implication of guilt or wrongdoing ends up on display for others, when the only offense may have been unusual (but not dangerous or criminal) behavior.

Other courts have similarly begun to recognize the emotional cost of these encounters. The Ninth Circuit awarded compensatory damages for the "excruciating pain, humiliation and ongoing embarrassment" that resulted from an officer's use of excessive force during a stop (*Tortu v. Las Vegas Metro. Police Dep't*, 2009, pp. 1086–87). Another court also awarded $200,000 to an individual who was apprehended on suspicion of larceny and assault and received injuries and suffered shame and humiliation during the resulting stop and detainment (*Mendoza v City of Rome* 1994).

While these cases were not brought by individuals with mental illness, it is not difficult to imagine that cases brought by such individuals would present a like set of circumstances that would equally allow for the probability of shame and humiliation during police stops. This would hold particularly true for individuals in mental health crisis who are dealing with officers who have received no training in this type of interaction. As Linda Hartling and Evelin Lindner point out elsewhere in this book, "vulnerable individuals navigate 'war zones' of insecurity fueled by systemic humiliation" (Hartling and Lindner, Chap. 2, this work, manuscript, p. 25).

Therapeutic Jurisprudence

One of the most important legal theoretical developments of the past 25 years has been the creation and dynamic growth of TJ (Wexler 1990); Winick and Wexler 2006). Therapeutic jurisprudence presents a new model for assessing the impact of case law and legislation, recognizing that, as a therapeutic agent, the law that can have therapeutic or antitherapeutic consequences (Perlin 2009, p. 912). Therapeutic jurisprudence asks whether legal rules, procedures, and lawyer roles can or should be reshaped to enhance their therapeutic potential while not subordinating due process principles (Perlin 2008). David Wexler clearly identifies how the inherent tension inherent in this inquiry must be resolved: "the law's use of mental health information to improve therapeutic functioning [cannot] impinge upon justice concerns" (Wexler 1993, p. 21). An inquiry into therapeutic outcomes does not mean that these can be used to diminish civil rights and civil liberties (e.g., Perlin and Lynch 2015, p. 213).

Using TJ, we "look at law as it actually impacts people's lives" (Winick 2009, p. 535) and assess law's influence on "emotional life and psychological well-being" (Wexler 2000, p. 45). One governing TJ principle is that "law should value psychological health, should strive to avoid imposing anti-therapeutic consequences whenever possible, and when consistent with other values served by law should attempt to bring about healing and wellness" (Winick 2003, p. 26).

Therapeutic jurisprudence has been described as "a sea-change in ethical thinking about the role of law...a movement towards a more distinctly relational approach to the practice of law...which emphasises psychological wellness over adversarial triumphalism" (Brookbanks 2001, pp. 329–30). In doing this, it supports an ethic of care.

One of the central principles of therapeutic jurisprudence is a commitment to dignity (Perlin 2013a, pp. 214–15). As noted earlier, Professor Amy Ronner describes the "three Vs": voice, validation, and voluntariness, arguing:

> What "the three Vs" commend is pretty basic: litigants must have a sense of voice or a chance to tell their story to a decision maker. If that litigant feels that the tribunal has genuinely listened to, heard, and taken seriously the litigant's story, the litigant feels a sense of validation. When litigants emerge from a legal proceeding with a sense of voice and validation, they are more at peace with the outcome. Voice and validation create a sense of voluntary participation, one in which the litigant experiences the proceeding as less coercive. Specifically, the feeling on the part of litigants that they voluntarily partook in the very process that engendered the end result or the very judicial pronunciation that affects their own lives can initiate healing and bring about improved behavior in the future. In general, human beings prosper when they feel that they are making, or at least participating in, their own decisions (Ronner 2002, pp. 94–95; see also, Ronner 2008, p. 627).

It is necessary to consider Professor Ronner's prescriptions in the context of what we know about dignity and to contextualize all of this with the notion of dignity. Professor Carol Sanger has suggested that dignity means that people "'possess an intrinsic worth that should be recognized and respected,' and that they should not be subjected to treatment by the state that is inconsistent with their intrinsic worth" (2009, p. 415). A notion of individual dignity generally articulated through concepts of autonomy, respect, equality, and freedom from undue government interference was at the heart of a jurisprudential and moral outlook that resulted in the reform, not only of criminal procedure, but of the various institutions more or less directly linked with the criminal justice system, including juvenile courts, prisons, and mental institutions (Miller 2004, p. 1569 n. 463).

CONCLUSION

It is unfortunate that this area remains underdiscussed, underresearched, and, ultimately, regarded as secondary. Courts, even when presented with the opportunity to make decisions that comport with TJ and can decrease stigma, shame, or humiliation, routinely continue to ignore those opportunities.

By way of example, a district court in Montana has ruled that a local police chief's failure to provide sufficient crisis intervention training and to have procedures in place to ensure that an officer trained in crisis intervention techniques was present on the scene, did not result in police officers' alleged use of excessive force on the arrestee, nor did it deprive the arrestee of his right to medical treatment after arrest (based on a failure-to-train claim under 42 U.S.C. § 1983, the Federal Civil Rights Act (*Peschel v. City of Missoula* 2009).

The Eighth Circuit has ruled that an arrestee was not denied reasonable accommodations in violation of the Americans with Disabilities Act (ADA) by police failure to use their crisis intervention training after an incident in which officers received information that the arrestee had assaulted his mother and where they had observed his "aggressive and irrational behavior," and subsequently repeatedly used a stun gun against the arrestee, who went into cardiac arrest and died (*DeBoise v. Taser Intern., Inc.* 2014; also e.g. *Garczynski v. Bradshaw* 2009) (absent a constitutional violation, the court would not address an estate's claim that the failure of the sheriff's office to implement a crisis intervention training program violated the decedent's Fourth Amendment rights).

Programs that target directly the possible sources of shame and humiliation—such as crisis intervention with its focus on de-escalation, thereby providing dignity in interactions with police—will remain underutilized until more legislators, judges, and people in daily contact with those with mental illness recognize the significant deleterious effects that repeated instances of shame or humiliation can have on this population.

There is no denying that the vicious cycle of arrest-institutionalization-release-repeat of persons with mental disabilities for "nuisance crimes" has created both a public health and a correctional institutional crisis. There is also no denying that there are proven ways of significantly remediating this state of affairs, through the greater use of the "Memphis Model" of policing and the greater deployment of "Crisis Intervention Teams." This is no longer news.

But there is also no denying that the subtext to the current state of affairs—the shame and humiliation that is part and parcel of the cycle we discuss here, both abetted by police practices that create more shame and more humiliation and that blind themselves to the long-term impact of what is regularly done—is rarely discussed or considered in the public debate over this issue. We discuss it here in the hopes that it raises public awareness of the depth of the underlying problems and in the hopes that the behaviors in question can change. We believe that if we embrace the tenets of therapeutic jurisprudence—and that we acknowledge how the principles articulated by Professor Ronner (voice, validation, and voluntariness) must be incorporated into any new policy we craft—we will have taken a major step toward remediating this situation. By way of example, the use of TJ can help us rise above/refuse to accept the "legitimacy of the attempted debasement" to which we referred above. And this will enable us to "transform systemic humiliation into systemic dignity" (Hartling and Lindner, Chap. 2, this volume, p. 17).

To return to our title, the persons about whom we write—persons with mental disabilities who are entrapped in two systems that frequently exacerbate the underlying problems—often, in Dylan's words, "wander off in shame." We hope the thoughts we express in this chapter can help put an end to this.

NOTE

1. For examples of shaming sanctions, see Perlin and Weinstein (2014, pp. 20–21) (citations omitted):

    1. A warning sign placed on the front door of a child molester's home following his release from jail, reading "No children under the age of [eighteen] allowed on these premises by court order."
    2. A witness who committed perjury in court being ordered to wear a sign in front of the courthouse which read: "I lied in court. Tell the truth or walk with me."
    3. A convicted thief being ordered to place an ad at least four inches in height and bearing the felon's photograph in the newspaper following his release from prison reading: "I am a convicted thief."
    4. Convicted drunk drivers being ordered "to wear pink hats during their performance of community service projects or to affix bumper stickers to their vehicles warning others of their crime."

5. Prison inmates who expose themselves in the presence of female guards being forced to wear pink uniforms.
6. A burglary victim being allowed to take something of like value out of the burglar's home.
7. A convicted purse snatcher being forced to wear tap shoes while out in public.

REFERENCES

Acquaviva, G.L. 2006. Mental Health Courts: No Longer Experimental. *Seton Hall Law Review* 36: 971–1013.
Bagenstos, S.R. 2012. The Past and Future of Deinstitutionalization Litigation. *Cardozo Law Review* 34: 1–52.
Bernstein, A. 1997. Treating Sexual Harassment with Respect. *Harvard Law Review* 111: 445–526.
Brett, S. 2012. "No Contact" Parole Restrictions: Unconstitutional and Counterproductive. *Michigan Journal of Gender and Law* 18: 485–493.
Brookbanks, W. 2001. Therapeutic Jurisprudence: Conceiving an Ethical Framework. *Journal of Law and Medicine* 8: 328–341.
Compton, M.T., et al. 2006. Crisis Intervention Team Training: Changes in Knowledge, Attitudes, and Stigma Related to Schizophrenia. *Psychiatric Services* 57: 1199–1202.
———. 2014. The Police-Based Crisis Intervention Team (CIT) Model: II. Effects on Level of Force and Resolution, Referral, and Arrest. *Psychiatric Services* 65 (4): 523–529.
Cooper, V.G., A.M. Mclearen, and P.A. Zapf. 2004. Dispositional Decisions with the Mentally Ill: Police Perceptions and Characteristics. *Police Quarterly* 7: 295–310.
Coyne, L. 2012. Can Shame Be Therapeutic? *Arizona Summit Law Review* 7: 539–561.
Cucolo, H.E., and M.L. Perlin. 2017. Promoting Dignity and Preventing Shame and Humiliation by Improving the Quality and Education of Attorneys in Sexually Violent Predator (SVP) Civil Commitment Cases. *Florida Journal of Law & Public Policy*. (forthcoming).
Deane, M.W., et al. 1999. Emerging Partnerships Between Mental Health and Law Enforcement. *Psychiatric Services* 50: 99–101.
DeBoise v. Taser Intern., Inc., 760 F.3d 892 (8th Cir. 2014).
Dylan, B. 1967. I am a Lonesome Hobo. Accessible at http://bobdylan.com/songs/i-am-lonesome-hobo/
Fisk, C.L. 2001. Humiliation at Work. *William and Mary Journal of Women & Law* 8: 73–95.

Fletcher, G. 2003. Thinking About Eden: A Tribute to Herbert Morris. *QLR* 22: 1–21.

Floyd v. City of New York, 959 F. Supp. 2d 540 (S.D.N.Y. 2013).

Fradella, H.F., and R. Smith-Casey. 2014. Criminal Justice Responses to the Mentally Ill. In *Criminal Justice Policy,* ed. S.A. Mallicoat and C. Gardiner, 201–224. Thousand Oaks: Sage.

Garczynski v. Bradshaw, 573 F.3d 1158 (11th Cir. 2009).

Green, T.M. 1997. Police as Frontline Mental Health Workers: The Decision to Arrest or Refer to Mental Health Agencies. *International Journal of Law and Psychiatry* 20: 469–486.

Grisso, T., and P.S. Appelbaum. 1995. The MacArthur Treatment Competence Study. III: Abilities of Patients to Consent to Psychiatric and Medical Treatments. *Law and Human Behavior* 19: 149–174.

Hartling, L.M., and T. Luchetta. 1999. Humiliation: Assessing the Impact of Derision, Degradation, and Debasement. *Journal of Primary Prevention* 19: 259–278.

http://www.humiliationstudies.org

http://www.thearc.org/document.doc?id=4925

http://www.wweek.com/portland/article-6212-why_did_james_chasse_jr_die.ht

http://www1.nyc.gov/assets/criminaljustice/downloads/pdf/annual-report-complete.pdf

Katz, J. 2014. Elements of Shame. In *The Widening Scope of Shame,* ed. M.R. Lansky and A.P. Morrison, 231–260. New York City: Routledge.

Klein, D.C. 1991. The Humiliation Dynamic: An Overview. *Journal of Primary Prevention* 12: 93–121.

Kondo, L. 2004. Advocacy of the Establishment of Mental Health Specialty Courts in the Provision of Therapeutic Justice for Mentally Ill Offenders. *American Journal of Criminal Law* 28: 255–336.

Lazare, A., and W.S. Sogg. 2001. Shame, Humiliation and Stigma in the Attorney-Client Relationship. *Practical Lawyer* 47 (4): 11–21.

Leasure, S.L. 2012. Criminal Law—Teenage Sexting in Arkansas: How Special Legislation Addressing Sexting Behavior in Minors Can Salvage Arkansas's Teens' Futures. *University of Arkansas Little Rock Law Review* 35: 141–164.

Lynch, A.J., and M.L. Perlin. 2017. "Life's Hurried Tangled Road": A Therapeutic Jurisprudence Analysis of Why Dedicated Counsel Must Be Assigned to Represent Persons with Mental Disabilities in Community Settings. *Behavioral Sciences and the Law* 35: 353–363.

Massaro, T.M. 1991. Shame, Culture, and American Criminal Law. *Michigan Law Review* 89: 1880–1944.

———. 1997. The Meanings of Shame Implications for Legal Reform. *Psychology, Public Policy and Law* 3: 645–704.

———. 1999. Show (Some) Emotions. In *The Pasions of the Law,* ed. S. Bandes, 80–122. New York City: New York University Press.

Mendoza v City of Rome, 872 F. Supp. 1110 (N.D.N.Y. 1994).

Miller, E.J. 2004. Embracing Addiction: Drug Courts and the False Promise of Judicial Interventionism. *Ohio State Law Journal.* 65: 1479–1576.

Miller, W.I. 1993. *Humiliation & Other Essays on Honor, Social Discomfort, & Violence.* Ithaca: Cornell University Press.

Murphy, S., et al. 2012. Crisis Intervention for People with Severe Mental Illnesses. *Cochrane Database of Systematic Reviews* 5. Accessible at http://www.ncbi. nlm.nih.gov/pmc/articles/PMC4204394/

Netter, B. 2005. Avoiding the Shameful Backlash: Social Repercussions for the Increased Use of Alternative Sanctions. *Journal of Criminal Law and Criminology* 96: 187–215.

Nussbaum, M.C. 2004. *Hiding from Humanity: Disgust, Shame, and the Law.* Princeton: Princeton University Press.

Panzarella, R., and J.O. Alicea. 1997. Police Tactics in Incidents with Mentally Disturbed Persons. *Policing: An International Journal of Police Strategies & Management* 20: 326–338.

Perlin, M.L. 2008. "Everybody Is Making Love/Or Else Expecting Rain": Considering the Sexual Autonomy Rights of Persons Institutionalized Because of Mental Disability in Forensic Hospitals and in Asia. *Washington Law Review* 83: 481–512.

———. 2009. "His Brain Has Been Mismanaged with Great Skill": How Will Jurors Respond to Neuroimaging Testimony in Insanity Defense Cases? *Akron Law Review* 42: 885–916.

———. 2013a. *A Prescription for Dignity: Rethinking Criminal Justice and Mental Disability Law.* Burlington: Ashgate Publ.

———. 2013b. "There Are No Trials Inside the Gates of Eden": Mental Health Courts, the Convention on the Rights of Persons with Disabilities, Dignity, and the Promise of Therapeutic Jurisprudence. In *Coercive Care: Law and Policy,* ed. B. McSherry and I. Freckelton, 193–217. New York City: Taylor & Francis.

———. 2013c. "Wisdom Is Thrown into Jail": Using Therapeutic Jurisprudence to Remediate the Criminalization of Persons with Mental Illness. *Michigan State University Journal of Medicine and Law* 17: 343–371.

———. 2017. "God Said to Abraham/Kill Me a Son": Why the Insanity Defense and the Incompetency Status Are Compatible with and Required by the Convention on the Rights of Persons with Disabilities and Basic Principles of Therapeutic Jurisprudence. *American Criminal Law Review* 54: 477–519.

Perlin, M.L., and A.J. Lynch. 2015. How Teaching About Therapeutic Jurisprudence Can Be a Tool of Social Justice, and Lead Law Students to Personally and Socially Rewarding Careers: Sexuality and Disability as a Case Example. *Nevada, Law Journal* 16: 209–225.

———. 2016a. "Had to Be Held Down by Big Police": A Therapeutic Jurisprudence Perspective on Interactions Between Police and Persons with Mental Disabilities. *Fordham Urban Law Journal* 43: 685–711.

―――. 2016b. "In the Wasteland of Your Mind": Criminology, Scientific Discoveries and the Criminal Process. *Virginia Journal of Criminal Law* 4: 304–360.

―――. 2016c. "Mr. Bad Example": Why Lawyers Need to Embrace Therapeutic Jurisprudence to Root Out Sanism in the Representation of Persons with Mental Disabilities. *Wyoming Law Review* 16: 299–323.

Perlin, M.L., and H.E. Cucolo. 2017. "Tolling for the Aching Ones Whose Wounds Cannot Be Nursed": The Marginalization of Racial Minorities and Women in Institutional Mental Disability Law. *Journal of Gender, Race & Justice* 20: 431–458.

Perlin, M.L., and J. Douard. 2008–09. "Equality, I Spoke That Word/As If a Wedding Vow": Mental Disability Law and How We Treat Marginalized Persons. *New York Law School Law Review* 53: 9–29.

Perlin, M.L., and N.M. Weinstein. 2014. "Friend to the Martyr, a Friend to the Woman of Shame": Thinking About the Law, Shame and Humiliation. *Southern California Review of Law & Social Justice* 24: 1–50.

―――. 2016–2017. "Said I, 'But You Have No Choice'": Why a Lawyer Must Ethically Honor a Client's Decision About Mental Health Treatment Even If It Is Not What S/He Would Have Chosen. *Cardozo Public Law, Policy & Ethics Law Journal* 15: 73–116.

Peschel v. City of Missoula, 686 F. Supp. 2d 1092 (D. Mont. 2009).

Ronner, A.D. 2002. Songs of Validation, Voice, and Voluntary Participation: Therapeutic Jurisprudence, *Miranda* and Juveniles. *University of Cincinnati Law Review* 71: 79–114.

―――. 2008. Learned-Helpless Lawyer: Clinical Legal Education and Therapeutic Jurisprudence as Antidotes to the Bartleby Syndrome. *Touro Law Review* 24: 601–696.

Sanger, C. 2009. Decisional Dignity: Teenage Abortion, Bypass Hearings, and the Misuse of Law. *Columbia Journal of Gender and Law* 18: 409–499.

Scheff, T.J. 1998. Community Conferences: Shame and Anger in Therapeutic Jurisprudence. *Revista Jurídica U.P.R.* 67: 97–119.

Schneider, C.D. 1977. *Shame, Exposure and Privacy.* New York City: W.W. Norton & Co.

Schnittker, J., M. Massoglia, and C. Uggen. 2012. Out and Down: Incarceration and Psychiatric Disorders. *Journal of Health and Social Behavior* 53: 448–464.

Schug, R.A., and H.F. Fradella. 2015. *Mental Illness and Crime.* Thousand Oaks: Sage.

Schwartz, J. 2012. What Police Learn from Lawsuits. *Cardozo Law Review* 33: 841–894.

Steadman, H.J., et al. 2000. Comparing Outcomes of Major Models of Police Responses to Mental Health Emergencies. *Psychiatric Services* 51: 645–649.

Svensson, R., et al. 2013. Moral Emotions and Offending: Do Feelings of Anticipated Shame and Guilt Mediate the Effect of Socialization on Offending? *European Journal of Criminology* 10: 22–39.

Teller, J.L., M.R. Munetz, K.M. Gil, and C. Ritter. 2006. Crisis Intervention Team Training for Police Officers Responding to Mental Disturbance Calls. *Psychiatric Services* 57: 232–237.

Torrey, E.F. 1995. Jails and Prisons–America's New Mental Hospitals. *American Journal of Public Health* 85 (12): 1611–1613.

Tortu v. Las Vegas Metro. Police Dep't, 556 F. 3d 1075 (9th Cir. 2009).

Trager, O. 2004. *Keys to the Rain: The Definitive Bob Dylan Encyclopedia.* New York City: Billboard Books.

Wagner, L.A. 2009. Sex Offender Residency Restrictions: How Common Sense Places Children at Risk. *Drexel Law Review* 1: 175–209.

Warner, M. 1999. *The Trouble with Normal: Sex, Politics and the Ethics of Queer Life.* Cambridge, MA: Harvard University Press.

Washington v. Lambert, 98 F.3d 1181 (9th Cir.1996).

Watson, Amy C., and Anjali J. Fulambarker. 2012. The Crisis Intervention Team Model of Police Response to Mental Health Crises. *Best Practices in Mental Health* 8 (2): 71–81.

Wexler, D.B. 1990. *Therapeutic Jurisprudence: The Law as a Therapeutic Agent.* Durham: Carolina Academic Press.

———. 1993. Therapeutic Jurisprudence and Changing Concepts of Legal Scholarship. *Behavioral Sciences and the Law* 11: 17–29.

———. 2000. Practicing Therapeutic Jurisprudence: Psycholegal Soft Spots and Strategies. In *Practicing Therapeutic Jurisprudence: Law as a Helping Profession,* ed. Daniel P. Stolle et al., vol. 45. Durham: Carolina Academic Press.

Winick, B.J. 2003. A Therapeutic Jurisprudence Model for Civil Commitment. In *Involuntary Detention and Therapeutic Jurisprudence: International Perspective on Civil Commitment,* ed. Kate Diesfeld and Ian Freckelton, 2–54. Farnham: Ashgate Press.

———. 2009. Foreword: Therapeutic Jurisprudence Perspectives on Dealing with Victims of Crime. *Nova Law Review* 33: 535–543.

Winick, B.J., and D.B. Wexler. 2006. The Use of Therapeutic Jurisprudence in Law School Clinical Education: Transforming the Criminal Law Clinic. *Clinical Law Review* 13: 605–632.

Wurmser, L. 1981. *The Mask of Shame.* Baltimore: Johns Hopkins University Press.

Ziel, P. 2005. Eighteenth Century Public Humiliation Penalties in Twenty-First Century America: The "Shameful" Return of "Scarlet Letter" Punishments in *U.S. v. Gementera. BYU. Journal of Public Law* 19: 499–522.

CHAPTER 9

Systemic Humiliation in Families

Connie Dawson

In Chap. 2 of this volume, Hartling and Lindner ask "Can humiliation be transformed?" Yes, of course it can be transformed. The transformation is under way in areas such as restorative justice and reconciliation programs and in communities who are coming together to address common problems. There is a growing expectation that a person's voice should be heard. Fewer are in denial of how labeling and marginalizing people and groups gives rise to revenge and rage, undermining the health of whole societies.

As a recognition of the effects of humiliation on the quality of relationships between and among individuals and groups grows, so too does the impulse to move to more workable, effective, and respectful ways of coming together. As an awareness of the limitations of dominant-subordinate relationships grows, so too does the realization that better, more dignifying ways of conducting relationships exist.

Historically, the art of domination has been woven into the fabric of most organizational structures we experience today. Control battles are a natural extension of relationships based on horizontal and vertical differentiation. Someone has to win and someone has to lose. Someone is right and someone is wrong. Blaming others to avoid taking personal responsibility flourishes. The dynamic created by such beliefs and

C. Dawson (✉)
Portland State University, Portland, OR, USA

© The Author(s) 2018
D. Rothbart (ed.), *Systemic Humiliation in America*,
https://doi.org/10.1007/978-3-319-70679-5_9

behaviors is antithetical to relationships based on dignity, respect, equity, and partnership.

The institution of the family is charged with preparing children to take their place as adults in the larger culture. This chapter addresses how cultures transmit operational structures from one generation to the next, for good or for ill.

Every family relies to some extent on implicit rules that are embedded within their operating system. For centuries the implicit rules served the need of parents who conceived their roles primarily as authority figures. Rather than strengthening the sound development and dignity of family members, the rules tended to undermine healthy development and independence, fostering a fear among family members of being excluded or left behind. Such rules tend to inhibit a child's sound emotional and moral development, impacting their self-image and identity.

In the 1980s, Drs. Merle Fossum and Marilyn Mason (Fossum and Mason 1986), at the St. Paul (Minnesota) Family Therapy Institute, noticed that client families in aftercare therapy following treatment for an addiction disorder held certain common but unexpressed assumptions about the rules that governed their family dynamics. Such rules are cast as normal, yet they do not appear on a chalkboard and refrigerator or in rulebooks. They are not discussed at all, but every family member knows them. Nevertheless, adherence to these implicit rules did not foster healthy relationships and were likely to provoke emotional distance, stress, pain, and rebellion. Briefly, the implicit rules are as follows (Dawson 2016):

Do and be right. Don't make mistakes.
Blame others to avoid exposure of the mistake.
Ignore the information your feelings provide.
Keep secrets and withhold information.
Be unclear and unaccountable to avoid blame.
Be in control of others and outcomes.
Deny reality. It is what you say it is.

The deployment of such rules tends to result in uneven, insecure, and unequal relationships, all of which are counterproductive for emotionally intelligent parenting.

The implicit rules are anchored in an internalized belief shared among family members that there is something wrong with them. For this reason,

Fossum and Mason call the rules that were unspoken and common among newly recovering families *shame-based.*

> We define shame in experiential terms. It is more than a loss of face or embarrassment. Shame is an inner sense of being completely diminished or insufficient as a person. It is the self judging the self. A moment of shame may be humiliation so painful or an indignity so profound that one feels one has been robbed of her dignity or exposed as basically inadequate, bad, or worthy of rejection. A pervasive sense of shame is the ongoing premise that one is fundamentally bad, inadequate, defective, unworthy, or not fully valid as a human being (Fossum and Mason 1986, 5).

In this chapter, I explain in the first section the supportive role rules play in a family system. In the second section the connection between implicit rules, shame, and humiliation that make the family more vulnerable to maladaptive definitions of self and relationships is explored. Next, "Parental Leadership Styles and Family Dynamics" relates implicit, shame-based rules to resultant family dynamics and offers explicit rules for improved family functioning. In the final section I recommend certain interventions intended to support a shift from rules and parenting styles based on humiliation to gain parental power to those based on the rules and parenting styles supportive of family environments and interactions based on dignity.

The Role of Rules in the Family System

The family is the primary transmission agent of a culture, teaching children prescribed values, beliefs, and proper norms of behavior. Because of its interconnecting elements, a system as a whole cannot be understood by examining an element in isolation from others. As it is with other organisms, family systems need to adapt to changing pressures and circumstances to survive.

A major difference between closed and open systems is how they react to change. The boundaries regulating incoming information in a closed system are rigid and tend to be isolating. A closed system persists in following a familiar pattern of functioning even though the system is under particular pressure to adapt to changing circumstances and new information. An open system considers and adjusts to new information and circumstances as well as supporting members in safely exploring ideas and experiences outside family boundaries (Miermont 1995). Depending on the permeability of family boundaries, new or incoming information may be considered and beliefs and behaviors adjusted, or new information may be rejected out of hand in deference to maintaining the status quo (Davidson 1983; Miermont 1995).

As the basic societal institution charged with the development and socialization of children, the family will ideally provide nurture (love and care) and structure (safety and protection). The family is a complex, emotionally based, and interactional system where members have a role to play and rules to respect (Bowen 1993). Humans need unconditional love to thrive and grow, communicated by word, touch, and deed, as they learn to love themselves and others. But nurturing is not enough. Children also need to learn limits, skills, and standards. They need to be safe, to learn healthy habits, to develop a sense of who they are and who others are, to learn values and ethics, to develop character, and to become responsible for themselves and to others. Parents need to convey messages that *You can do this; I will teach you how; you are capable.* The set of parenting skills supporting the development of these skills is called structure. If they take their charge seriously, parents do their best to accomplish positive child-rearing using the experience, knowledge, and skills familiar to them (Clarke and Dawson 1998).

Rule Formation

Each family leader adopts and develops a set of rules intended, at a minimum, to govern interactions in the system, which is crucial to its survival. The unseen power of family rules implemented by parents centers on patterns of control (Clarke and Dawson 1998). Rules are to families as bones are to bodies. Family rules and their consequential enforcement serve to support the family's mission of developing its structure. Rules are *meant* to:

Protect the family from threatening intrusions;
Teach limits and boundaries relative to personal safety;
Teach skills necessary for independence and interdependence; and
Provide the climate and environment where essential needs for nurturing can be met.

Clear family rules serve to distinguish between safe and unsafe, or acceptable and unacceptable, behavior. Rules and consequences that are *explicitly stated* can be modified as children develop and mature. A rule about not crossing the street alone applies until the child demonstrates that he's capable of crossing safely alone. A process of negotiation, initiated by either parent or child, results in expanding a boundary set by a rule or making the rule even tighter until the parent is satisfied the child applies the rule successfully. The bottom line of a successful negotiation results in a new rule, or boundary.

As it is with criminal laws, familial rules have a positive consequence for compliance and a negative consequence for non-compliance. A natural consequence of a behavioral choice is usually an effective negative consequence as long as it doesn't involve physical, and, occasionally emotional, harm. Failure to show up at work may result in a warning, or even two, but the job may be in jeopardy. In the home, a child's failure to do a weekly chore may result in a warning or two, but beyond that a logical consequence could be an automatic deduction from an allowance. The cost exacted is meant to discomfort the child and serve as a reminder to consider outcomes before making choices. The wise use of consequences to enforce rules respects a child's ability to think and the parent's belief in the child's ability to make decisions that are in their best interests. These are the qualities underlying discipline. Punishment, which is exacting a measure of pain with an expectation that behavior choices will change, is ineffective in the long run, as it tends to result in craftiness, vengeance, anger, and avoidance.

Choices in Parenting

"A caring family is grounded in positive relationships, and a critical basis for those relationships is parents' values and goals" (Elias et al. 1999, 26). The principles of emotionally intelligent parenting provide an example of a sound frame of reference underlying the development of the rules that guide a family's practices (Elias et al. 1999, 10–16). They are as follows:

Be aware of one's own feelings and the feelings of others.
Show empathy and understand others' point of view.
Regulate and cope positively with emotional and behavioral impulses.
Be positive goal- and plan-oriented.
Use positive social skills in handling relationships.

Of course, there are many families for which these principles are not adopted.

Perhaps the strongest source of parenting styles comes from behavior learned through one's own family of origin. Understanding a parent's past within their family of origin offers insight into their current parenting style. Parents typically carry the values, beliefs, and behaviors of their growing-up years into the families they create. For instance, even though a parent's own childhood experiences of being disciplined felt more like punishment than discipline, the parent is likely to draw upon their known repertoire of parental behaviors and assumptions and automatically apply to their children what was said or done to them (Siegel and Hartzell 2003; Wolynn 2016).

Swiss psychologist Alice Miller, who brought the impact of harsh parental practices to light (Miller 1997), wrote "Beaten children very early on assimilate the violence they endured, which they may glorify and apply later as parents, believing they deserved the punishment and were beaten out of love. This is why society's ignorance remains so immovable and parents continue to produce severe pain and destructivity—all in 'good will', in every generation" (www.alice-miller.com/en). Miller described psychological abuse as an insidious trauma because of the difficulty patients had recognizing it as such. A vestige of these harsh practices persists in the form of implicit rules either based on those of previous generations or created to meet current parental self-interest. Where such implicit rules are operational, positive relationships tend to be jeopardized, problems are unacknowledged or unsolved, and family harmony is jeopardized.

THE CONNECTION BETWEEN IMPLICIT RULES, SHAME AND HUMILIATION

The agent of humiliation and shame seeks to position socially the targeted individual or group in a lesser place or "in the dirt." The result is a self-sense of being defective, which in turn fosters a sense of relinquishing power to others. "You don't know anything; I know better." In such cases, humiliation functions as a strategy of control by impugning the worth and dignity of another person or group. The many acts of humiliation "hook" personal, internalized shame. People who have little internalized shame generally don't succumb to being humiliated. They are likely to recognize attempts to humiliate as unwanted, incongruent, unwise, unreasonable, and/or toxic and steer clear when it's not in their best interests to comply.

Just as being angry or sad is felt in the body, so too with shame. The well-documented physical cues of the shame experience begin with a slumping posture, with head down, and an alteration of behavior that is deemed unacceptable to authority figures. "Shame on you!" "You should be ashamed of yourself." Shaming tends to arrest an unacceptable behavior, at least for the time being. The shamed person hopes that the emotional pain ceases, even though the only way to do that is to "go away" by disassociating, as seen by the look of complete blankness or nothingness in the eyes. Feeling ashamed cuts off a connection and often renders the person helpless, at least momentarily. "I lost my ability to think. I sank. I retreated and hoped people wouldn't notice me."

Being ashamed is a feeling, along with others in the affect system (Sedgwick and Frank 1995; Kaufman 1989). Thomas Verny has documented the infant's sensitivity to emotion while in the womb and as a neonate (Verny 1983). As social psychologist pioneer Robert Zajonc explains, the primary purpose of the affect system is to pick up danger or threats to survival (Zajonc 1980). Some of those dangers are as follows: crying to signal a need and not having that need satisfied; emotionally unavailable, unresponsive caregivers; frequent breaks in care; birth and separation trauma; and unsafe people and environments. Infant fear resulting from failures of caregivers to respond appropriately is experienced by infants not as the failure of caregivers, but as their failure to signal their need effectively. These preverbal feelings of ineffectiveness can lead to a sense of internalized shame (Morrison 1998; Fosha et al. 2009).

Internalized shame might be called unearned, for the infant and young child did nothing to deserve it. They were merely engaged in normal developmental tasks which were not addressed positively. Further shaming experiences like name-calling, ridicule, disregard, discontinuity of care, physical and sexual abuse, perfectionistic expectations beyond a young child's ability, rejection, neglect, and abandonment are internalized by the child as their defectiveness, and the child necessarily develops adaptive defensive strategies to keep those perceived faults and inadequacies from being seen or known by others.

Beyond early childhood, shame serves as a cultural or societal warning against unacceptable behavior. "Shame on you" means "Stop what you're doing!" Shame can be useful for those with sufficient brain development to understand the line between approved and disapproved behavior, along with the consequences of stepping over the line. Breaking the rules carries penalties in the culture: humiliations like shunning, separation, isolation from the group, and, in some eras and some cultures, private or public flogging and other physical punishments. Staying within the lines is called self-control and breaking the rules can be called shame that is *earned.*

In adulthood, an inordinate amount of energy will be devoted to defending a perceived defectiveness or inadequacy from being known by others. Unconsciously, any perceived vulnerabilities must be controlled (Kaufman 1983).

Common Adaptations to Internalized Shame

Humans, fearing exposure of their so-called faulty selves, automatically strive to keep others from seeing their perceived defects. Three of the most common defenses against exposure of the defects are rage, contempt, and perfectionism (Kaufman 1983).

Adult rage is a distance-regulating device used to prevent exposure, conveying the message for others to back off. Rage has early developmental origins because of its function in regulating distance. Babies signal their needs by crying. Their cry quickly becomes touched with anger, which is geared to demand help. If that doesn't work, the baby escalates to rage, which is anger coupled with helplessness.

Contempt is literally turning away from being seen, cutting off an interaction. Contempt is a silent way of blaming the break on the targeted person while protecting the one administering the contempt from having to disclose a perceived vulnerability. Contempt fosters emotional abandonment.

Perfectionism means trying hard not to make mistakes. A mistake is interpreted as imperfection, which in turn is felt to reflect one's defects. Striving to look good in the eyes of others requires being outer-focused on what others need while failing to acknowledge personal self-care needs.

Parental Leadership Styles and Family Dynamics

In addition to the influence of explicit and implicit rules on family functioning and the internalization of shaming circumstances, the style of family leadership that parents employ functions as the delivery system of the rules and circumstances. Researcher and psychologist Diana Baumrind (1967) identified three styles of family leadership based on parameters of parental responsiveness (nurture) and parental demandingness (structure). She defined responsiveness as "the extent to which parents intentionally foster individuality, self-regulation, and self-assertion by being attuned, supportive, and acquiescent to children's special needs and demands" (Baumrind 1966, 410). Demandingness is defined as "the claims parents make on children to become integrated into the family whole by their maturity demands, supervision, disciplinary efforts and willingness to confront the child who disobeys" (Baumrind 1966, 411).

Equipped with their generational parenting legacies, family leaders determine the rules and use the style of parenting that suits their beliefs and experience. The *authoritative* style (high warmth and high control) is where the leadership is seen as having knowledge and experience while expecting family members to share responsibility for family functioning. Children are expected to respect family rules and parents are responsive to children's needs. Studies show that children reared in families with authoritative leadership develop a realistic and positive sense of themselves, are more confident, and are better equipped to conduct their own lives.

Another parenting style is *authoritarian* (low warmth and high control), where the leader dictates how members are to function, usually without much input from individual members. Children reared under authoritarian leadership are not encouraged to do their own thinking or to challenge family leadership; they are expected to do what the leader says. An authoritarian leader seeks to dominate. Discussion, when it occurs, ends with a winner and a loser, and every thought or opinion is judged and labeled good or bad. If the leader's requests, edicts, or mandates fail to result in compliance, escalating manipulations are employed, including deal-making, coercion, threats of abandonment, and threats of, or actual, violence (Grolnick 2003).

The third parenting style is *permissive*, where leaders have a low value on control, either too much (indulgent) or too little (neglectful) value on warmth, and have few expectations of members. Parents employing this style of leadership place very few restraints on their children and pay little attention to monitoring children's activities.

In *Life Beyond Shame, Rewriting the Rules*, Dawson (2016) introduces seven implicit shame-based rules, each containing the following four elements:

(a) The implicit rule and its *directive*, or assumed meaning
(b) The impact on *family dynamics* that flows from each implicit rule
(c) The replacement dignity-based explicit rule supporting authoritative parenting
(d) Opportunities for moving toward adopting the replacement rule

Substituting Explicit for Implicit Rules

Rule One: Do and be right.

Directive: Be morally, intellectually, and socially right. Don't make mistakes. Regard yourself and others harshly for errors in judgment and performance.

Family Dynamics: Difficulty deciding what and who is right with no clarity offered.

Use of name-calling and labeling, ridicule, negative and unwanted teasing, comparisons to others, chronic criticism of personhood, use of global words (never, always).

Members develop defensive postures to protect themselves.

Members feel unsafe and off balance.

Thinking primarily of self and others only in terms of extremes: right/wrong, good/bad, either/or, win/lose.

Being hypocritical. (Do as I say, not as I do.)

Being judgmental of self and others.

Being confused by mixed messages. (Come here/go away.)

Fixed beliefs and the perception of fixed beliefs that inhibit addressing problems.

Dynamics facilitate more separateness than connection, more fear than love and respect.

Public perceptions take precedence over individual needs.

(What will the neighbors think?)

Replacement Rule: **Learn and then learn again from your mistakes.**

Undertake a personal review of shaming incidents, expecting to gain insight into the people and purpose behind them.

Opportunities: Research origins of unearned shame.

Change personal shame into guilt wherever possible.

(Tangney and Dearing 2002)

Use apology, restitution, and making amends to restore valued relationships.
Be open to new mentors and new information.
Exercise understanding and compassion for self and others.

<u>*Rule Two:*</u>	Blame
Directive:	*When you make a mistake or get blamed for something, pass the blame elsewhere.*
Family Dynamics:	*Keeping others off balance by member's attempts to maintain control.*

Presence of accusations and faultfinding.
Character assassinations.
Sarcasm being used to minimize and discredit.
Use of contempt, disinterest or disregard.
Mutual accusations.
Making excuses, false reasons.
Initiating and perpetuating rumors.
Difficulty in accepting inability to control decisions, thinking and behaviors of others.
Accepting blame that is misplaced.
Reactively using blame to cover failures of responsibility.
Reduced motivation to initiate or try again for fear of failure.

Replacement Rule: **Accept responsibility for your decisions and behaviors.**

Opportunities: *Assess consequences of over-functioning on behalf of others and under-functioning for self.*
Review childhood experiences to become aware of possible early origin of personal defensive postures and patterns; assess contemporary need to continue them.
Practice taking responsibility while allowing others to assume their part.
Notice the effect on self-esteem and the pride of taking responsibility and following through.

Rule Three:	*Ignore feelings, yours and others'.*
Directive:	*Do not acknowledge your feelings about what's going on.*
Family Dynamics:	*Denial of another's feelings and the information they provide is a "Don't exist" and/or "Don't trust yourself" message.*
	Members tend to be insecure.
	Feelings of groundedness may be absent.
	Family may feel (and be experienced by others) as fake, weird, boring, and either overly even/uneven, or distracted.
	Whenever expressions of feelings are discounted or even dangerous, denial and discrediting become safer options.
	Denial of feelings leads to distorted perceptions of people and circumstances.
	Difficulty in using feelings accurately to assess personal needs.
Replacement Rule:	**Pay attention to your feelings. Acknowledge them and use the information they provide to identify what you need.**
Opportunities:	*Recover and develop personal abilities to express and rely on affective information.*
	Become personally aware of universal feelings, such as mad, sad, glad, scared, and exploring how they provide critical information about circumstances and people.
	Acknowledge the contribution of feelings to the development of social skills, self-awareness, self-regulation, self-soothing, empathy, motivation, and compassion.
	Reclaim or build trust in the information the body's affective system provides.
	Listen carefully and with interest, to family and individual stories of struggle and celebration. Focus on feelings to better learn the personal impact (meaning) of experiences.

Rule Four:	*Keep secrets.*
Directive:	*Do not raise the issue or ask questions about whatever might jeopardize the status quo.*
Family Dynamics:	*Keeping secrets (and telling lies) protects a person's perceived shame from exposure (criticism, judgment, etc.) and temporarily avoids unwanted consequences.*
	Withholding information that might be used by another to improve their quality of life.
	Protecting the family's public image and community standing.
	Protecting family's internal self-image.
	Creates distance in relationships.
	Develops a false or uncertain sense of reality.
	Keeping secrets hidden tends to undermine a sense of personal integrity.
	Members have a sense that something is missing because of inconsistencies and incongruence between word and deed. Members become suspicious and engage in careful, edited communication, holding their own secrets inside..
Replacement Rule:	**Tell your truth in the most respectful and likely receivable way, after first recognizing your own.**
Opportunities:	*Review family history of the effects of exposed secrets.*
	Evaluate personal secrets; consider the possible negative and positive outcomes of moving to revisit and resolve them.
	Examine the damage withholding truth or telling lies does to one's self- image and feelings of rectitude.
	Knowing and speaking one's truth generally augments a sense of personal power.

Rule Five:	*Be unclear and unaccountable.*
Directive:	*Don't communicate clearly. Be wary of commitments, promises, and agreements.*
Family Dynamics:	*Failure to keep commitments, promises, and agreements is a hallmark of untrustworthiness.*

Failure to account for the consequences of family decisions and actions may translate to disrespect of authority figures in general.

Incongruence between intention and action.

Criticism, when correction or change is called for, tends to be aimed at personhood instead of helpful teaching or problem solving.

Rule enforcement ranges from rigid to lax and changes at the whim of leaders.

Criticism regarding undesirable behavior may signal the leaders' inability to offer or support alternatives.

Family members avoid being accountable to avoid judgment or punishment.

Capricious changing of standards, boundaries, or expectations leads to frustration, uncertainty, and reactivity in dealings with authority figures.

It may be dangerous to be accountable.

Family develops a language of irresponsibility to avoid being clear and accountable.

Conflicts occurring in contexts based in the previous four rules are difficult to resolve and frequently intractable

Replacement Rule: **Be clear and accountable for your agreements and to your commitments.**

Opportunities: *Be clear about who is responsible for what.*

Clarify boundaries, standards, and consequences, thereby allowing members to make decisions in their best interests.

Take an authoritative approach to parenting and supervising.

Promote predictability and security in systems.

Members can learn and practice dependability and confidence in themselves and with others.

Identify problems and address or solve them.

Rule Six:

Directive:

Family Dynamics:

Be in control.

Manipulate, threaten, coerce, and use whatever works to get what you need.

Failure to discriminate between what is controllable and what is not. Family members are compliant, defiant, or passive to the methods of control exercised by leaders.

Behaviors related to emotional pain like depression, anxiety and social isolation are evident.

Control-seeking behaviors are geared toward being secure in uncertain, dismissive, or fearful environments.

The experience of rigid controlling behaviors generates high levels of stress.

Family leadership tends to be authoritarian, permissive, or uninvolved.

Leaders control by withholding information members might use to improve their quality of life..

Needs of members are often overlooked or addressed inappropriately.

Shaming is frequently used to bring members into compliance with dictates of family leadership figure(s).

A world view of win or lose dominates conflicts of needs, beliefs, values, and behaviors.

Persistence of a generalized anxiety or fear of losing control

Replacement Rule:

Opportunities:

Ask for what you need. Be willing to negotiate.

Positive control means being in charge of children's safety and protection until they mature into taking responsibility for themselves.

Be responsible for yourself and to others.

Develop the ability to identify and clarify the difference between needs, wants, and desires.

Establish a supportive environment where members are encouraged to enhance their abilities and implement personal goals.

Democratize the system; members' input is valued.

Establish a climate of openness and personal responsibility.
Cast off and replace historical erroneous beliefs based on shame.
Practice forgiveness of self and others.

Rule Seven: *Deny reality*
Directive: *What's going on is not really going on. Accept discrepant behaviors and occurrences as normal.*
Family Dynamics: *Denial prevents problem-solving.*
Living in contexts where reality is discounted is emotionally and physically dangerous.
Problems are called unsolvable. (Nothing changes anyway.)
Family members are troubled attempting to account for discrepancies between their reality and the reality of others in the same situation.
Members can be risk-aversive because of a generalized fear of failure and subsequent exposure of being unworthy.
Members may not have confidence in data, uncertain of its reliability.
Where a climate of staying stuck in distress prevails, opportunities to succeed are ignored or unrecognized.
Members who accept the family mantra of maintaining the status quo, no matter the existence of new information, opportunities, or pain, often do so reflexively, without being aware of it.
Replacement Rule: **Pay attention to what is true. Keep in touch with your own reality and check out your reality with others you trust.**
Opportunities: *Move toward identifying and solving problems instead of denying them.*
Members' confidence in themselves is strengthened as their realities are more closely matched with others they trust.

Family stress is reduced as solutions to problems are identified and worked through.
Knowing when to trust self and others increases personal power.
Members move in discrete steps from denial of a problem to empowerment to solve it. (Clarke and Dawson 1998)

Physical pain is the body's way of signaling a problem that needs solving. The person with a high tolerance for pain may not respond until the problem is so demanding and the symptoms so debilitating that a solution becomes extremely remote. In like manner, a person or group with a high degree of tolerance for emotional pain, such as chronic stress, may tend to deny the existence of a problem and stay stuck until the family explodes, implodes, or disintegrates. As therapist Esther Perel writes, "Stuck is when stability goes rigid. If you were to think systemically, you would say *every* system traverses stability and change. If there is too much stability, you fossilize and you go stuck. If there is too much change you can go chaotic. So stuck is the extreme version of stable" (Perel 2013).

Families in pain are paralyzed by rigid policies and practices. Perhaps the goal is finding a midpoint between stability and change that more nearly balances the warmth and control features of authoritative parenting.

CHANGING THE DYNAMICS OF SYSTEMIC HUMILIATION IN THE FAMILY

Every family unit lives according to its unique culture. A realization among family members of the cultural dimension of their interaction can serve as a point of departure for learning to respect and dignify one another while adapting to constantly changing circumstances. Each family will inevitably be challenged to navigate its own internal cultural diversity, including differences in ethnic or national heritage, gender, physical ability, sexual orientation, religious beliefs and practices, and so on. The family must also account for and accommodate the various inborn biologically derived differences between and among parents and children. The family is itself a learning laboratory in cultural integration.

Borrowing from the field of intercultural organizational development, several concepts might serve as guides to encourage a move from cultural blindness to cultural synergy. The goal is to improve family security (trust), cohesion, and connectedness by encouraging respect for diversity within the unit (Adler and Gunderson 2008). The combination of knowledge and respect for diversity helps to avoid problems in the system and translates into the strongest preparatory climate for positive functioning in the culture.

If family therapists seek to transform a family's reliance on implicit shame-based rules to explicit rules based on dignity, the Developmental Model of Intercultural Sensitivity (DMIS), developed by Milton Bennett, provides a useful paradigm (Bennett 1993). The DMIS is divided into two sets of stages describing movement from a closed system to an open one. In Ethnocentrism (characterized by stages of denial, defense, and minimization), people unconsciously experience their own cultures as central to reality. They tend to avoid the idea of cultural difference, seeing that as a threat to the reality of their own cultural experience. In Ethno-relativism (the stages of acceptance, adaptation, and integration), people consciously recognize that all behavior exists in a cultural context, including their own.

Briefly, in the first stage of denial:

> people have not yet constructed the category of 'cultural difference.' To them, the world is completely their current experience of it, and alternatives to that experience are literally unimaginable. People of other cultures…seem less human, lacking the 'real' feelings and thoughts of one's own kind. Cultural strangers exist as simpler forms in the environment to be tolerated, exploited, or eliminated as necessary. This is the default position of normal socialization (Bennett 1993, 219).

If denial is one extreme of intercultural sensitivity, integration is its polar opposite. In the integration stage, people are able to "perceive events in cultural context to include their own definitions of identity. For these people, the process of shifting cultural perspective becomes a normal part of self, and so identity itself becomes more fluid" (Bennett 2001, 13). This may describe a family whose members know and respect one another's differences and similarities and have come to respect and value one another without judgmental comparisons.

Interventions into Systemic Humiliation in the Family

A system changes in two ways: (1) individual parameters change in a continuous manner but the structure of the system does not alter (first-order change) and (2) the system changes qualitatively and in a discontinuous manner (second-order change). Second-order change occurs with changes in the body of rules governing their structure or internal order (Watzlawick et al. 1974). The resilient family adapts or changes in both ways. An individual may change behaviors, challenging others in the system to adapt, and the rules governing the family's internal order may be modified. However, an underlying mandate for secrecy is carried in the implicit rule that makes a shame-based family reluctant to self-identify as needing help because it reveals they didn't do something "right." Making way for change in the family system involves coming out of denial that a legacy of multigenerational, unearned, internalized shame may be related to family pain (Tangney and Dearing 2002). This suggests the importance of raising awareness of how families, as a matter of legacy, unwittingly deploy implicit rules that humiliate instead of treating self and others as worthy.

The process of protecting and maintaining denial is called *discounting* (Schiff et al. 1975). Discounting is making something more, less, or different from the way it really is. "Our perceived inability to do something or understand what is going on is usually based on some old personal decision about our lack of power" (Clarke and Dawson 1998, 150). There are four steps in the process of coming out of denial—first, overcoming denial of the problem's existence; second, overcoming denial of the problem's seriousness; third, realizing that solutions exist; and fourth, accepting one's personal power to solve the problem, which leads to the empowerment to address it.

With permission to acknowledge a problem, families need a variety of community resources that back up remediation, many already in existence. A necessary corollary to public education is the identification and availability of well-prepared and easily accessible professionals with skills in parent education and couples and family therapy. Specialists in facilitating enhanced communication skills and such strategies as mediation, conflict resolution, reconciliation, and restorative justice activities help families operationalize and strengthen newly implemented changes. Ultimately, the development of community-based family education centers or networks could provide a reliable and trustworthy presence for families seeking or attracted to improvement.

CONCLUSION

A family's reliance on the implicit rules and permissive or authoritarian parenting styles tends to undermine the dignity of family members. Dealing correctively with humiliation in a culture begins with recognizing the efficacy of an authoritative parenting style in ways that satisfy the need for both respectful authority and warmth and care. Replacing the traditional implicit rules with the replacement explicit rules facilitates a shift in family beliefs, interactions, and relationships.

Families can change the norms that create emotional distress; they can improve upon their values, beliefs, and behaviors. Evelin Lindner, founder of the Human Dignity and Humiliation Studies Network, gives systemic change in families a powerful boost when she says "Love, mature strong forceful love, informed by the appropriate concepts of courage and competence, is needed at the personal level as much as the global institutional level. Firm love is but another word for survival" (Lindner 2010, 11). Inasmuch as the family is the first place where love is experienced, it plays a pivotal role in changing broader negative trajectories based on humiliation and violence. After all, love is in the doing.

REFERENCES

Adler, N., and A. Gunderson. 2008. *International Dimensions of Organizational Behavior*. Mason: The Thomson Corporation.

Baumrind, D. 1966. Effects of Authoritative Parental Control on Child Behavior. *Child Development* 37 (4): 887–907.

———. 1967. Child Care Practices Anteceding Three Patterns of Preschool Behavior. *Genetic Psychology Monographs* 75 (1): 43–88.

Bennett, M.J. 1993. Towards Ethnorelativism: A Developmental Model of Cultural Sensitivity. In *Education for the Intercultural Experience*, ed. R.M. Paige, 2nd ed. Yarmouth: Intercultural Press.

Bennett, M. 2001. *Developing Intercultural Competence for Global Leadership*. Portland: The Intercultural Development Research Institute.

Bowen, M. 1993. *Family Therapy in Clinical Practice*. London: A Jason Aronson Book, Roman & Littlefield, Publishers, Inc.

Clarke, J.I., and C. Dawson. 1998. *Growing Up Again: Parenting Ourselves, Parenting Our Children*. Center City: Hazelden Foundation.

Davidson, M. 1983. *Uncommon Sense: The Life and Thought of Ludwig Von Bertalanffy*. Los Angeles: J. P. Tarcher.

Dawson, C. 2016. *Life Beyond Shame: Rewriting the Rules*. Bloomington: Balboa Press.

Elias, M.J., S.E. Tobias, and B.S. Friedlander. 1999. *Emotionally Intelligent Parenting: How to Raise a Self-Disciplined, Responsible, Socially Skilled Child*. New York: Harmony Books, Crown Publishers, Inc.

Fosha, D., D.J. Siegeland, and M.F. Solomon, eds. 2009. *The Healing Power of Emotion*. New York: W. W. Norton & Co.

Fossum, M., and M. Mason. 1986. *Facing Shame: Families in Recovery*. New York: W. W. Norton & Co.

Grolnick, W.S. 2003. *The Psychology of Parental Control: How Well-Meant Parenting Backfires*. Mahwah: Lawrence Erlbaum Associates.

Kaufman, G. 1983. *The Dynamics of Power: Building a Competent Self*. Cambridge, MA: Schenkman.

———. 1989. *The Psychology of Shame: Theory and Treatment of Shame-Based Syndromes*. New York: Springer Publishing.

Lindner, E. 2010. *Gender, Humiliation, and Global Security: Dignifying Relationships from Love, Sex, and Parenthood to World Affairs*. Santa Barbara: Praeger.

Miermont, J. 1995. *The Dictionary of Family Therapy*. New York: Wiley-Blackwell.

Miller, Alice. 1997. *The Drama of the Gifted Child: The Search for the True Self*. New York: Basic Books.

Morrison, A.P. 1998. *The Culture of Shame*. New York: Random House.

Perel, E. 2013. The Secret to Desire in a Long Term Relationship. https://www.ted.com/talks/esther_perel_the_secret_to_desire_in_a_long_term_relationship. Accessed 12 July 2016.

Schiff, J.L., et al. 1975. *Cathexis Reader: Transactional Analysis, Treatment of Psychosis*. New York: Harper and Row.

Sedgwick, E.K., and A. Frank, eds. 1995. *Shame and Its Sisters: A Silvan Tomkins Reader*. Durham: Duke University Press.

Siegel, D.J., and M. Hartzell. 2003. *Parenting from the Inside Out*. New York: Jeremy P. Tarcher/Putnam.

Tangney, J.P., and R. Dearing. 2002. *Shame and Guilt*. New York: The Guilford Press.

Verny, T. 1983. *The Secret Life of the Unborn Child*. New York: Dell Books.

Watzlawick, P., J.H. Weakland, and J.H. Fisch. 1974. *Change: Principles of Problem Formation and Problem Resolution*. New York: W. W. Norton & Company.

Wolynn, M. 2016. *It Didn't Start with You*. New York: Viking, Penguin.

Zajonc, R.B. 1980. Feeling and Thinking: Preferences Need No Inferences. *American Psychologist* 35: 157–193.

CHAPTER 10

Madness, Violence, and Human Dignity: Transforming Madness for Dignified Existence

David Y. F. Ho

Many people yearn for and actively seek extraordinary experiences, good and bad. William James (1920/2008) once wrote to his family:

> I'm glad to get into something less blameless, but more admiration-worthy. The flash of a pistol, a dagger, or a devilish eye, anything to break the unlovely level of 10,000 good people—a crime, murder, rape, elopement, anything would do (p. 43).

"A devilish eye, elopement, and rape" conjure up romantic-sexual fantasies, in an ascending order of salaciousness. Fantasies of a violent nature are also abundant; "anything would do" is really scary.

To associate madness and violence seems natural enough. Have we not seen enough of mass shootings by mentally disturbed individuals in America, for instance? I will, however, argue that this association is misconstrued. And what does madness have to do with human dignity? My answer is, "Everything." The present chapter is an attempt to defend this answer. The world has long wanted to expunge madness from dignified

D. Y. F. Ho (✉)
Formerly Director of the Clinical Psychology Programme,
University of Hong Kong, Hong Kong

© The Author(s) 2018
D. Rothbart (ed.), *Systemic Humiliation in America*,
https://doi.org/10.1007/978-3-319-70679-5_10

existence. But is it possible? And even if the answer is yes, which I doubt, is it desirable?

Advocates of human dignity have long championed the rights of the disadvantaged or disenfranchised, minority or ethnic groups subject to systemic abuse or violence by another, and so forth. In comparison, people with mental disorders have not received the attention they deserve in human dignity and humiliation studies. Throughout history, mentally disordered persons have suffered systemic stigmatization, ostracism, and illtreatment (cf. Perlin and Lynch, Chap. 8, this volume). What is lesser known is the mistreatment they have received, yes, at the hands of psychiatrists (e.g., overmedication, lobotomy, indiscriminate use of electric shock therapy).

In order to pay greater attention to the plight of the mentally disordered, I will draw on my firsthand experiences from both being a "doctor" (clinical psychologist) and a "patient." I have had my share of extraordinary experiences, which I did not actively seek. They simply occurred spontaneously, inexplicably, and unpredictably during 20 episodes of mood disorder I have had—all of exuberance and none of depression. In terms of psychiatric nomenclature, my condition may be characterized as a unipolar mood disorder with only hypomanic and/or manic episodes. This condition is highly atypical; common mood disorders are characterized by episodes of depression or by bipolar mood swings alternating between unusual elevation and depression. (Incredibly, one occurrence coincided with the final stage of writing this manuscript.)

Even now, I cannot switch the episodes on or off at will. But I continue to value them as life-enriching experiences (Ho 2016). After the occurrence of so many episodes of "madness," it is hardly surprising that the question should arise: "Am I mad or enlightened?" Johnson and Friedman (2008) have discussed the challenges psychological diagnosticians face when dealing with religious, spiritual, or transpersonal experiences that may range from healthy to psychopathological. The present rejoinder adduces evidence from my own self-studies (Ho 2014a, 2014b, 2016) to spell out the conditions under which madness may be rendered benign, even transformed in the service of human dignity.

In what follows, first I clarify the key construct of this chapter, namely, human dignity. To justify the claim that human dignity is ecumenical and all inclusive, an excursion into the debate between cultural-ethical universalism and relativism is unavoidable. This debate informs the arguments advanced in this chapter, in which the implicit tensions between universalism and relativism pervade. Second, I refute the claim that madness and violence are necessarily connected; mentally disordered or disabled persons are more likely the recipients, rather than perpetrators, of humiliation or violence. Third, I argue that madness may be rendered benign if and when its violent forms of expression are kept under control. Finally, I reexamine the history of violence committed in the name of religion and, more fundamentally, the duality of good and evil in religious or ideological fanaticism. I attempt to distinguish between the good from the evil directions in which religiosity, coexisting with madness, may take: in other words, between benign and malignant madness. I frankly admit that making such a distinction is based on ethical, rather than psychiatric, grounds. My arguments summate to support my thesis that it is possible to retain a measure of madness in dignified living (i.e., madness-in-dignity) and of dignity even in a state of madness (i.e., dignity-in-madness).

Construct Explication

The focus here is to clarify the use of three major terms in this chapter: "madness," "violence," and "human dignity." Obviously, I am using the term "madness" rather loosely. "Madness" is a nontechnical term that refers, in a broad sense, to mental disorders or abnormal conditions. It lacks specificity and does not refer to a specific disorder. Madness connotes insanity, frenzy, and severity: For instance, psychosis is madness, but typically we would not refer to a common anxiety disorder, which is mild in relative terms, as madness. In sum, without further specification, madness is used broadly to refer to the more severe forms of mental disorders in this chapter.

The expression of violence takes many forms: subtle-indirect or open-direct; verbal, physical, or both; individual or collective; occasional or repetitive; planned or unplanned; random or institutional. Violence is especially vicious when it is targeted toward a specific cultural or ethnic group, intentionally, systemically, and systematically (e.g., genocide and ethnic cleansing). Against such an extreme affront to human dignity, humanity has declared, "Never again"! Even when it is expressed lesser forms, violence humiliates and, therefore, threatens human dignity. In this chapter, we are more concerned with collective, systemic, and institutional (though not necessarily planned) than with individual forms of violence. Accordingly, analysis at the macro-sociopolitical level is more applicable than at the micro-psychological level. (See other chapters, this volume, for detailed analyses.)

To explicate the key construct in this chapter (and of this book), human dignity is essential to the development of my arguments. Here, I simply state that human dignity is characterized by the following five defining attributes.

1. Human dignity is an inalienable right, based on the intrinsic worth of the human person. Therefore, no one should be deprived of dignity. Unlike social status, prestige, face, and the like, it does not have to be earned. It is not respect because, without self-respect, respect by others can hardly be taken for granted. It is not entitlement, the right to be guaranteed benefits under a government program, because human dignity goes beyond tangible benefits. More fundamentally, human dignity does not derive from governmental authority; rather, the exercise of governmental authority itself has to be based on respect for human dignity.

2. Human dignity is a cardinal or core value underlying diverse aspects of life. A loss of dignity would result in a significant decrease in the overall quality of life and a gain in dignity would give greater substance to a good life. What would life be like without dignity?

3. Human dignity is relational. It is not anchored in the isolated individual person, but in relations between persons: If your dignity is threatened or damaged, so would mine be; equally, if your dignity is secure, I would feel more secure about mine. An important implication follows: Collectively, the total gain or loss of human dignity for humankind is greater than the summation of human dignity over individuals.

4. Human dignity is all inclusive. It is applicable to all without exception, without regard to age, gender, ethnicity, disability or incapacitation, and physical or mental condition.

5. Human dignity is universal, based on belief in the unity of humankind. Universality does not negate but allows for ethnic-cultural pluralism. Accordingly, we acknowledge that concrete expressions of human dignity may vary in different ethnic-cultural contexts. However, universality does negate social norms and practices (e.g., ethnic cleansing) that, under specific historical, political, or cultural conditions, result in great harm to human dignity.

Minimal material conditions (e.g., food, shelter, safety) have to be met for dignified living. Threats to dignified living may come from natural calamities, from human action or inaction, or from a combination of natural and artificial causes. For instance, human activities may lead to natural calamities through environmental disregard; and inaction may fail to prevent unnecessary loss of dignity after the occurrence of calamities. Accordingly, conservationist values are essential to the preservation of human dignity. They constitute an extension of civic virtues from society to nature, simply because the destruction of the environment on a global scale by human activity will eventually erode the foundation of civil societies.

DIALECTICAL TENSION BETWEEN THE PARTICULAR AND THE UNIVERSAL

Universality or ecumenicity is one of the cardinal principles underlying the affirmation of human dignity. Yet, we must make a critical point explicit here: Ecumenicity must not degenerate into the kind of pluralism that allows for "anything goes." Inherent in pluralism is the dialectical tension between two tendencies: diversity and unity. Diversity without unity leads to factionalism; unity without diversity is boring uniformity. I have stated categorically that human dignity is universal. This invites disputation because many may argue that, as a value, human dignity is subject to various historical and sociocultural interpretations. A revisit to the age-old debate between universalism and particularism is thus unavoidable.

The tension between the particular and the universal is as old as the social sciences. Norms, beliefs, and values supposedly shared by virtually all known cultural groups, albeit not necessarily in the same manner, are *cultural universals*. Those shared by only a cultural group or related groups (e.g., the ethic of filial piety in Confucian cultures) are *culture specific*. (See the Appendix for an imaginary debate between relativist Dr. R and universalist Dr. U centered on the question: Is human dignity universal or culture specific?)

The thesis of *universality* presupposes the existence of core values shared by the majority of cultural traditions, although their concrete expression may take different forms. It entails the identification and extraction of commonalities across cultures. Values such as love, courage, justice, and wisdom may be identified as plausible universals because they are rooted in the world's great philosophical-religious teachings and are upheld in virtually all cultural traditions. Conceived at a high level of abstraction or generality, universals allow for cultural variation in interpretation and expression. Nonetheless, universals imply that there are irreducible standards for human conduct. To a universalist, many cultural practices (e.g., foot binding in traditional China) present an affront to human dignity.

Social scientists who adhere to *cultural relativism* refute this implication. Standards, they claim, are subject to temporal and geographical variations; what is right or wrong, normal or abnormal, is relative to the cultural group in question at a specific period in history. Moreover, to pass judgment on the cultural practices of another group is to commit ethnocentrism or, more precisely, culturocentrism, considered as a cardinal sin. Cultural relativists prefer to rely on the concept of *deviance*: What is deviant in one cultural group may be accepted even as standard practice in another, and vice versa. Viewed in this light, madness is a manifestation of deviance, not of mental derangement.

In conclusion, we affirm the dialectical synthesis between unity and diversity. Intercultural fertilization enriches our understanding of human dignity as an ecumenical ideal. This ideal, diversity within unity, is both principled and tolerant: Ecumenicity without tolerance succumbs to absolutism; unprincipled ecumenicity absorbs unwanted elements and risks becoming tainted. The tension between principled discernment and tolerance drives its further development. A major task lies ahead of us: to identify and catalog commonalities as well as differences in conceptions of human dignity among the world's philosophical, religious, and cultural traditions.

ARE MADNESS AND VIOLENCE NECESSARILY CONNECTED?

Does mental disturbance or abnormality necessarily lead people to become prone to violence? Let me first draw on my experience in a huge state mental hospital where I lived and worked as a clinical psychologist for some five years in the 1960s. Back then, state mental hospitals were places of hopelessness, where inmates were locked up in smelly wards and given no effective treatment. The one I worked in was a monstrosity with more than 5,000 inmates. My experience led me to question if there was a pervasive or necessary connection between madness and violence. Contrary to common perception, the hospital was a quiet, peaceful place. I saw little physical violence among patients, but mostly passivity, resignation, and despair that resulted from being institutionalized to the hospital milieu. The patients were not perpetrators of violence; rather, they were victims of humiliation and institutional "violence"—an affront to human dignity. Such institutionalization is common to *total institutions* (e.g., armies, prisons, ecclesiastical institutions) in which workers or inmates perform most of their daily functions within the same geographical location under an authoritarian social structure (Goffman 1961). Typically, the mentally disordered who are not (or not yet) institutionalized receive no better treatment either. Perlin and Lynch (Chap. 8, this volume), for instance, have forced upon public consciousness the humiliating consequences of shaming and shameful arrest policies of urban police departments in their treatment of persons with mental disabilities.

Elsewhere, American society is full of physical violence (e.g., bullying and gang fights), in contrast to the hospital grounds I have described. The violence seems everywhere, in virtual reality as in real life, among normal people. Mass shootings by the mentally disturbed do occur, with alarming regularity. But to attribute the loss of lives to madness is to turn a blind eye to a more fundamental question: Does the loss of lives result purely from the mad people who have guns, or more from the normal people who oppose gun control? This line of questioning leads to an uncomfortable thought: Human tragedies result more from failures of the normal to prevent their recurrence than from actions of the abnormal.

Madness-in-Dignity and Dignity-in-Madness

My firsthand experiences during episodes of madness lend further credence for negating the putative connection between madness and violence (Ho 2014a). Rather, they point to a dialectical relation between madness and spirituality: Each may transform, and be transformed by, the other. This statement requires explanation. First, I explicate the construct of spirituality as follows:

1. Spirituality addresses existential or transcendent issues, such as those concerning one's relations with others and one's place in the cosmos. The conviction that life is meaningful and purposeful is quintessential to spirituality.

2. Spirituality is located in the domain of cardinal or superordinate values underlying all aspects of life, such as respect for life and love of humanity.
3. Spirituality is characterized by self-reflectiveness, and is hence meta-cognitive, in nature.

In my conception, discontent with ordinary existence is the mother of spirituality. The reason is that spiritual fulfillment goes above and beyond ordinary existence conditioned by the biological and sociocultural givens in which a person is situated. It entails reaching for the highest ideal, that is, the realization of human potential to its fullest. It finds expression in different religious-philosophical traditions: in Christianity, to be Christlike and bear the sufferings of humankind on one's shoulders; in Buddhism, to have "the heart of a bodhisattva," filled with compassion; in Daoism, to be sage-like, selfless, spontaneous, living in harmony with nature and society; in Confucianism, to reach self-realization as the ultimate purpose in life through continual self-cultivation; and in Marxism, to struggle for the liberation of humankind from social injustice in the form of class exploitation and oppression. In sum, the paths to spirituality are many, grounded in different beliefs and ideals.

In terms of a dialectical relation, the transformation of spirituality entails harnessing the creative forces of madness; and the transformation of madness entails receiving the healing effects from spirituality. The idea of harnessing goes beyond coexisting with madness. Coexistence is like living at the foot of an active volcano, not knowing when it will explode. Harnessing madness is more radical: The creative forces of madness are made subservient to spirituality to drive its further development. The healing forces of spirituality temper the volatility of madness and keep it from causing harm or destruction. Self-reflection and self-monitoring, both indicative of metacognitive functioning, play a crucial role in this dialectical process. Even in the depth of madness, I would frequently ask myself, "Am I mad or enlightened?" This has helped me greatly to deflate my supreme self-confidence, keep in touch with reality, and avoid causing more harm to myself or others.

In this way, spirituality and madness coexist in a dialectical relation. Spirituality without a measure of madness is devoid of energy; madness without spirituality loses its redeeming value. Spirituality derives creative energy from madness to reach new heights; madness receives the healing, calming effects of spirituality to become benign. Thus, it is possible to retain a measure of madness in dignified living (i.e., madness-in-dignity) and of dignity even in a state of madness (i.e., dignity-in-madness).

This dynamic conception means that madness may continue to be intertwined with spirituality, not something to be expunged from the mind. A dialectical relation entails tension and conflict. Many psychologists (e.g., Carl Rogers) tend to regard inner conflicts as negative and self-consistency as positive for mental health. Self-consistency is manifest in congruence between the real self and the ideal self. By this count, ironically, psychopaths are the most congruent and thus mentally healthy! The notion of self-consistency may lead to a sterile conception of human functioning in which conflicts have no place. Conflicts are, however, a source for change, adaptation, and creativity in the process of their resolution.

I am humbled by how arduous the process can be; failures persist even after having had plenty of opportunities for learning from 20 episodes of madness. When spiritual forces prevail, unpleasant memories do lose their destructiveness and madness becomes more benign. Thus, I have had limited success: experiencing moments of serenity, most ironically, during episodic madness and when spiritual forces augmented during madness carry into normal times. These extraordinary experiences have informed me on spirituality in clinical practice (Ho 2014b).

MADNESS IN CULTURAL CONTEXT

In Western psychology, the healthy self is conceived as stable over time; it is a coherent, integrated, and unitary whole. In Eastern thought, Daoism and Buddhism in particular, the notion of selflessness is central to the conception of selfhood (Ho 1995). During episodes of madness, there were moments when I experienced transcendent states of emptiness in which the self appeared to have vanished.

Buddhist ideas of self-emptying or no-mind emptiness refer in a positive light to a state of mind emptied of self and its thoughts and cravings (Ho 1995, 2014a) and should not be confused with spiritual emptiness. Moreover, differences in conceptions of selfhood between the East and the West entail the need to guard against uncritical viewing extraordinary experiences (e.g., selfless self) in pathological terms. I would argue further that expanding our conceptions of selfhood opens more doors to life enrichment in the West as well.

To experience the selfless self or the empty mind is to go beyond, not supplant, the normal and healthy. In a similar vein, the achievement of impulse control is a prerequisite to experiencing the extraordinary, which implies overcoming repression and gaining access to the unconscious. If what comes out are unchecked rampant impulses and raw destructiveness, the result would be horror. Digging deeply into my own self, I see a preponderance of positives (e.g., love of humanity) over the negatives (e.g., hateful violence), and I foresee no horror when impulses are expressed in magnified intensities. Early in one of my episodes of madness, I wrote in my diary that Eros without Thanatos is "safe." But a reversal of this preponderance raises the specter of madness wedded to evil. Witness the horrid destructiveness to the world that mad psychopaths, exemplified by Adolf Hitler, have wrought.

It is important to distinguish between thoughts, words, and deeds in terms of impulse control. This is especially important when repression vanishes, as in my case, and access to the unconscious is unhindered. Impulses are harmless as long as they remain in the domain of thought. This is a fundamental viewpoint in psychoanalytic theory—in sharp contrast with Confucian ethics, which insists on keeping thoughts "correct" and "pure." Psychoanalysis is predicated on the total eradication of all restrictions on thought: Nothing is unthinkable. Now, to dare to think the unthinkable is the fountainhead of creativity. Thought control suffocates it. As long as we exercise adequate control over the expression of our impulses in words or in deeds, madness may be rendered benign. And the attainment of an ideal, madness-in-dignity, as well as dignity-in-madness, may be in sight.

ARE MADNESS AND EVIL NECESSARILY CONNECTED?

In recent decades, the association of madness and violence has been strengthened by human bombers in the Middle East and elsewhere who blow innocent people and themselves up in the name of God or Allah. This compels us to reassess the connection between madness and evil. At the same time, we must also reexamine the long history of violence committed in the name of religion and, more fundamentally, the duality of good and evil in religious or ideological fanaticism.

Psychopathology of Religious Luminaries

The duality of good and evil looms large in religiosity. In this chapter, I attempt to differentiate between the good from the evil directions in which religiosity, coexisting with madness, may take: in other words, between benign and malignant madness. Religiosity and spirituality are distinct, though overlapping, concepts. A major difference concerns the propensity toward violence. Religiosity may carry with it potential perils of dogmatism, cultism, extremism, or, worse, fanaticism. Because religious experiences pertain to the ultimate questions of life, the danger of their occurrence in violent forms rings a grave alarm. The likes of evil cults ending in mass suicide and religious militants who murder in the name of God are magnified consequences of violent tendencies wedded to religious fervor. In contrast, spirituality has an inherent immunity to guard itself against these perils, because of its propensity toward humility, contemplativeness, and self-reflection. Exemplars of spirituality (e.g., prophets, mystics, Arhats) may be tormented by self-doubt or guilt; they may be given to self-denial—but not to suicide bombing or other forms of wanton outbound aggression.

Like religiosity and spirituality, religiosity and madness are overlapping concepts. Logically, this implies that neither is a necessary or sufficient condition for the other. It is possible to be religious without being mad or be mad without being religious, be neither, or be both. The last category, being both religious and mad, may comprise only a minority, but an important minority. Religion may enter into madness in the form of hallucinations or delusions with religious content. In some cases, these psychiatric symptoms are merely by-products of madness; they disappear with its termination. In other cases, symptoms with religious content form the core of madness—that is to say, religion is now wedded to madness, a highly incendiary condition. In still other cases, and these are the most interesting of all, religiosity takes on a life of its own, coexisting with madness, and transforms the person's life in two possible directions, one toward the good and the other toward evil. When that happens, we may witness the arrival of a new prophet or another monster. That is why a study of the psychopathology of religious luminaries throughout the ages may be so illuminating.

An account of great leaders of religious movements, Gautama, Jesus, Muhammad, St. Francis of Assisi, George Fox, and many others, reveals some recurrent patterns. Their career paths are tortured paths, characterized by most, if not all, of these elements: a triggering event leading to intensive religiosity; intense, fierce inner struggle; isolation and solitude; being a voice in the wilderness, figurative or literal; self-denial, to an extreme; temptations of great force, typically of lust for sex or power, that are eventually overcome; experience of enlightenment; preaching to increasingly larger multitudes; rejection by orthodoxy or, worse, being branded as a heretic and persecuted; surviving persecution; and, finally, recognition as a religious leader.

My experiences pale in significance compared with those of religious luminaries. Willful hallucinations, such as those of mine, are under the control of the hallucinator and should not be construed as pathological. The psychopathology of my madness is circumscribed and relatively tame; in particular, paranoid ideation is absent. I have no ambition to be a religious leader. I just yearn to lead a good life. Not so with the great religious leaders of the world: Together, they manifest a museum of psychiatric symptoms (e.g., hallucinations, delusions of grandeur). Whereas genius tends to be associated with manic depression, religiosity-spirituality tends to be associated with paranoia. Medical authors have long adduced biblical evidence to allege that no less a leader than Jesus suffered from paranoia. Albert Schweitzer (1913/2011), the renowned medical missionary to Africa, wrote his doctoral thesis, entitled *The Psychiatric Study of Jesus*, to refute this allegation.

George Fox and Quakerism: A Tortuous Road Toward Dignity

No one to my knowledge, however, has come out for a psychiatric defense of George Fox, who founded Quakerism (later called the Religious Society of Friends) in seventeenth-century England. For this reason, I have chosen Fox as a case study of how religious fervor wedded to madness need not lead to more, but rather to less, violence in the world. Fox was a troubled and searching youth drawn to religious concerns. He was shocked by what he saw as the failure of the "professors," that is, the professing Christians, to live their beliefs. At age 19, Fox left home on a spiritual quest, during which he challenged religious leaders everywhere to answer his questions. Nowhere did he find satisfaction. In 1647, having "forsaken all the priests" and in despair, he heard a voice, saying, "There is one, even Christ Jesus, that can speak to thy condition." To Fox, this was a direct, immediate, and transforming experience of God. It was to become the heart of his message and ministry, marking the beginning of the Quaker movement. Predictably, Fox was persecuted. He was imprisoned eight times. He suffered cruel beatings and deprivation. But he was an indomitable figure. Nothing would drive him to detract from his dogged persistence to spread his message. His *Journal* and other writings continue to be the basic works of Quakerism.

Anyone who succeeds in leading a religious movement into maturity, surviving untold hardship and persecution, has to be a religious genius. The probability of success, though statistically significantly different from zero, is still near zero. But Fox was also a mad genius. A reading of his *Journal* makes clear that Fox was a deeply disturbed man. Paranoid ideation leaps out from the pages. As a clinical psychologist, I detect one extremely disturbing aspect in Fox's case: his obedience to, and acting out, hallucinatory commands attributed to some external authority. An excerpt from his *Journal* (as quoted in James, 1902/2002, emphasis added):

> The word of the Lord came to me, that I must to thither [to the city of Lichfield].... Then was I commanded by the Lord to pull off my shoes. I stood still, for it was winter: but the word of the Lord was like a fire in me. So I put off my shoes.... Then I walked on about a mile, and as soon as I got within the city, the word of the Lord came to me again, saying: Cry, 'Wo to the bloody city of Lichfield!' So I went up and down the streets, crying with a loud voice, Wo to the bloody city of Lichfield! ... As I went thus crying through the streets, there *seemed* to me to be a channel of blood running down the streets, and the market-place *appeared* like a pool of blood.... After this a deep consideration came upon me, for what reason I should be sent to cry against that city, and call it the bloody city! ... *afterwards* I came to understand, that in the Emperor Diocletian's time, a thousand Christians were martyr'd in Lichfield. So I was to go, without my shoes, through the channel of their blood, and into the pool of their blood in the market-place, that I might raise up the memorial of the blood of those martyrs (pp. 12–13).

What if the commands had been of a more violent-destructive sort? The use of the words *seemed* and *appeared* suggests an awareness of the distinction between appearance and the real thing. The "deep consideration" is a clear indication of a self-reflective mind (or metacognition) at work. The word "afterwards" is significant, for it informs us that the crucial historical information about Lichfield comes after the actions. The martyrs' blood then gives Fox's actions perfect rationalization and elevation to the status of religiosity.

His *Journal* also reveals a total commitment to his religious quest; indifference to his physical and, more significantly, social costs that the quest entails. To Fox, how others perceive and react to his actions are irrelevant. Surely, here is a mark of egomania. But is there anything evil in his actions? The answer is no. That is the critical question that may differentiate religiosity from evil. To conclude, Fox is a religious genius, paranoid but not evil. William James (1985) says, in *The Varieties of Religious Experience*:

> A genuine first-hand religious experience like this [of George Fox] is bound to be a heterodoxy to its witnesses, the prophet appearing as a mere lonely madman. If his doctrine prove [sic] contagious enough to spread to any others, it becomes a definite and labeled heresy. But if it then still prove [sic] contagious enough to triumph over persecution, it becomes itself an orthodoxy; and when a religion has become an orthodoxy, its day of inwardness is over: The spring is dry; the faithful live at second hand exclusively and stone the prophets in their turn (p. 270).

Great religious leaders share some common attributes: They have charisma; they have an unshakable belief in their own righteousness; they have a singularity of purpose, to spread their message or doctrine; their determination is resolute, even ruthless, and no sacrifice is too great a price to pay to reach their goals. Contagiousness comes from the combination of these attributes. Now the same combination is found in the leaders of evil cults, of whom there are few examples more destructive and revolting than James Jones. Moreover, if religiosity is extended to the larger domain of ideology, then we may easily find men of genius who are both mad and evil, of whom Adolf Hitler must lay claim to being the Führer. How can benign madness and malignant madness be differentiated?

Duality of Good and Evil

Judgments of good and evil are made, not on psychiatric or scientific, but on ethical grounds. So the severity of psychiatric disturbance, if any, is irrelevant. Though fully capable of acting in naughty, mischievous, even out-of-bound ways, I confess that I lack the capacity to do evil. This I count as a blessing. Less inclined to inflict pain on others than to hold myself responsible for wrongdoings, I find it easier to forgive others than to forgive myself. This I now count as a liability.

"Every tree is known by its fruit": This provides a hint on how we may proceed. Suppose we look at two trees, Fox and Hitler, and see how they are known by their fruits, Quakerism and Nazism. Suddenly, the contrasts cannot be sharper at every turn. Nazism is too well-known to require an introduction. For now, a brief introduction to Quakerism will suffice. Early Quakers were so named because they were said to tremble or quake with religious zeal. The nickname Quaker stuck, now devoid of its original derisiveness. Quakers are also known as Friends, belonging to the Religious Society of Friends. Quakerism was a radical movement against hollow formalism, for a return to the original gospel truth, in the aftermath of the Protestant Reformation. George Fox, the leader, believed that the Scriptures must be read in the same Spirit that inspired those who wrote them. He and his followers rejected the ecclesiastical authority of their day. Their movement represented a call to return to the original, primitive Christianity. Predictably, Quakers were branded as heretics and persecuted. Quakerism has survived but has shown resilience in preserving its original intentions, not to become itself orthodoxy. Today, the friendly Quakers, no longer quaking, may be seen doing their work for peace and the betterment of humankind everywhere.

The central beliefs of Quakerism are at once simple and deceptively simple. Simple, because they are stated in simple words, accessible to most people. Deceptively simple, because deeper meanings rooted in Quaker traditions and the "testimonies" of exemplary Quakers cannot be understood in words alone. They have to be lived, witnessed in the deeds of daily life. Without getting too deeply into Quaker theology, I find this core belief to be the most illuminating: There is an indwelling Seed, Christ, or Light (which may be interpreted as metaphors) within all persons that, if heeded, will guide them and shape their lives. From this simple idea springs a wealth of spiritual implications.

The core belief is a statement of ecumenicity: The Light is within *all* persons, that is, everywhere. It erases, therefore, the artificial divide between the secular and the religious, so that all of life may be lived in the Light. Each person I meet is potentially inspired and inspirational. When I shun or reject one, I deprive myself of an inspirational channel to spirituality; when I embrace one, I enrich myself spiritually. What a creative and powerful idea! God is directly accessible to all persons without the need of intermediary priest or ritual. Quakerism rejects, therefore, ecclesiastical authority and "empty forms" of worship (e.g., set prayers, words, and rituals). All persons are to be equally valued. No wonder Quaker organization is an ultimate democracy.

Buddhism and Quakerism share much in common. Of the world's major religions, Buddhism stands out in its appeals: nonviolence, compassion, and respect for life in all its forms. Through supreme effort, a person has the potential to reach enlightenment. This idea is truly radical, for it implies the possibility of altering the cosmic flow of events, namely, breaking the cycle of births and rebirths, through conscious self-direction. In sum, both Buddhism and Quakerism are champions of human dignity.

With this brief introduction to Quakerism, we are now better positioned to make a judgment. The fruits of Fox may be found in Quakers' humanitarian mission of service outreach, programs of education social action; the fruits of Hitler are death by the millions, unprecedented destruction, and the Holocaust. Quakers were victims of persecution; Nazis persecuted innocent victims. Quakers are led by love; Nazis are consumed by hate. Quakers do not have a creed, but "testimonies" expressed in individual lives and collective actions; Nazis have *Mein Kampf* as their bible. Quakerism is inclusionary, tolerant of diversity; Nazism is exclusionary, obdurate in its insistence on racial purity. Quakers believe that each person has the divine potential to be guided by an indwelling Light or Truth, without the need for intermediary priests; Nazis demand absolute obedience to the Führer. Quakers believe in self-direction and self-determination; Nazis excel in mind control. Quakers are pacifists; Nazis are warmongers. Quakers value the individual man, woman, and child equally, without distinction; Nazis believe in Aryan superiority. The Quaker Way of decision-making and governance is not the rule of the majority, but a deliberate process of resolving differences, in which the opinion of each single person is respected and heard; Nazi governance is the embodiment of totalitarianism, where the voice of the Führer drowns out all others.

To conclude, benign and malignant madness can be differentiated on the basis of directional actions toward good or evil taken by a mad person. Yes, we may identify mad geniuses who have acted as champions of human dignity throughout history. Again, madness may be linked to good rather than to evil, to peace rather than to violence, and to human dignity rather than to degradation.

CONCLUSION

Among the defining attributes of human dignity are universality and total inclusiveness. Accordingly, it is applicable to all without exception—without regard to disability or incapacitation, physical or mental condition. Our major thesis is that it is possible, even desirable, to retain a measure of madness in dignified living (i.e., madness-in-dignity) and of dignity even in a state of madness (i.e., dignity-in-madness). Arguments in support of this thesis rest on, firstly, establishing that mental abnormality does not necessarily lead people to become prone to violence, and, secondly, making a distinction between benign madness and malignant madness based on ethical, rather than psychiatric, grounds. Malignant madness causes suffering to the sufferer and those around him. If wedded to evil, as in the case of Hitler and his gang of psychopaths, it has no redeeming value; it serves only to magnify suffering and threaten human dignity. Benign madness is devoid of evil and may be harnessed to enhance dignified existence.

The creative energy of madness may be harnessed for dignified existence, given that several preconditions are met (Ho 2016). The first is the capability for self-reflectiveness that enables one to be aware of and monitor the extraordinary state in which one finds oneself. The second is an intact sense of self, without which, paradoxically, selflessness can hardly be attained. The third is adequate impulsive control, without which the destructive forces of madness may get out of control. Finally, most important of all is the preponderance of love over hate, for its reversal would raise the horrid specter of madness wedded to evil. Even when these preconditions are met, sustained effort is needed to transform madness in the service of life enrichment. And without ever having been mad, there may be a limit on how such transformation can be accomplished.

Appendix

To a universalist, "objectionable" practices abound. Foot binding in China, practiced for centuries to make women more "attractive," is one. Female genital mutilation is still practiced widely in Middle Eastern countries. Often referred to as female circumcision, it comprises all procedures involving partial or total removal of the external female genitalia or other injuries to the female genital organ, whether for cultural, religious, or other nontherapeutic reasons. Another example should be added, if only to avoid the impression that different norms exist only between ethnic or cultural groups: abortion as murder, a position held vehemently by the pro-life camp in opposition to the pro-choice camp in the United States. We should also take note that all examples cited entail the female body and sexuality. Is this purely coincidental? Can we avoid taking a stand on the ethical issues they bring?

Before deciding on whether we agree with relativism or universality, let us witness an imaginary debate between relativist Dr. R and universalist Dr. U. At the end, we will be better informed on where we stand on the issues. Here, we need to make explicit a distinction between two related, but distinct, issues of this debate, the cultural and the ethical. At stake is the question: Is human dignity universal or culture specific?

Debate

Dr. U: Misguided cultural or religious pluralism can corrupt into moral relativism, a curious and dangerous position denying that there are irreducible standards for human conduct. Moral relativism poses a threat to ecumenicity, which affirms universalistic values and principles. Thus, tension exists between the embracement of diversity and the threat that this embracement may pose. Indiscriminate admittance of cultural or religious beliefs and practices may be as deadly as embracing the Medusa.

Dr. R: Universalistic doctrines of morality disregard cultural diversity. In contrast, ethical relativism allows any culture to define what it regards as right or wrong. As a cultural relativist, I reject the idea of universal norms, simply because there are no norms accepted in or common to all cultures. As an ethical relativist, I refute the idea that cultural values may be ranked on primitive-to-advanced or bad-to-good dimensions. In particular, I reject the notion of a pathogenic culture or subculture in which its social pathologies or mental disorders are rooted in some of its cultural norms. Cultural relativism leads to ethical relativism: There is no way to reach consensus across cultures; or to decide if one set of norms or values is better, or worse than another.

Dr. U: We may stand our argument on its head, and affirm general, culturally invariant principles by challenging ethical relativists to negate them: Can you name a single culture that rejects appropriate behavior, and affirms deviant behavior, defined according to its own norms? Alternatively, can you think of a single exception to the universal principle that all cultures affirm appropriate behavior, and negate deviant behavior, according to its own definition of what is appropriate and what is deviant? Similarly, it is both possible and necessary to formulate general, higher-order ethical principles according to which lower-order principles may be judged.

Dr. R: You are treading toward the issue of *ethical relativism.* Universalistic doctrines of morality disregard cultural diversity; in contrast, ethical relativism allows any culture to define what it regards as right or wrong. Throughout history, universalism has sometimes assumed the form of absolutistic doctrines, which have not served humanity well. The rise of relativism parallels the decline of the absolute.

Knowledge is power; absolutistic knowledge is tyrannical power. The institutionalization of absolutistic knowledge confers upon its possessor absolutistic authority and control over others. Absolutism should prod us to become aware that knowledge can indeed be a dangerous thing.

Dr. U: To say that absolutistic doctrines have not served humanity well sounds like a universalistic, not relativist, statement!

You imply that any set of values is as good as another for humankind when you reject the idea that some cultural norms may be pathological and hence pathogenic. In so doing, you remove the motivation for cultural change for the better. But cultures do change and benefit from inter-cultural fertilization. Take foot binding, for instance. Chinese people now look back on it as a backward practice that oppressed women. The world is moving toward the idea that there are fundamental values, such as human rights, even if consensus on defining those values has not been achieved.

Are cultural relativists simply amoral or immoral as well? Cannibalism is repugnant, but not evil or pathological. But female genital mutilation, which violates the rights of women to health and sexual fulfillment, flies in the face of the idea of progress. Violation of human rights, ethnic cleansing, genocide, and other forms of terrorism are plainly heinous. To deny that some cultural norms may be unethical or pathological opens the door to condone all these practices. Beware that ethical relativism may be used inadvertently to silence critics and paralyze action in defense of human dignity.

Dr. R: By documenting cultural variation, cultural relativism provides ammunition for ethical relativism, which promotes toleration, if not acceptance, of cultural values that diverge from one's own. Tolerance of diversity is what the world needs more of.

Dr. U: Extreme cultural relativism can amount to *incommensurability*, the absence of common conceptions and perspectives. Incommensurability means that there is no common ground, and hence no possibility, for communication or mutual understanding between divergent cultures, leading to misunderstanding, even mistrust. Not an appetizing position to take at all.

Dr. R: Not all cultural relativists take such an extreme position. Ethical relativism champions diversity and counters uniformity. It has a rightful place particularly in this age of globalization when the identities of many cultures are under threat.

In 2008, the Australian government made a historic apology to the Aboriginal people for a six-decade policy of forced resettlement. In the early 1900s, thousands of mixed-race children were taken from their families and sent to live in orphanages, mission homes, or Caucasian households. Now, this is truly the mark of a civilized nation. Will the Government of the United States apologize to African and Native Americans?

Dr. U: I'm for it. But note that you have raised ethical relativism to universal status: Acceptance of cultural diversity is a universal principle. This contradicts relativism, which disallows universal principles!

Dr. R. I have no problem with accepting ethical relativism as a universal principle. Each culture is free to define for and by itself what is good and what is bad, *except* to disallow other cultures the same privilege.

Dr. U: Embodied within your refined version of cultural relativism is a universal principle: All cultures are equal. There is simply no way to escape from universality. Consider now the logic of self-application in the case of ethical relativism. You assert that there is no way to decide if one set of values is better or worse than another. Ethical relativism is a set of values, and so is universalism. Then, on what grounds can you negate universalism and affirm ethical relativism?

Dialectical Synthesis

The ideal is diversity within unity: That would be the end result of continuing the dialogue in which Dr. R and Dr. U are engaged. Universalism in keeping with pluralism allows for, even welcomes, culturally diverse understandings of human dignity. Closely allied with universalism is equifinality, which entails the idea that the same ultimate goal may be reached from different paths. Anyone is at liberty to define his own chosen path for leading a dignified life, *except* to disallow others the same privilege. In principle, there may be as many developmental paths as there are individuals.

REFERENCES

Goffman, E. 1961. *Asylums: Essays on the Social Situation of Mental Patients and Other Inmates*. New York: Doubleday Anchor.

Ho, D.Y.F. 1995. Selfhood and Identity in Confucianism, Taoism, Buddhism, and Hinduism: Contrasts with the West. *Journal for the Theory of Social Behaviour* 25: 115–139.

———. 2014a. *Enlightened or Mad? A Psychologist Glimpses into Mystical Magnanimity*. Lake Oswego: Dignity Press.

———. 2014b. A Self-Study of Mood Disorder: Fifteen Episodes of Exuberance, None of Depression. *Spirituality in Clinical Practice 1*, 297–299. https://doi.org/10.1037/scp0000040.

———. 2016. Madness May Enrich Your Life: A Self-Study of Unipolar Mood Elevation. *Psychosis: Psychological, Social and Integrative Approaches 8*, 180–185. https://doi.org/10.1080/17522439.2015.1135183.

James, W. 1985. *The Varieties of Religious Experience*. Cambridge, MA: Harvard University Press.

———. 2002. *The Varieties of Religious Experience: A Study of Human Nature* (Centenary ed.). London: Routledge. (First Published in 1902).

———. 2008. *The Letters of William James* [Electronic book]. New York: Cosimo. (Original Work Published 1920).

Johnson, C.V., and H.L. Friedman. 2008. Enlightened or Delusional? Differentiating Religious, Spiritual, and Transpersonal Experiences from Psychopathology. *Journal of Humanistic Psychology* 48: 505–527.

Schweitzer, A. 2011. *The Psychiatric Study of Jesus: Exposition and Criticism*. Trans. C.R. Joy. Whitefish: Literary Licensing. (Original Work Published 1913).

Notes on Contributors

Connie Dawson, a former counselor educator at Portland State University, has coauthored several books on parenting and development. Dr. Dawson has been an attachment-oriented therapist working especially with adoptive and foster families. In 2017, she received a Distinguished Alumni Award from the College of Education and Human Development at the University of Minnesota.

Tony Gaskew, PhD., is Associate Professor of Criminal Justice, Director of Criminal Justice, and Founding Director of the Prison Education Program at the University of Pittsburgh (Bradford). He is the author of over 30 publications focusing on race, crime, and justice, including his latest book, *Rethinking Prison Reentry: Transforming Humiliation into Humility*.

Linda M. Hartling, PhD., is the Director of Human Dignity and Humiliation Studies and coleader of the World Dignity University initiative and Dignity Press. She holds a doctoral degree in clinical/community psychology and is the past Associate Director of the Jean Baker Miller Training Institute, at the Wellesley Centers for Women at Wellesley College.

Professor David Y. F. Ho served as Director of the Clinical Psychology Program at the University of Hong Kong. He has authored numerous scholarly contributions in psychiatry, psychology, sociology, and education, and was the first Asian to serve as President of the International Council of Psychologists (1988–1989).

© The Author(s) 2018
D. Rothbart (ed.), *Systemic Humiliation in America*,
https://doi.org/10.1007/978-3-319-70679-5

Karina V. Korostelina is a Professor at the School for Conflict Analysis and Resolution at George Mason University. She conducts research on dynamics of identity and power, identity-based conflicts, history education, and resilience. A recipient of 39 fellowships and grants, she has edited six books, authored nine books and numerous articles.

Evelin G. Lindner has a dual education as a Medical Doctor and a Psychologist, with a PhD in Medicine (Dr. Med.) and a PhD in Psychology (Dr. Psychol.). She is the founding president of Human Dignity and Humiliation Studies, the cofounder of the World Dignity University initiative, and a nominee for the Nobel Peace Prize in 2015, 2016, and 2017.

Alison J. Lynch is a staff attorney with the New York State Protection and Advocacy Program, focusing on issues related to individuals with mental illness and criminal justice. Prior to practicing law, Alison studied neuroscience and psychology, and has published several articles focusing on the intersection of these topics in the law.

Joseph V. Montville is Director of the Program on Healing Historical Memory at George Mason University. A former career diplomat he spent 23 years in the Arab world and the State Department; he defined the concept of "Track Two," nonofficial diplomacy. Educated at Lehigh, Harvard, and Columbia, in 2008 the International Society of Political Psychology gave Montville its Nevitt Sanford Award for "distinguished professional contribution to political psychology."

Michael L. Perlin is Professor of Law Emeritus at New York Law School and cofounder of Mental Disability Law and Policy Associates. He has written 31 books and nearly 300 articles on all aspects of mental disability law. Previously, he was a Deputy Public Defender and director of the Division of Mental Health Advocacy in N. J.

Dr. David Ragland is a native of St. Louis, Missouri and cofounder for the Truth Telling Project of Ferguson. He is a Visiting Professor at Pacifica Graduate Institute, and his most recent research is a chapter entitled "Radical Truth Telling from the Ferguson Uprising: An Educational Intervention to Shift the Narrative, Build Political Efficacy, Claim Power and Transform Communities," for Wiley Press. David is an active public intellectual, frequently writing for the *Huffington Post* and *PeaceVoice*; he also is called upon for presentations and workshop facilitations nationally.

Arthur Romano is an Assistant Professor at the School for Conflict Resolution and Analysis. He is a scholar-practitioner whose research and applied interests include global educational movements, the use of transformative and experiential education in communities affected by violence and nonviolence education. Dr. Romano has designed and implemented experiential educational programs in Asia, Africa, and Central America on peace and conflict resolution related themes. He codeveloped the Diversity Matters Now workshop series, which explores issues related to identity and peace-building in colleges and universities across the United States.

Daniel Rothbart is a Professor of Conflict Analysis and Resolution at the School for Conflict Analysis and Resolution, George Mason University. Professor Rothbart specializes in identity-based conflicts, civilians in war and the symbols of violence, with an extensive publication record on these topics. He is currently exploring the power of moral emotions—shame, humiliation, and compassion—as central to protracted conflicts and their resolution. Professor Rothbart is codirector of the Program on Prevention of Mass Violence. He also chairs the Sudan Task Group, which is an organization that seeks to build long-term peace in Sudan.

Solon Simmons is former Vice President for Global Strategy and current associate professor in conflict analysis and resolution at George Mason University. A sociologist by training, Solon has broad interests in political culture, narrative, media, political ideas, symbolic politics, ethics, and public opinion as these relate to deep seated and intractable moral conflicts. He is the author of *The Eclipse of Equality: Arguing America on Meet the Press* and is currently working on a book on the significance and promise of the Nobel Peace Prize as it relates to modern values.

INDEX[1]

A

Addiction disorder, 196
African Americans, 10, 59–62, 64,
  68, 69, 82, 83, 86–90, 92,
  94, 99, 107, 109–111,
  119, 121, 127,
  149–151, 184
American elites, 76, 82
American greatness, 77

B

Baldwin, James, 5, 12, 131, 133, 148
Biden, Vice President Joe, 65, 81, 99
Black, 5, 7, 11–13, 26, 30, 58, 82,
  87, 89, 94, 98, 107–125, 127,
  128, 131–168
Black cultural privilege (BCP),
  13, 133–142
Black lives matter, 83, 84, 86, 152
Blossom Plan, 59

Boehner, John A., 64, 67
Brown, Michael, 10, 13, 58,
  59, 61–64, 69, 150–154, 159
Brown Jr., Michael, 61, 153, 168n2
Brown v. Board of Education, 58
Buddhism, 224, 231, 232

C

Capitalism, 78, 79
Charlottesville, Virginia, 12
Civil rights movement, 4, 78, 119
Class political, 75
Clay, Lacy, 62, 70n2
Climate crisis, 19
Clinton, Hillary, 10, 65, 85,
  87, 88, 90–96, 100
Coates, Ta-Nehisi, 5
Compassion, 13, 132, 134,
  140, 205, 206, 224, 231
Conflict analysis, vi, 80, 127

---

[1] Note: Page numbers followed by 'n' refer to notes.

Made in United States
North Haven, CT
05 February 2022

15706019R00143